# Women Street Photographers

PRESTEL

MUNICH · LONDON · NEW YORK

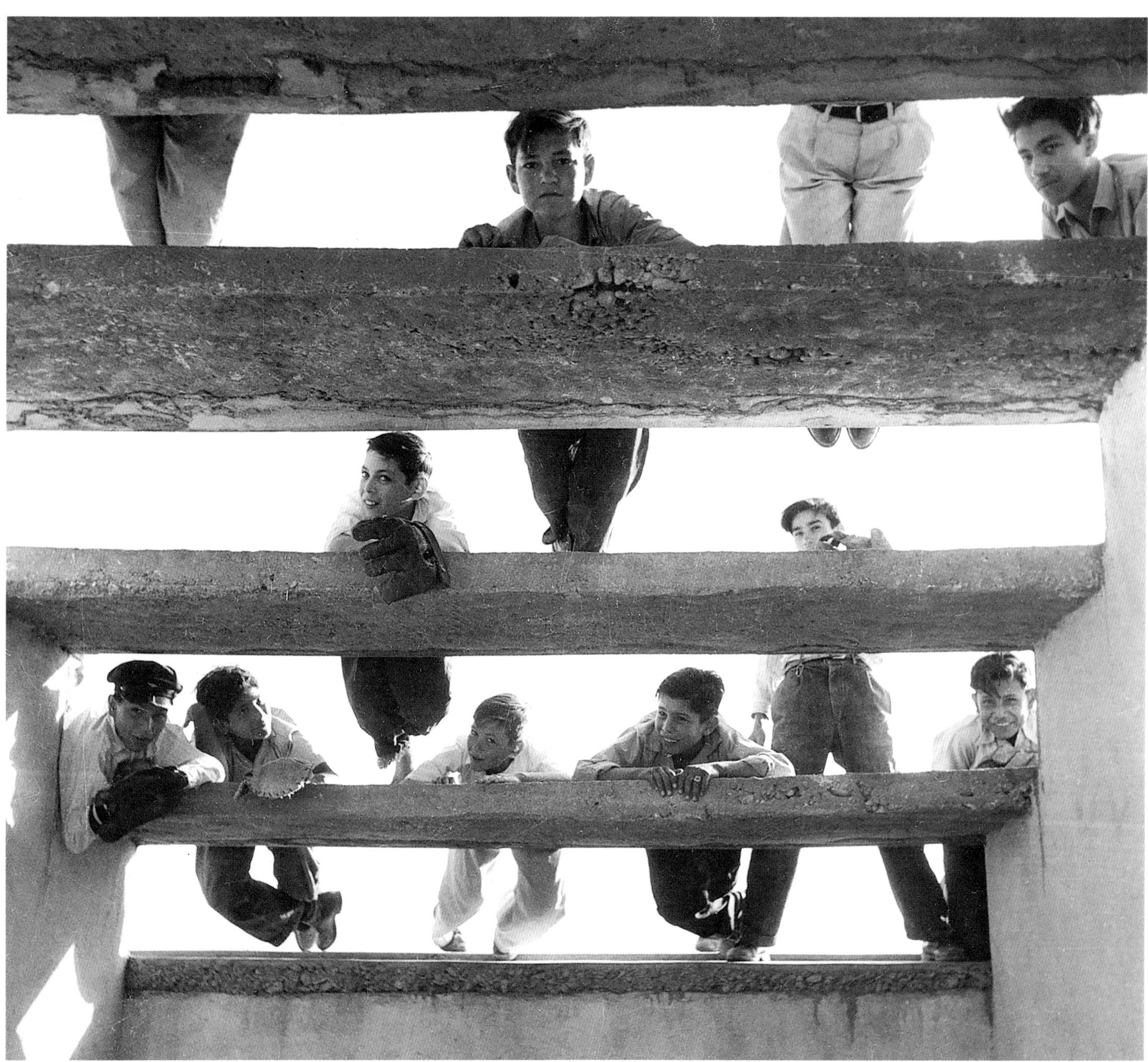

Lola Alvarez Bravo, *Los gorrones*, 1955

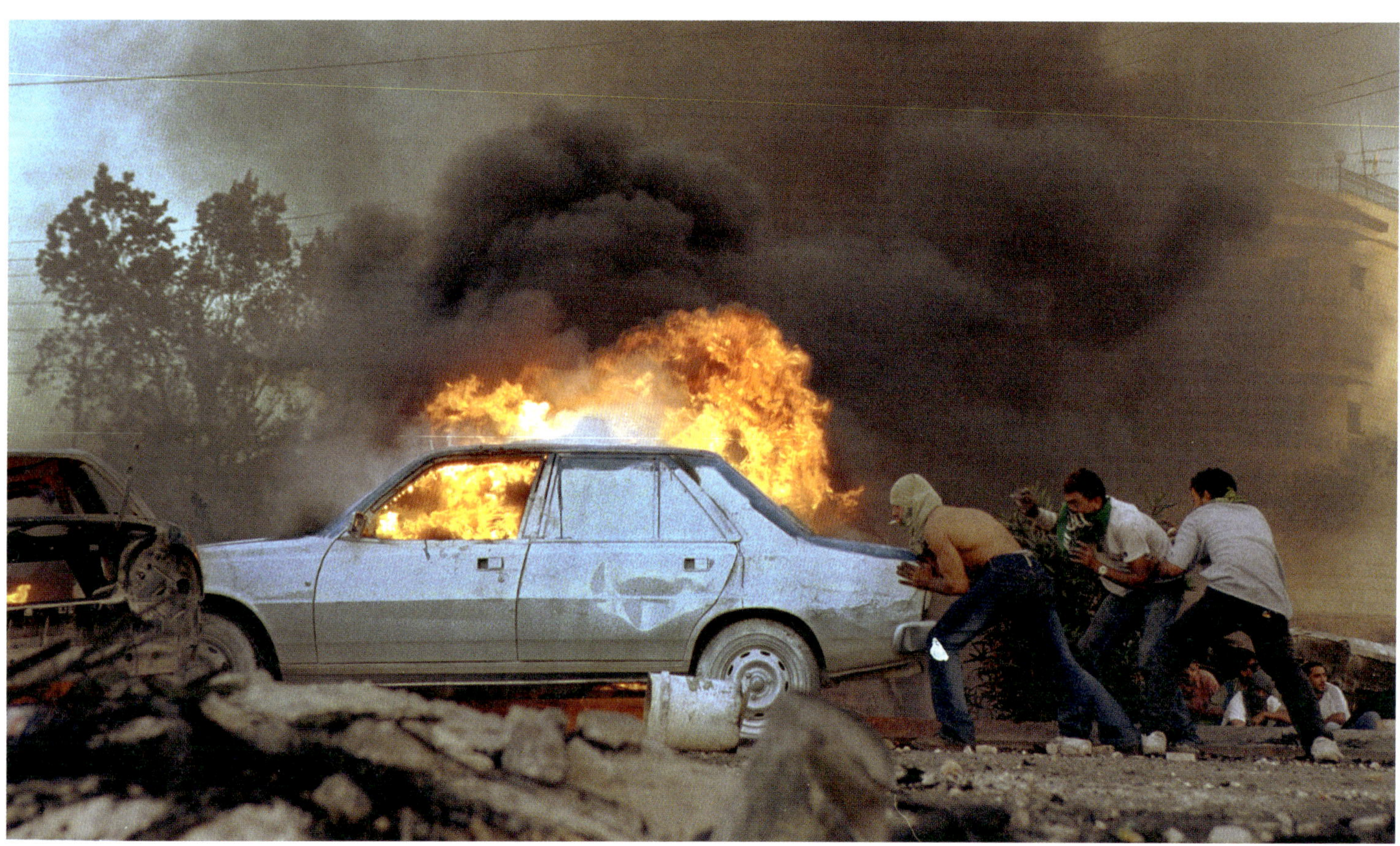

Palestinian protesters hide from
Israeli soldiers behind a burning car in
Ramallah, Palestine. October 11, 2000.
The image was taken just before
the photographer took shelter in a
nearby building, witnessing the local
wedding ceremony described here.

# FOREWORD by Ami Vitale

I began my career covering conflicts. I was a twenty-six-year-old woman and put myself in places like Kosovo, Angola, Gaza, Afghanistan, and, later, Kashmir. My reason for going, I told myself, was to document the brutality of conflict. I thought the most powerful stories were large global events driven by violence and destruction. I took on the life of the jet-setting photojournalist, graduating to covering the conflict in Israel and Palestine, and coming to many realizations about my craft while amid the rubble and chaos of a region fuelled by animosity. But this proximity to destruction became all too close one day when my life was spared only by a fortuitous fault with my camera battery. Two Israeli soldiers had been taken to a police station in Gaza where an angry mob took over. I was running to document the scene when the batteries in my camera fell out. The moment I stopped to pick them up, a nearby helicopter fired a missile and vaporized the building to which I was running. It saved my life. I should have been inside that building doing what I thought I should be doing: getting close to the action.

Covering some of the world's most volatile communities left me awed by more intimate, overlooked, and seemingly "everyday" scenes. I was taught to react to events and be close to the action, but I slowly learned that it can be the less dramatic moments that best convey the human experience. One day, as I was walking back to my hotel in the West Bank city of Nablus, I heard music from a nearby building. I wandered up some dark stairs and found a Palestinian couple dancing together. It was their wedding ceremony and they were surrounded by all the people who loved them. Outside, a brutal conflict was unfolding, but here, in the middle of it all, was this captivating expression of love. It was a profound and simple moment that reminded me it was not enough only to cover the conflict raging outside; we must also find the quieter stories that remind us of our shared humanity.

I now work as a photojournalist exploring subjects from animal conservation to the role of women in fighting climate change, and when I look back on my experiences of photographing conflict, I wonder how I got through them. They were sometimes unimaginable, often lonely, and occasionally utterly terrifying. Working as a female photographer during times of conflict brought its own set of problems: I've been harassed and threatened, and learned quickly that I have to be thoughtful about how and where I work. No picture is worth my own personal safety.

What has slowly emerged throughout my photographic career is that we have an obligation to illuminate the things that unite us as human beings. We must learn to recognize the unacknowledged moments of intrigue, humor, and beauty that can be seen on every street in the world—during both normal, everyday life and in exceptional, heightened circumstances. My camera empowered me from a young age and later, I came to realize, also gave me the ability to share and amplify other people's stories. What was at first my passport to engage with the world eventually became my tool for changing it. Photography reminds us of our deep connections to one another and can also be a means of creating awareness and understanding across cultures; it is a way of making sense of what connects us in the world we share.

# INTO THE WORLD by Melissa Breyer

On November 7, 1800, a decree was issued in Paris requiring women to obtain a permit in order to wear pants in public. The French writer George Sand (the penname of Amantine Lucile Aurore Dupin) defied the order by donning men's attire and freely roaming the streets, sans permit. Once outfitted in her grey wool garb and boots, Sand felt "secure on the sidewalks," she wrote in her autobiography. "I flew from one end of Paris to the other. It seemed to me that I could have made a trip around the world … No one knew me, no one looked at me, no one found fault with me; I was an atom lost in that immense crowd."[1]

At a time when "proper" women would have risked disgrace by being out alone—their place was in the home, after all—Sand was reveling unescorted in the streets. She was a secret female counterpart to the male flâneur, the man of leisure who strolled the boulevards to cultivate what Honoré de Balzac called "the gastronomy of the eye."[2] Although Sand's medium was the pen, her peripatetic explorations of 1830s Paris helped pave the way for those who would eventually take their cameras and roam the streets to capture the goings-on of public life: women street photographers.

***

Not long before Sand was flying around Paris, a French inventor by the name of Nicéphore Niépce was looking for a way to make images without having to draw them. In 1826, he had the idea to use a device popular in the Renaissance, the camera obscura, to create a projection upon a treated pewter plate. Left alone for eight hours, the sun etched the view onto the surface, resulting in the world's first photograph. The image reveals a tangle of rooftops and buildings. It is a rustic thing,

all texture and shapes, with few details—yet it is hard to overstate its importance.

With photography still in its nascent stage, Sarah Anne Bright and Constance Fox Talbot were experimenting with the medium in Britain. They both made photographs in 1839—and each has alternately been credited with having been the first woman to do so. In 1843, amateur botanist Anna Atkins created a book entitled *Photographs of British Algae*, composed entirely of cyanotype impressions. It was the first book ever to be photographically printed and illustrated.

Photography's early years were filled with tinkering and rife with images of nature and simple scenes. It was not until the French artist and chemist Louis-Jacques-Mandé Daguerre came up with his namesake daguerreotype in 1839 that the world had its first commercially successful photographic process.

At this point innovations in photography were most notably taking place in the West—our focus here, given street photography's strong Western roots—but that is not to say that photography was not happening elsewhere. Europeans brought daguerreotype cameras to China as early as the 1840s, for instance, and soon thereafter Chinese photo studios were developing their own style of photographic representation. In India, daguerreotype cameras were available in Calcutta a year after their invention and by the 1870s, Indian photographers were opening commercial studios.

Daguerre had used his new process to create the first known photograph of a human in the late 1830s. The image, captured on a silvered copper plate, reveals a scene of Boulevard du Temple in Paris. Strolling figures passed by too fleetingly to be registered by the plate's long exposure, but a man getting his boots shined remained still for long enough to be immortalized forever in the historic image. Would it be a stretch to call this the first street photo?

Defining "street photography" is not for the faint of heart and has given rise to much debate. It was neither codified in a manifesto nor formally clarified early on. As described by the *Encyclopaedia Britannica*, street photography is "a genre of photography that records everyday life in a public place ... Street photographers do not necessarily have a social purpose in mind, but they prefer to isolate and capture moments which might otherwise go unnoticed."[3]

While the discourse over what comprises street photography may endure into eternity, the body of work by Staten Island resident Alice Austen could serve as a model for the genre itself. She was ten years old in 1876 when her uncle gave her a camera and she spent the next fifty years making more than 7,000 photographs, processing them herself in a second-floor closet turned into a darkroom. A bicycle enthusiast, she cruised the streets with fifty pounds of gear in tow, seeking subjects to photograph. She took photos of anything and everyone who interested her, from the high life of Staten Island, to the street sweepers, suspenders sellers, postmen, policemen, fishmongers, organ-grinders, shoeshine boys, and newsgirls of lower Manhattan. What she was doing all the way back then is not very different from what street photographers are doing today. [Fig. 1]

***

[Fig. 1] Alice Austen, *Street Cleaner, Twenty-Fourth Street*, 1896

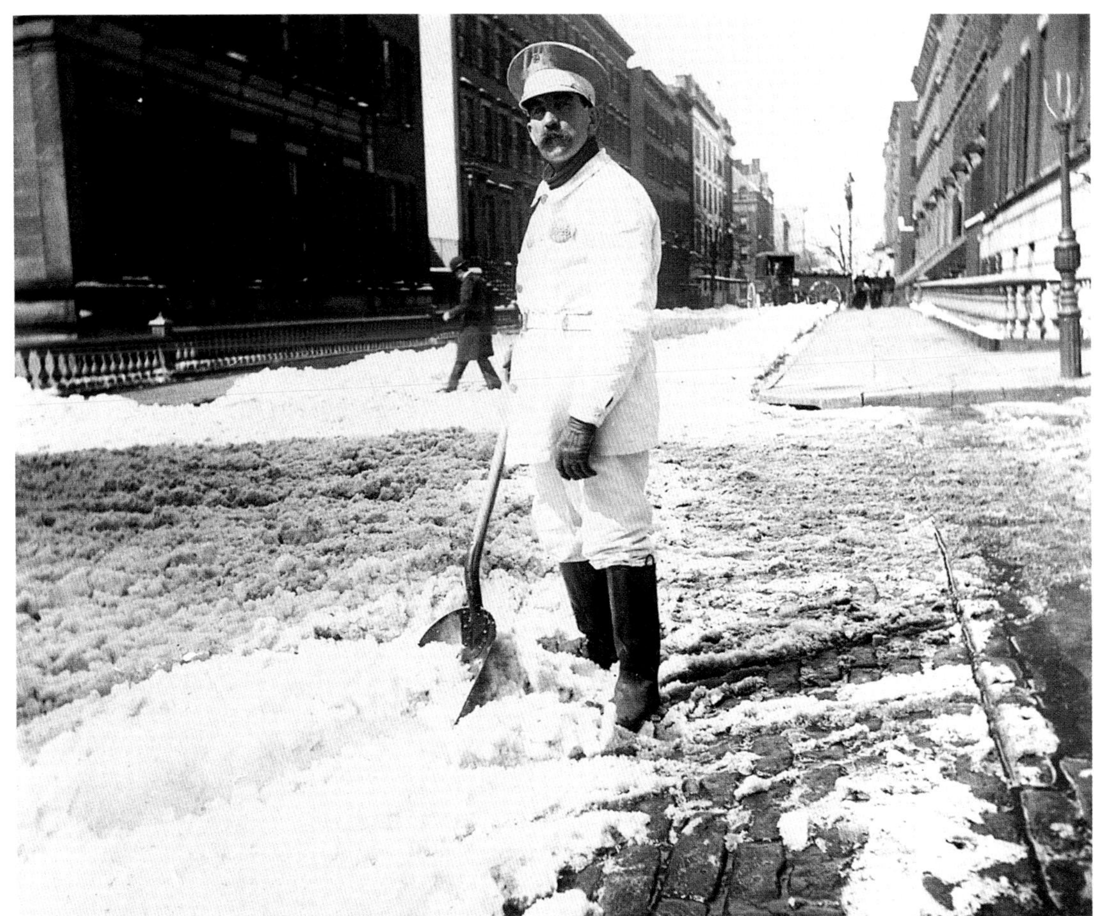

1   George Sand, trans. Thelma Jurgrau, *Story of My Life: The Autobiography of George Sand* (SUNY Press: New York, 1991), pp. 893, 904–5.

2   Honoré de Balzac, *The Philosophy of Marriage*, Part 1 [1828] (Outlook Verlag: Frankfurt am Main, 2019), p. 25.

3   Naomi Blumberg, "Street Photography," in *Encyclopaedia Britannica*, online at britannica. com, August 6, 2014.



INTO THE WORLD

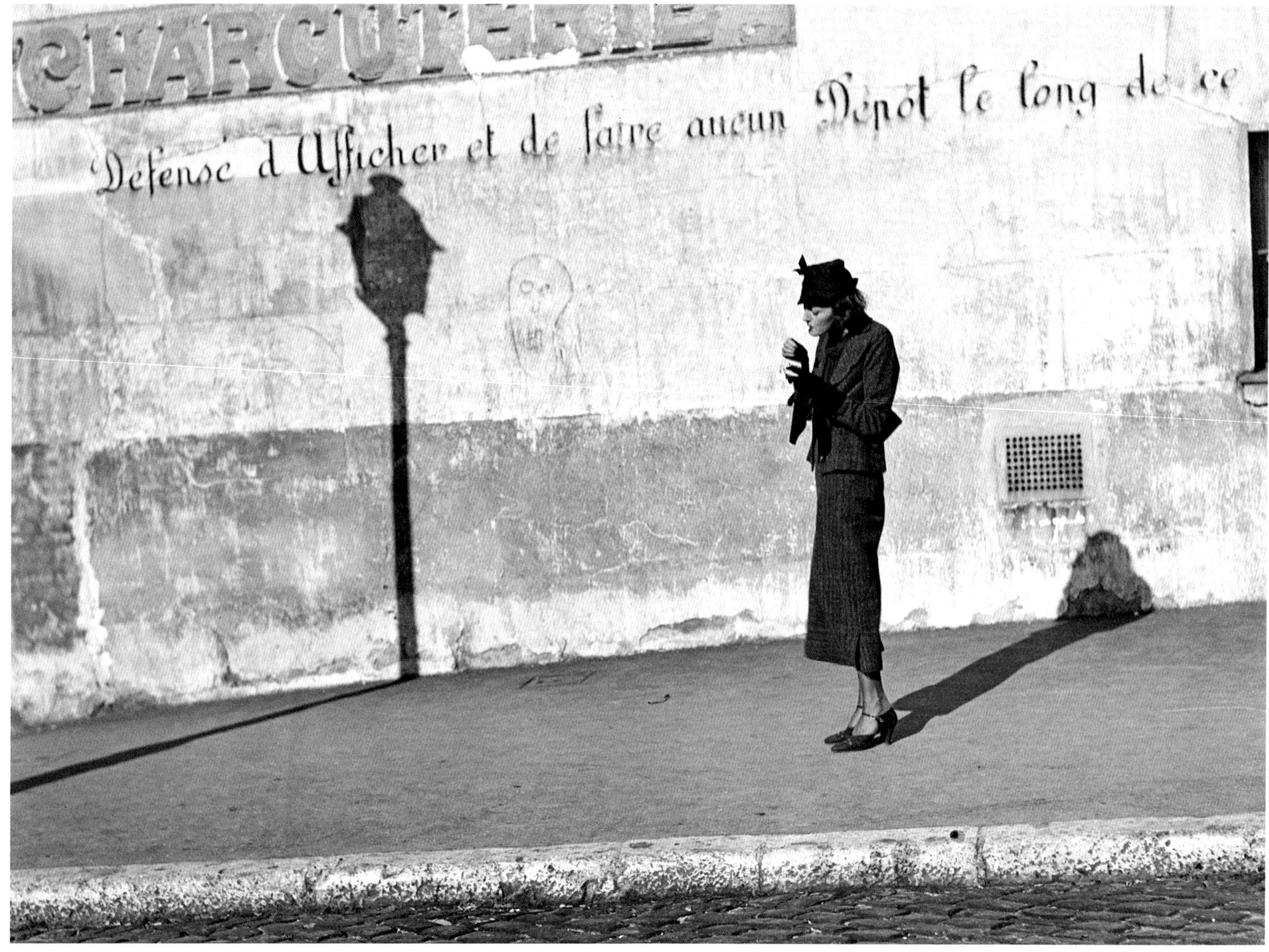

[Fig. 2] Marianne Breslauer,
*Défense d'Afficher*, Paris, 1937

Photography took a leap forward when George Eastman introduced the Original Kodak camera in 1888. Small enough to hold in the hands, the fixed-focus camera came loaded with a one-hundred-exposure roll of film. Now, rather than having to struggle with cameras that used a glass-plate negative for each exposure, photographers could shoot with a simple and portable machine. Eastman Kodak's introduction of the Brownie in 1900 made photography yet more accessible and affordable.

However, the new cameras didn't have the quality required by professional photographers, which is why Jessie Tarbox Beals, dressed in the typical street-skimming dresses and large hats of the day, lugged around her cumbersome large-format camera, along with a tripod and the requisite gear. Beals was hired by the *Buffalo Inquirer* as a staff photographer in 1902, making her America's first female news photographer. While most women photographers at the time were photographing friends at home or making portraits in the studio, Beals was out in the world taking photos of real life, and with moxie. She even taught herself to use flash powder, making her the first female night photographer. And her influence was not lost on the world. As the Library of Congress notes, "Her courageous example encouraged other women to pursue photography."[4]

Although the technological advances in photography were becoming more available globally, gender roles in some parts of the world meant that many women were far from being able to buy a camera and freely roam the streets (as is still the case today). But in the United States, the 1920s and '30s gave rise to a number of historic women photographers whose work informed what we now call street photography. There was Berenice Abbott, who strove to document a changing New York City; photojournalist Margaret Bourke-White, who in 1930 became the first Western professional photographer allowed into the Soviet Union; and of course Dorothea Lange, who left her San Francisco portrait studio to join the government's Resettlement Administration. Her work included some of the most enduring photographs we have today, including her *Migrant Mother, Nipomo, California* of 1936, which has become one of the most famous photographs in history.

During this period a group of early women pioneers of street photography emerged, coaxed forward by another advance in technology. In 1925, Leica launched the company's first commercially available 35mm camera. It was small and equipped with fast shutter speeds and well-crafted lenses, affording those making candid photographs in public a discreet way to do so with high-quality results.

In Paris, photographer Ilse Bing bought the new camera in 1929, her subsequent work earning her the moniker "Queen of the Leica." And it was a Leica that Helen Levitt purchased in 1935 after being inspired by the work of street photography pioneer Henri Cartier-Bresson. Levitt's images of New York City's children and life in the poorer neighborhoods started appearing in magazines by 1939, and by 1943 she had a solo exhibition at MoMA. She would spend the next forty years walking the streets to catch, as the *New York Times* described, "fleeting moments of surpassing lyricism, mystery and quiet drama."[5] Echoes of Levitt's influential work can still be felt in photographs being made today.

Meanwhile, in Paris, German-born Marianne Breslauer spent the late 1920s and '30s focusing her lens on street scenes ranging from the homeless along the river Seine to the horseraces at Longchamp. Breslauer spent her time walking through the streets, finding poetry in the mundane: one of the hallmarks of modern street photography. In a photo from 1937 she presents a sliver of a moment that would otherwise have gone unseen [Fig. 2]. In the image, an elegant figure in a hat lights a cigarette, with her glove and a matchbox in her hand.

4   Beverly W. Brannan, "Jessie Tarbox Beals (1870–1942): Biographical Essay," Library of Congress Prints and Photographs Division, January 2011, online at www.loc.gov.

5   Margaret Loke, "Helen Levitt, Who Froze New York Street Life on Film, Is Dead at 95," *New York Times*, March 30, 2009, online at nytimes.com.

The wall before which she stands is a chaos of text and texture, and acts as a screen for the shadow of a lamppost that takes on the look of cartoon-character companion. It was an unremarkable split second, made remarkable for having been frozen by Breslauer's camera.

In India, Homai Vyarawalla, known by her pseudonym Dalda 13, was recognized as the country's first woman photojournalist. Working from the 1930s onward, she was often seen riding her bicycle on the streets of New Delhi with a camera bag slung over her shoulder. A few years later, another Indian photographer, Li Gotami Govinda, would go on assignment in western Tibet to create one of the last records of life and culture there before the Chinese occupation.

It was also in the 1930s that Lola Alvarez Bravo began venturing out from her studio in Mexico City to start photographing what she called "the life I found before me."[6] Considered the first professional woman photographer in Mexico, Alvarez Bravo wore many hats in terms of her photography, but it was her personal work that pushed the boundaries for the time and place. The Center for Creative Photography, which owns her archives, describes how she moved "amongst the people along cluttered streets, observing them at work, in the marketplace, and at leisure, waiting for opportunities to capture informal moments in carefully composed scenes."[7]

And there was Vienna-born Lisette Model, who moved to New York City in 1938; just two years later, her work would be included in the inaugural exhibition of MoMA's Department of Photography. There is a certain energy in Model's candid photos—and with her proclivity for capturing the city's quirkier characters, the result is a unique dynamic that still feels relevant.

***

Western women in the 1930s had come a long way relative to the Victorian social constraints of their predecessors, and the Second World War would do much to nudge gender roles further forward. Women photographers were allowed entry into jobs formerly reserved for men. In New York, Ida Wyman, already interested in photography, got a job at Acme News Pictures at the age of sixteen. Here, she explains, "in an all-male environment, I became both their first mailroom 'girl' and their first 'girl' printer."[8] During her lunch breaks she would shoot her "picture stories" on the street, which she started showing to editors who were receptive to her work. She would go on to have a long career, noting, "Everyday life and where it was happening was what interested me."[9]

Similarly, when a knee injury forced Vivian Cherry out of work as a dancer in 1945, she took a job at a photo lab that was short on male staff. Working with prints sparked an interest in photography and she spent the rest of her long life taking an abundance of remarkable street photos. Cherry's admiration for Helen Levitt can be seen in her images of the city's children, but those are just a fraction of her body of street work, which offers iconic glimpses of New York City, from the Lower East Side to Harlem. [Fig. 3]

Millions of women joined the workforce during the war, and things would never quite be the same afterwards. In the United States, Rosie the Riveter offered a new vision of female strength and determination, and attitudes about "a woman's place"—the home—began to shift. When the war was over, most women were sent back to their abodes to resume domestic duties, but a new independence had taken hold. The genie was out of the bottle.

It is no coincidence that the postwar years welcomed in a new group of women who took to the streets to make photos. The 1950s saw Sabine Weiss creating compelling photos in Paris and Inge Morath shooting around the world.



INTO THE WORLD

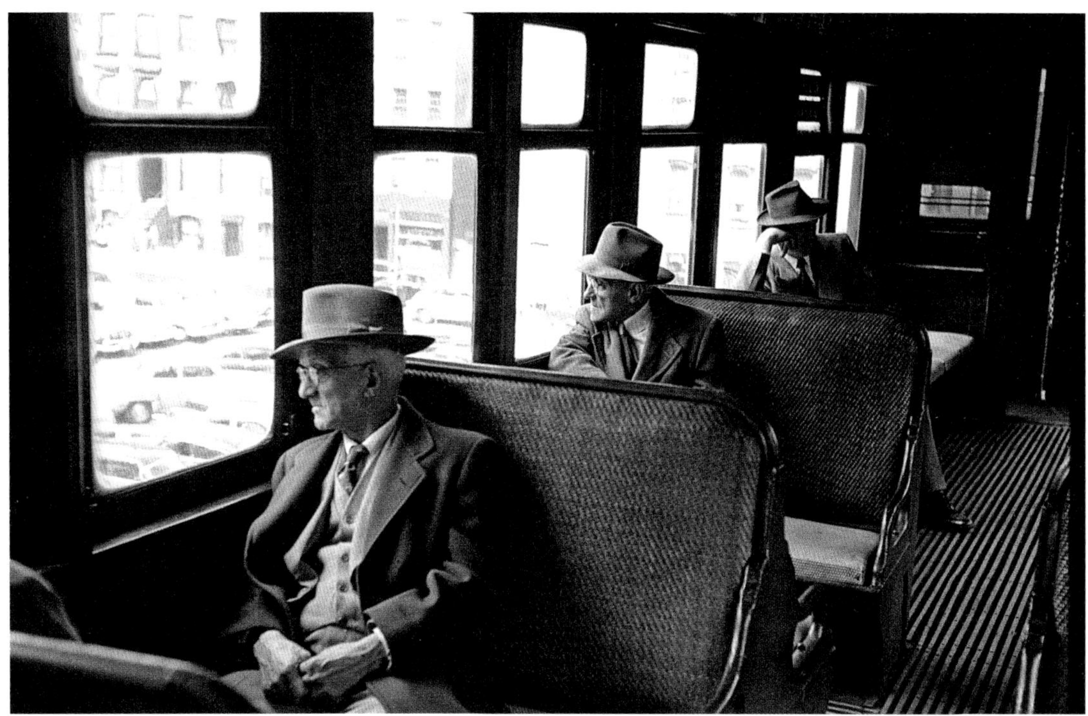

Diane Arbus was finding her photographic voice in New York City, and Eve Arnold became the first woman photographer to join Magnum Photos. In 1952, photographer Barbara Morgan co-founded *Aperture* magazine. It was also during this time that London-based Dorothy Bohm turned from the studio to street photography, where she would become an early adopter of color film and amass an illustrious body of work.

Although a new generation of women photographers was finding some measure of success and recognition, there were others who were more private in their endeavors. If it weren't for the accidental discovery of a massive collection of photographic work in a Chicago storage space, the world would never have known of Vivian Maier, the posthumous megastar who worked as a nanny. Starting in the 1950s, she took more than 100,000 photographs over the following decades, featuring the denizens of New York City, Chicago, and beyond—yet she shared her photography with very few people. Among the secret photos she took is one quiet masterpiece after the next. Her photos are edgy yet empathetic and reveal a keen eye and a sly sense of humor. Despite her unusual story and the issues of privacy that her discovery raises, Vivian Maier's distinct aesthetic has made her one of history's most prominent street photographers.

***

While the war inspired some new thinking about gender roles, the 1960s saw a seismic shift. In the United States, feminist author Betty Friedan wrote the seminal book *The Feminine Mystique* in 1963, the same year in which Gloria Steinem went undercover as a Playboy Bunny and wrote an exposé on Hugh Hefner's organization. The next year, Title VII of the Civil Rights Act became federal law, protecting women against discrimination in the workplace. And in 1966, the National Organization for Women (NOW) was founded to promote feminist ideals and lead societal change.

6   "Lola Alvarez Bravo," Center for Creative Photography, online at ccp.arizona.edu, accessed May 13, 2020.

7   Ibid. An example of her work can be seen opposite the contents page of this book.

8   "Ida Wyman: Artist Statement," Stephen Cohen Gallery, online at stephencohengallery.com, accessed May 13, 2020.

9   Ibid.

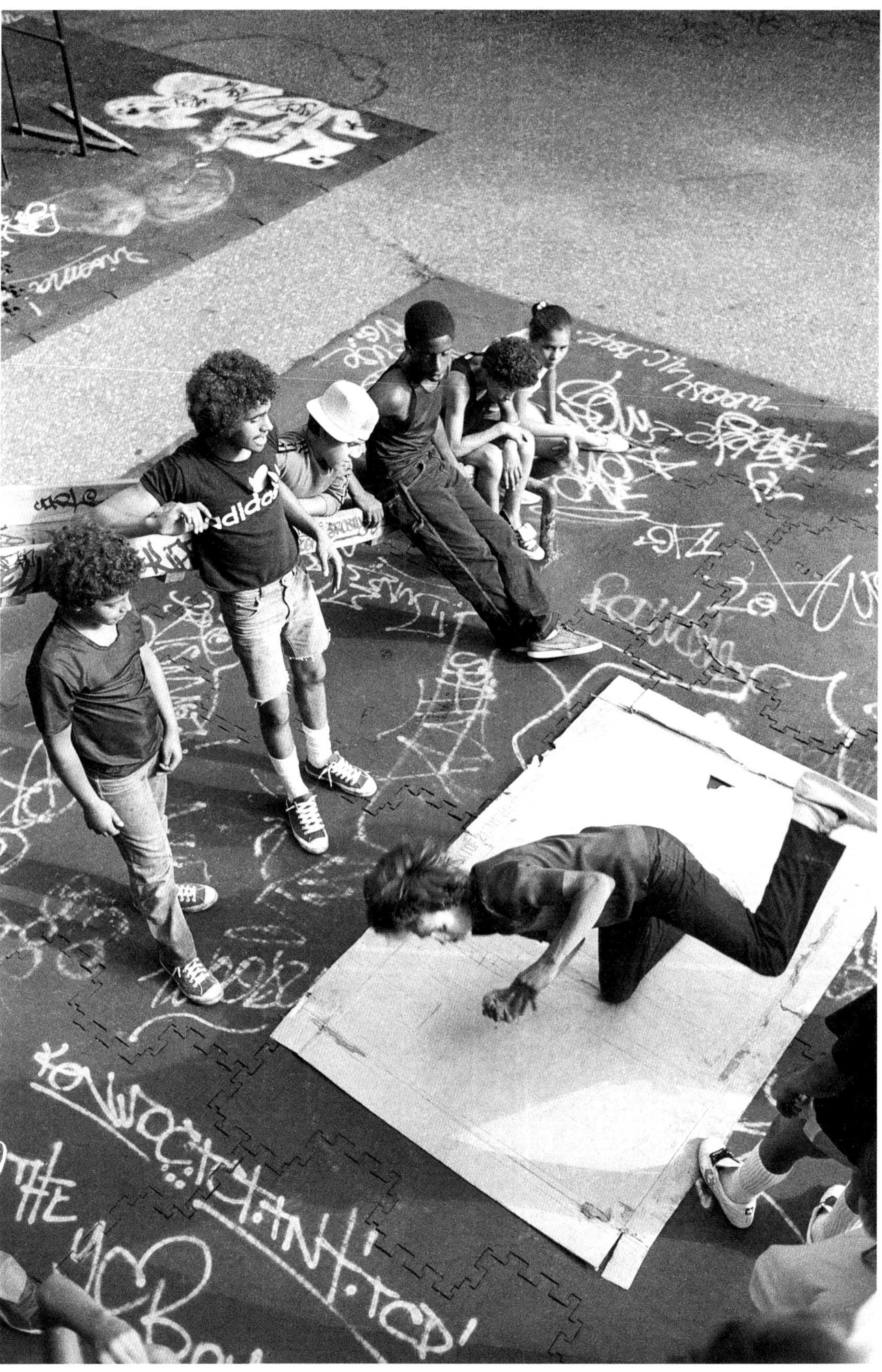



[Fig. 4] Martha Cooper,
*Cooper Rock Steady*, 1981



INTO THE WORLD

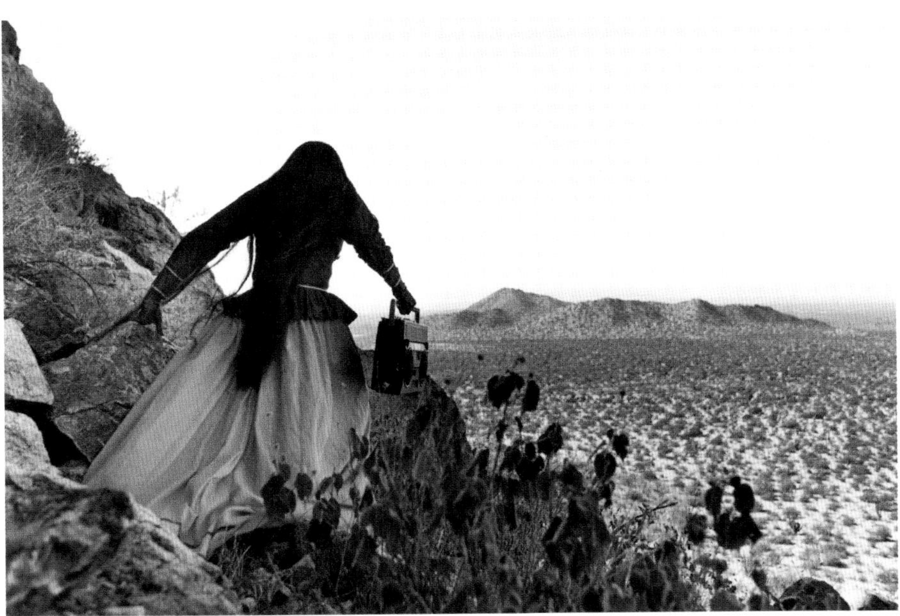



It was in this global context that Martine Franck's photography career took off in France, as did Ruth-Marion Baruch's in San Francisco. In Northern England, Shirley Baker was creating a remarkable archive of street photography that would span decades, while New York City became a magnet for a small cadre of women street photographers such as Jill Freedman and Mary Ellen Mark.

Mark started shooting the city streets in the mid-1960s and would eventually travel around the world creating her distinctively compassionate documentary and street images. "I remember the first time I went out on the street to shoot pictures," Mark once said. "I was in downtown Philadelphia and I just took a walk and started making contact with people and photographing them, and I thought: 'I love this. This is what I want to do forever.' There was never another question."[10] Her first book, *Passport*, was published in 1974, and she went on to publish twenty books in total.

By the early 1970s, Susan Meiselas was photographing strippers and had begun her long-running New York City project *Prince Street Girls*. Her work

has served as inspiration across genres. Martha Cooper moved to New York in 1975 and became—as she remains, almost five decades later—the premier documentarian of graffiti, street art, and their makers [Fig. 4]. Her photographs of furtively illustrated subway cars, and urban life in general, are iconic, offering time travel to anyone nostalgic for hand-painted trains, rather than ones fully wrapped in Target ads.

In 1979, Donna Ferrato arrived in New York City and began photographing the city's nightlife scene in legendary clubs such as Studio 54 and the swingers' paradise Plato's Retreat. The dichotic dynamic of New York City in the late 1970s and early '80s also set the stage for Meryl Meisler, who photographed the dizzy mania of Manhattan's disco scene by night while documenting the extreme urban decay of Bushwick, Brooklyn, by day—long before it became a hipster haven.

Elsewhere, Tish Murtha was focusing on youth unemployment and marginalized communities in Northern England, Graciela Iturbide was capturing the lives of Mexico's underrepresented native cultures, [Fig. 5] and Janet Delaney was exploring San Francisco's changing neighborhoods. And this is but a few of the women taking photos in public at the time, a group that would grow exponentially in the decades to come.

***

At this point in our story, everyone was still working in film, but then came the sea change that would dramatically alter the course of photography: the development of digital cameras. The first one was built in 1975 by an engineer at Eastman Kodak. Thirteen years later, in Japan, Fujifilm launched the world's first fully digital camera, which saved data to a memory card that could store five to ten photographs.

10  William Grimes, "Mary Ellen Mark, Photographer Who Documented Difficult Subjects, Dies at 75," *New York Times*, May 27, 2015, online at nytimes.com.

The digital camera revolution made photography more affordable and accessible than ever. It simplified some of the thinking and much of the process, and the introduction and expeditious evolution of the phone camera even more so. If the Original Kodak camera of 1888 marked the advent of amateur photography, digital cameras and phone photography propelled it into the stratosphere.

These developments would allow for millions of new photographers—by some estimates, more than 1.4 trillion photos were taken in 2019. Among them, an impressive new generation of women street photographers has emerged. While some contemporary women street photographers have been working for decades, and some choose to use film, the arrival of digital has made the genre much more accessible. Importantly, it has also made street photography much more global—particularly for women.

Whereas the earliest women photographers were primarily Western and often had to defy social mores— not to mention lug around fifty-pound cameras and process their images in second-floor closets—the dovetailing of women's liberation with new photographic technology has made the work of twenty-first-century street photographers decidedly more possible in many countries. Those of us who can freely and safely go out, unescorted, and shoot in public now have better access to the tools needed to document otherwise unnoticed moments of public life.

Despite this continuing increase in women around the world picking up a camera, women still remain under-represented in photography and other areas of the arts. When women are given platforms for their artistic work, it is often under the subcategory of their sex: "Women Artists," rather than just "Artists." In many artistic mediums, the inclusion of this caveat feels patronizing and irrelevant; a judgement of the artist's work tempered by their biographical background in a way not experienced by their male counterparts. However, with street photographers this acknowledgment feels not only necessary but celebratory; these images were not created in the safety of a studio, but on city streets and village backroads around the world, where in the past it has not always been possible for women to take photographs—and take up space. This book is an acknowledgment that we have finally started to move beyond this (albeit to different degrees in different areas); a celebratory roar for those individuals who have given a subversive spin to the historically male figure of the flâneur.

Now, when curators, collectives, festival organizers, and editors are asked about unequal representation, they can no longer claim, "There just aren't many women street photographers." These photographers have voiced their presence and are increasingly invited to participate. But when not included, we are taking history into our own hands. We go out into the world and take photographs, curate our own exhibits, form our own collectives, and create our own events. And now, we even write our own books.

# List of Photographers

 LIST OF PHOTOGRAPHERS

 LIST OF PHOTOGRAPHERS

 LIST OF PHOTOGRAPHERS

 LIST OF PHOTOGRAPHERS

# 1.

# Gulnara Samoilova

Once a year, I travel back to Russia to the Republic of Bashkortostan where I visit small villages and document the everyday lives of ordinary people. I always visit Sabantuy, an annual festival that takes place all over the region. It is my favorite place to photograph.

I was moved by the beautiful landscapes, kind and warm people, delicious food, and fascinating culture. I was especially struck by the resemblance of clouds to white cotton candy, and this concept immediately became part of my series *Cloud Eaters*. I spotted these two kids standing in the middle of a large grassy field and passionately eating the white cotton candy against a backdrop of fluffy clouds, as if they had just pulled those clouds from the sky. They didn't even notice me.

*Gulnara is a New York City-based fine art and street photographer, curator, and educator. She is the founder of the Women Street Photographers traveling exhibition, associated Instagram feed and artist residency. Her work is a part of major private and museum collections.*

GULNARA SAMOILOVA, Tatar/American

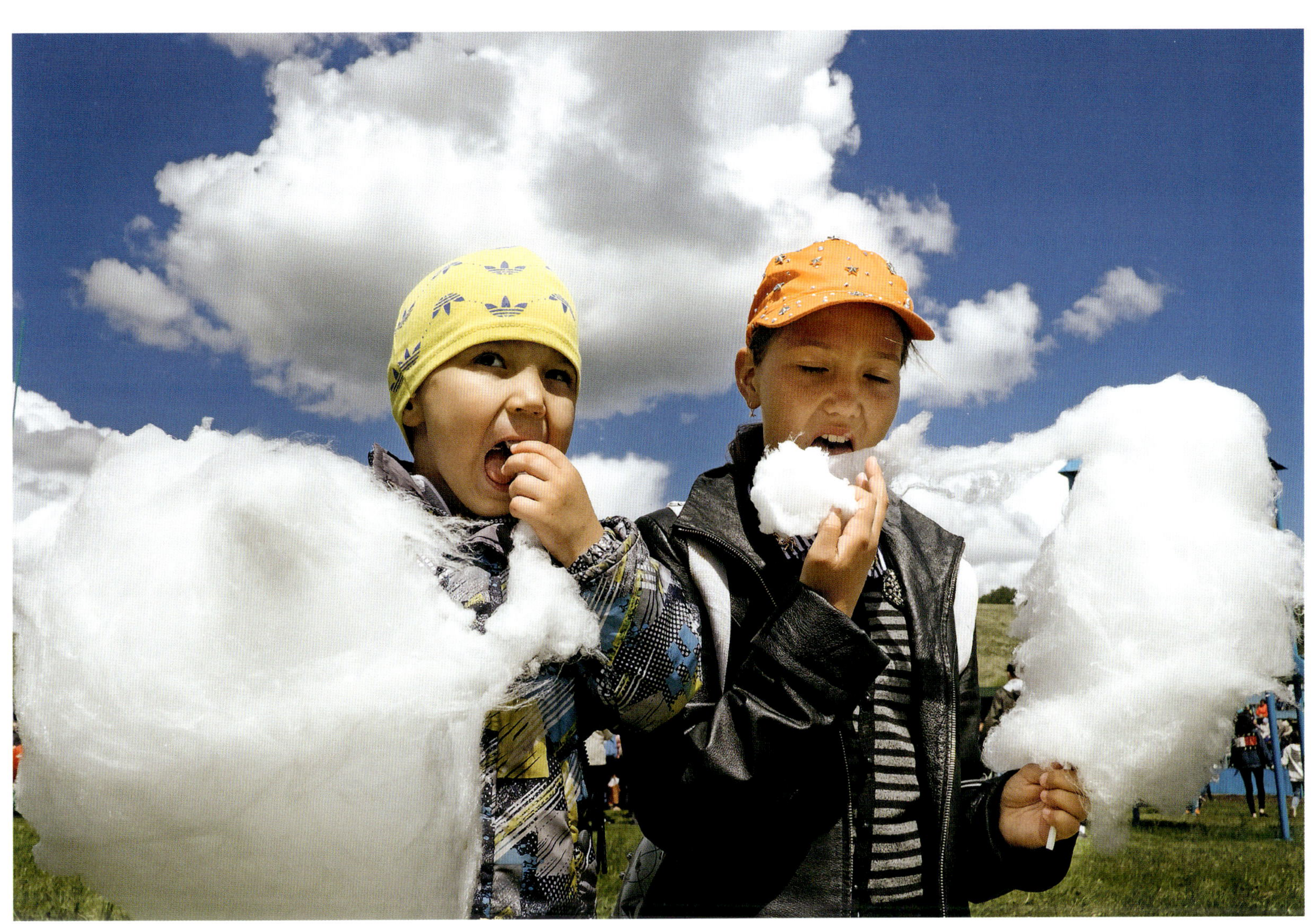

*Cloud Eaters*, Yermekeevo, Bashkortostan, 2018

# 2.

# Birka Wiedmaier

In Turkey it is common for couples who are getting married to have wedding portraits taken.

I watched this couple for quite some time while their pictures were taken on a small beach in the town of Şile. This scene was the one that fascinated me the most. Why was this boat chosen as the location? Why was she positioned like this?

It felt surreal to see the bride with her beautiful dress draped over this small boat, in contrast to her surroundings. She did not move much and waited to be given her flowers. Everything seemed to revolve around her; the groom can hardly be identified.

In the surrounding bedlam she is the anchor and definitely the center of attention.

*Birka is a Berlin-based photographer whose work has been exhibited in Moscow, London, Paris, New York, Kuala Lumpur, and other cities around the world. Her photographic journey started while living in Moscow. She is mainly self-taught and focuses on street photography.*

BIRKA WIEDMAIER, German

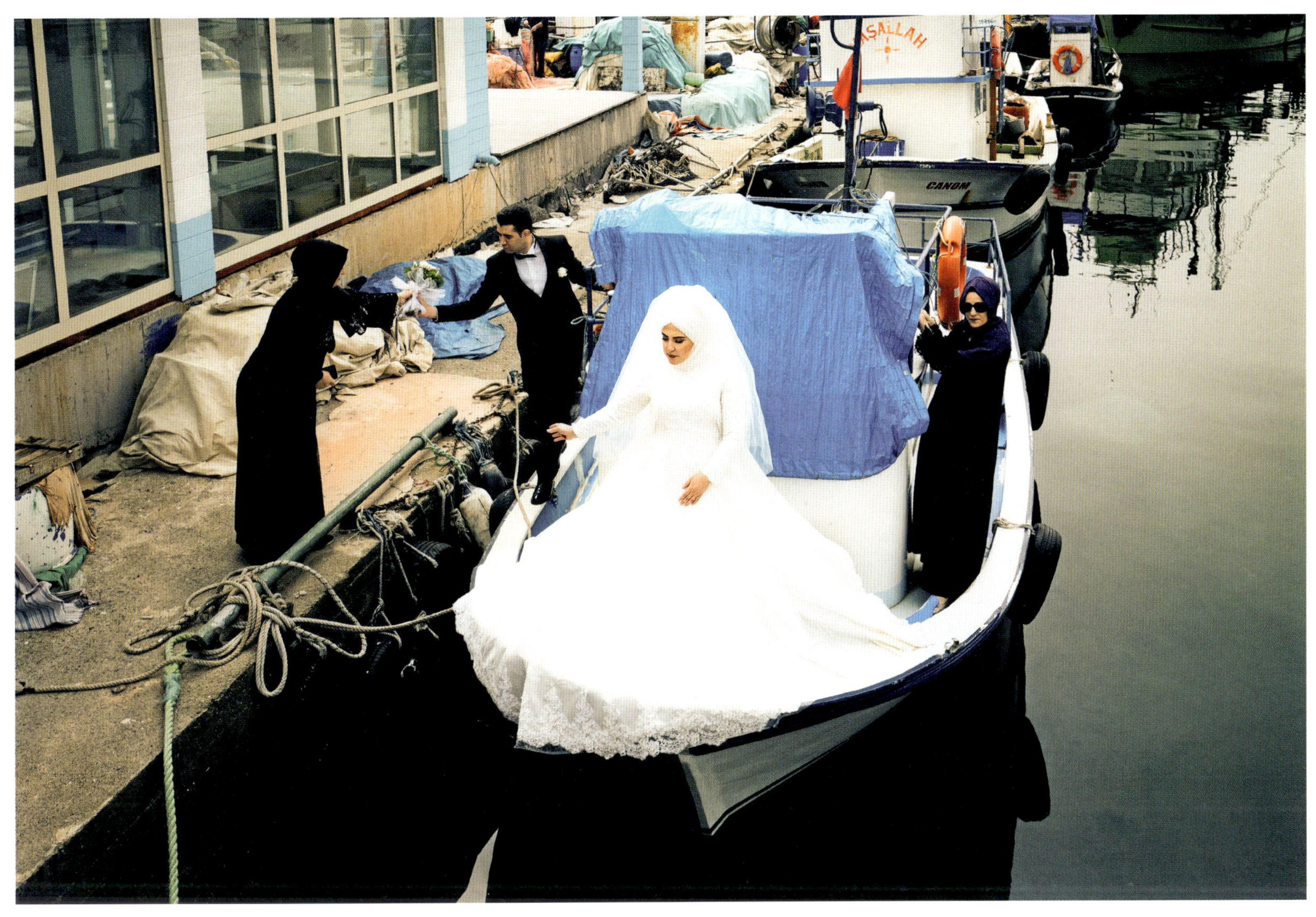

*Untitled*, Şile, Turkey, 2019

# Efrat Sela



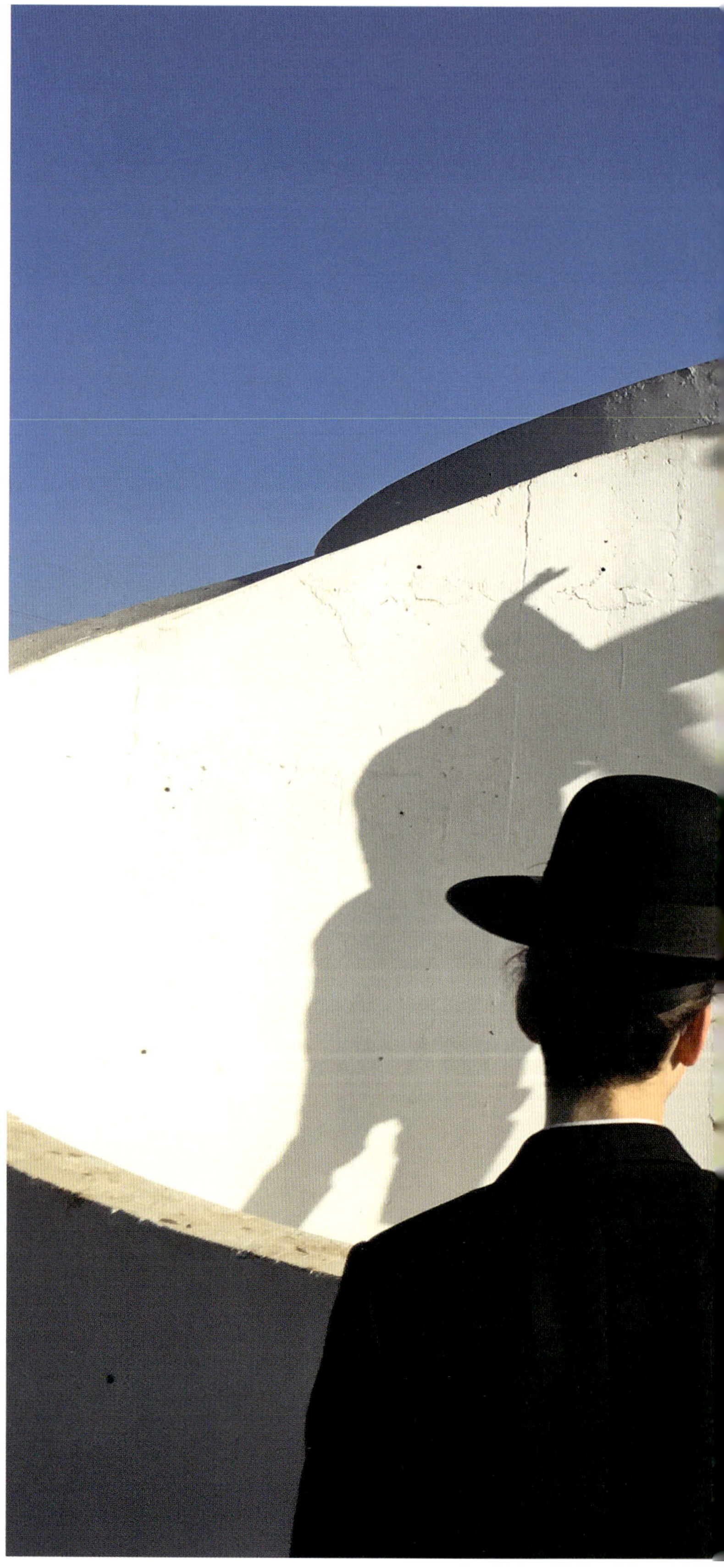

Early one Friday morning, I noticed from far away a group of ultra-Orthodox youth walking in the park. I walked toward them. The contrast was beautiful when they approached the *Serpentine* sculpture and started to climb it for fun; I was there to capture the moment.

*Efrat is a street and documentary photographer working in Israel. She is fascinated by the human experience in all its forms, looking for mankind's interaction within society and culture.*

EFRAT SELA, Israeli

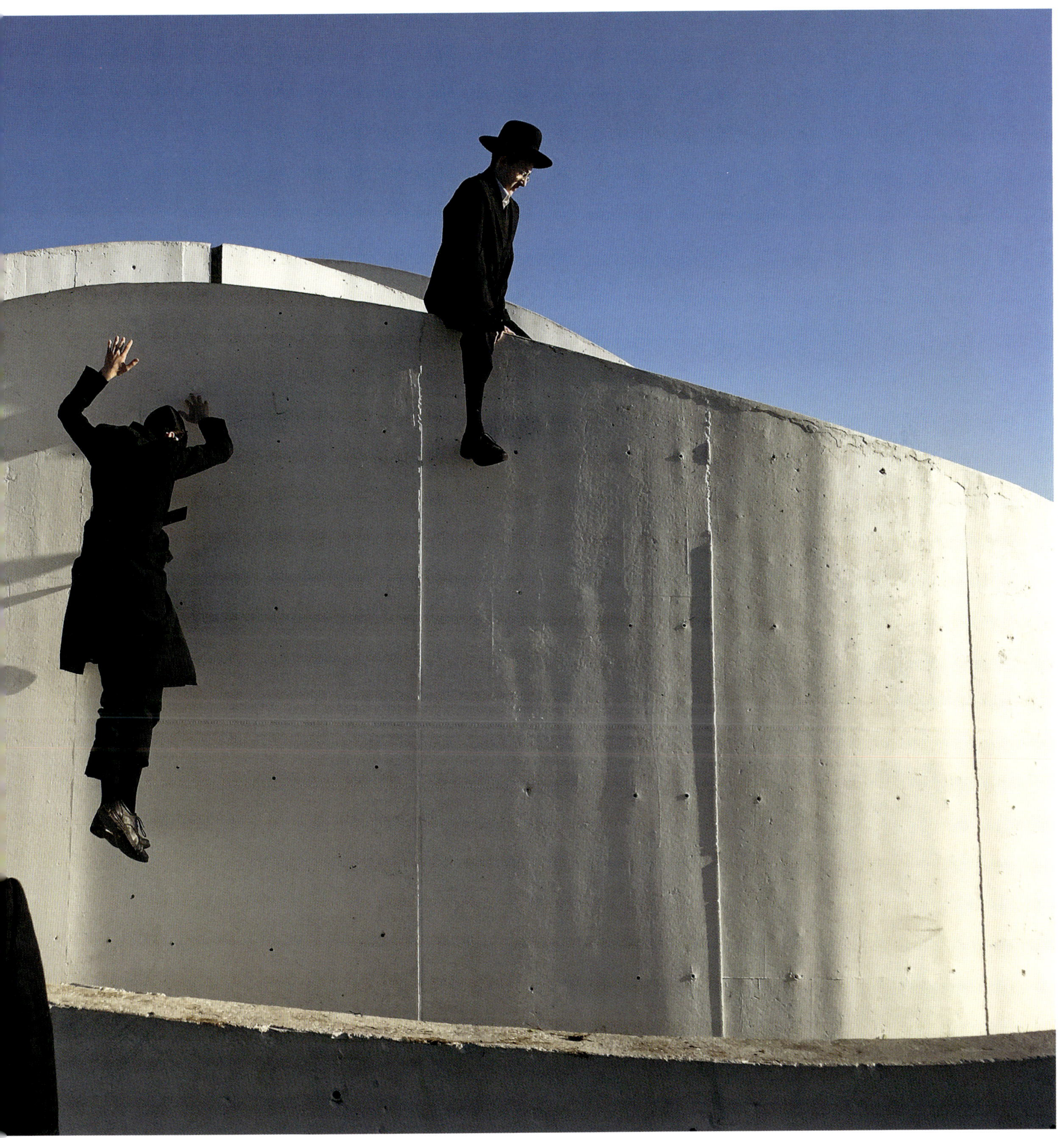

*The Serpentine*, Tel Aviv, Israel, 2017

# 4.

# Graciela Magnoni

This image is part of my series about the Punjabi homeland, on which I have been working since 2014. I saw these Sikh school boys inside a truck while I was driving behind them on a rural road. I was struck by the contrast between the delicacy of their manner, their well-kept uniforms, and the rural aspect of Punjab. I loved the fact that they were not wearing shoes. This could have been a choreographed advertisement for a fancy brand! But in fact it was a candid and spontaneous moment in bucolic Punjab. The boys were driving to a religious festival after school.

*Graciela moved into street photography after working for more than a decade as a press photographer in Brazil and the USA. She is currently working on a long-term project in Punjab on both sides of the Indian/Pakistani border.*

GRACIELA MAGNONI, Uruguayan/French

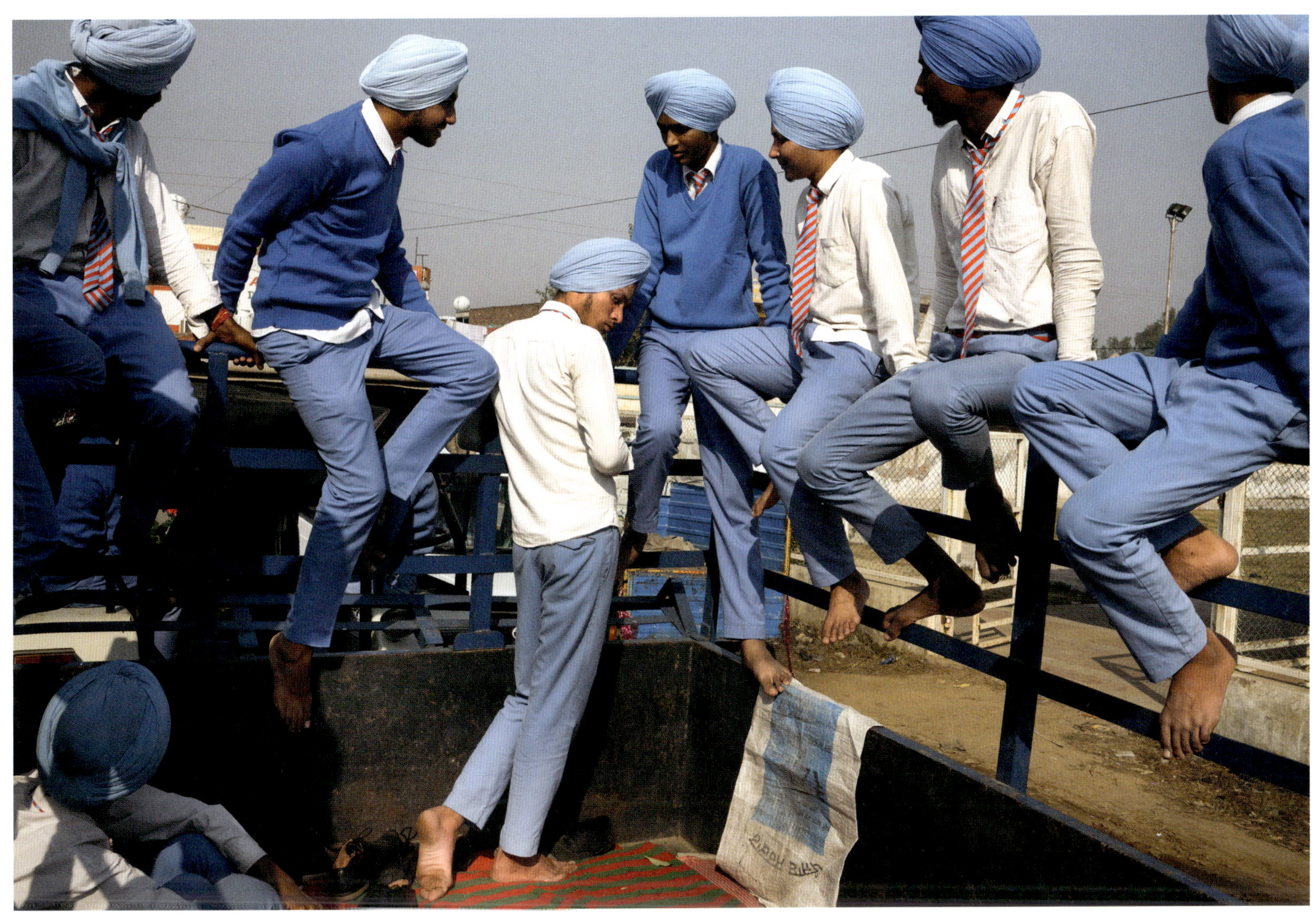

*Untitled*, Punjab, India, 2018

# 5.

# Karine Bizard

The ritual of shaving is one of the thousands of moments
I love to shoot on the banks of the Ganges in Varanasi.

When we made eye contact, I immediately grabbed
my camera. In less than a second he could have moved,
turned his eyes away, or closed them, but he didn't.

He maintained this intense and deep look, as if he were
"accepting the game." As serious, dark, and melancholic
they are, I see a smile in those eyes.

*After practicing as a defense attorney in Paris for thirteen
years, Karine moved into photography in 2017 and continues
to tell human stories.*

KARINE BIZARD, French

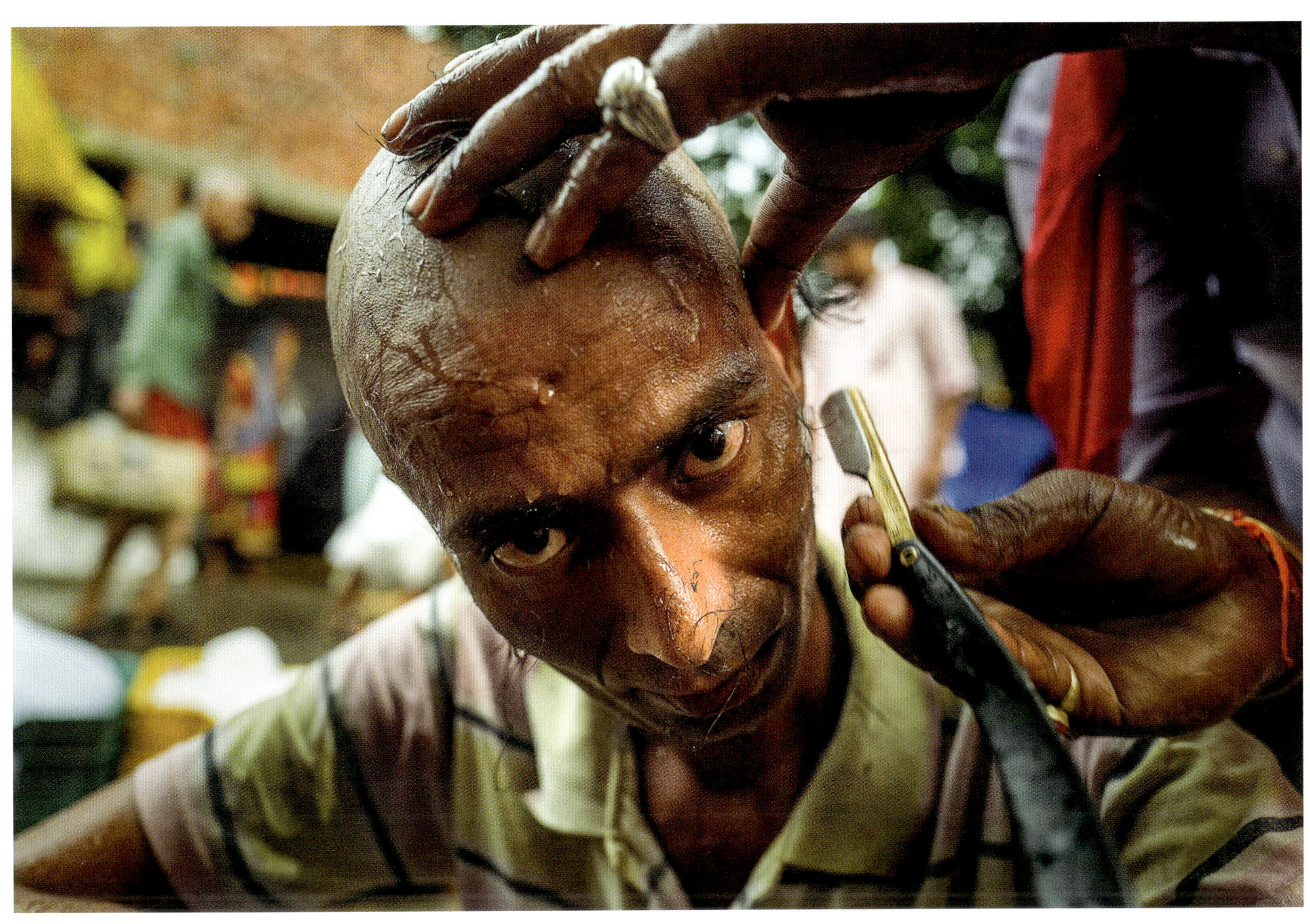

*The Look*, Varanasi, India, 2019

# 6

# Amy Touchette

What does a photographic subject look like? On the street—just like a camera—all you can know of a stranger is their exterior. What you can see is either strong enough to draw you in or too faint to get through to you. It determines the photographable from the unphotographable. Most visual clues on a person suggest their character. On rare occasions like this, such pieces of information suggest a past event. They provide viewers with a space to imagine the person's story and connect with them.

*Amy is a Brooklyn-based photographer who explores themes of social connectedness through street portraiture. Trained at the International Center of Photography, where she now teaches, she is represented by ClampArt in New York City.*

AMY TOUCHETTE, American

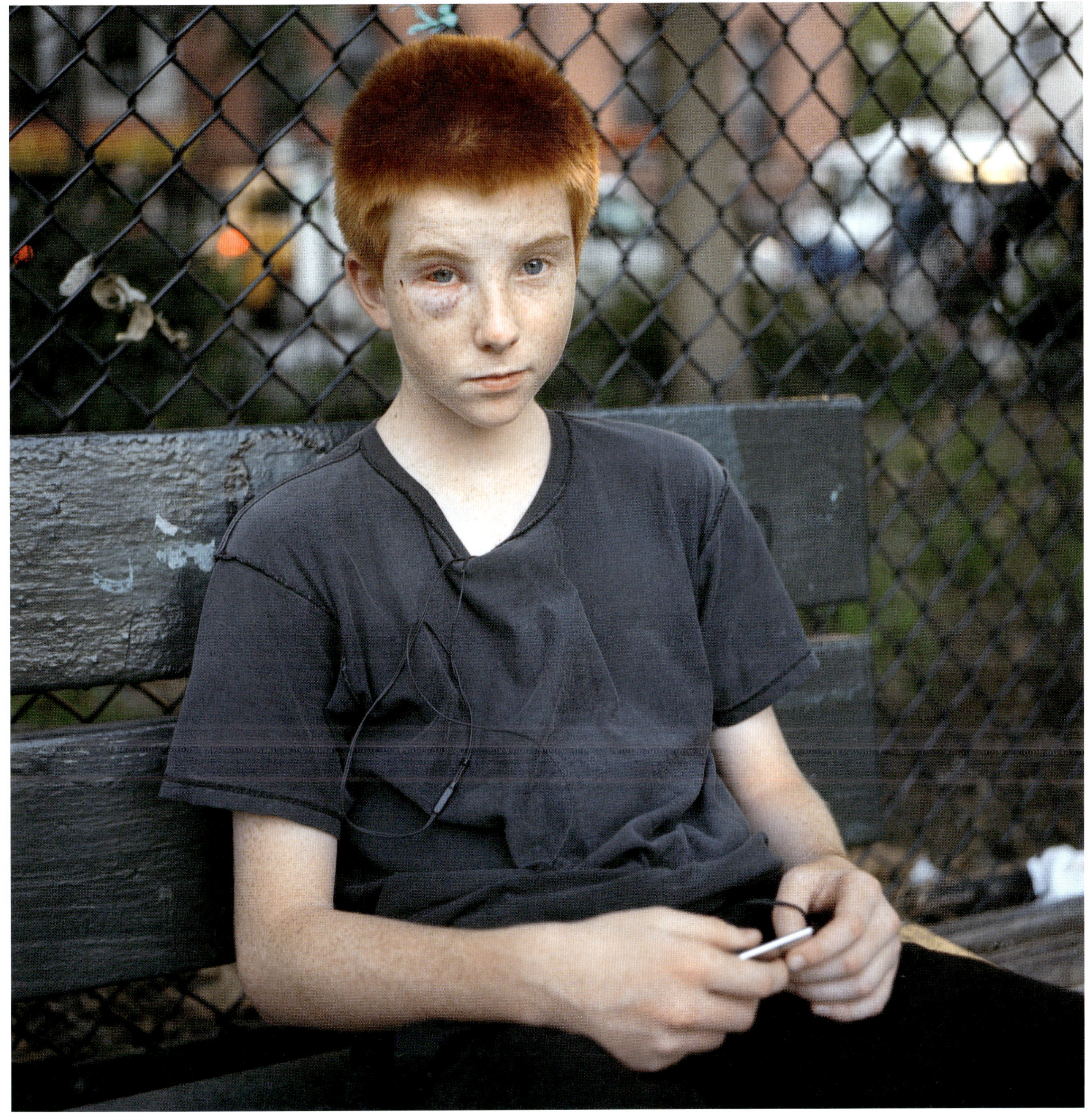

*New York Young, No. 11*, New York City, USA, 2011

# 7

# Suzan Pektas

This photo is part of my *She* series, in which I explore deeper intimate relationships between myself and my subjects. I scrape off their known identities and work with them as anonymous beings. The focus is on the mutual and natural interaction between the object and the subject, the one looked at and the one looking at. They are usually female and in their thirties, which is a special period in which one develops a certain level of maturity. Women can switch between different identities fast while sustaining their integrity. Under a veil of mystery, a unique blend of power and sensibility often defines women. Their body language drags me into a surreal world, feeding my fantasies and dreams. This fascinates me on different levels—a mixture of dreams and reality.

*Suzan is an Istanbul-based independent photographer mostly focusing on the identity of individuals in relation to their environments. Her current projects concentrate primarily on women, urban transformation, and immigration.*

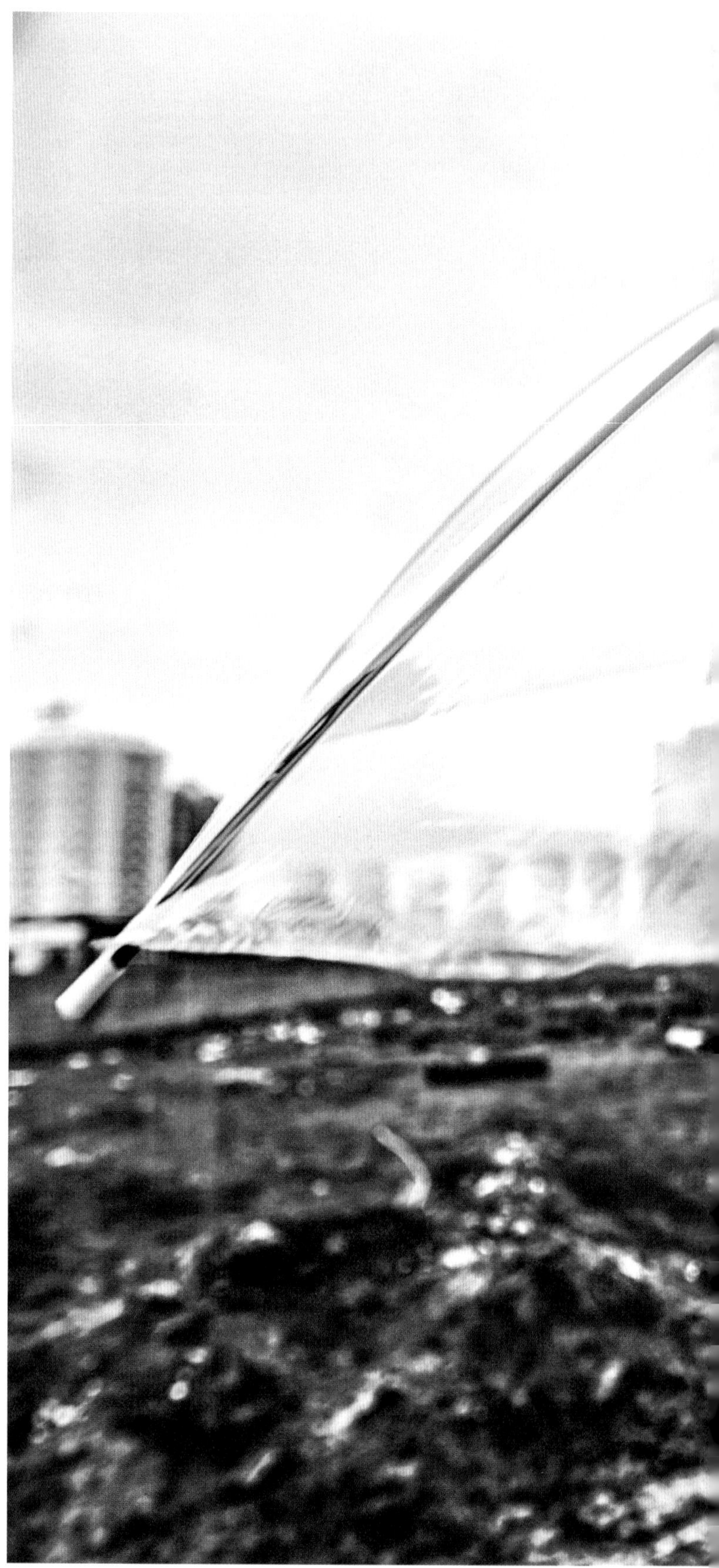

SUZAN PEKTAS, Turkish

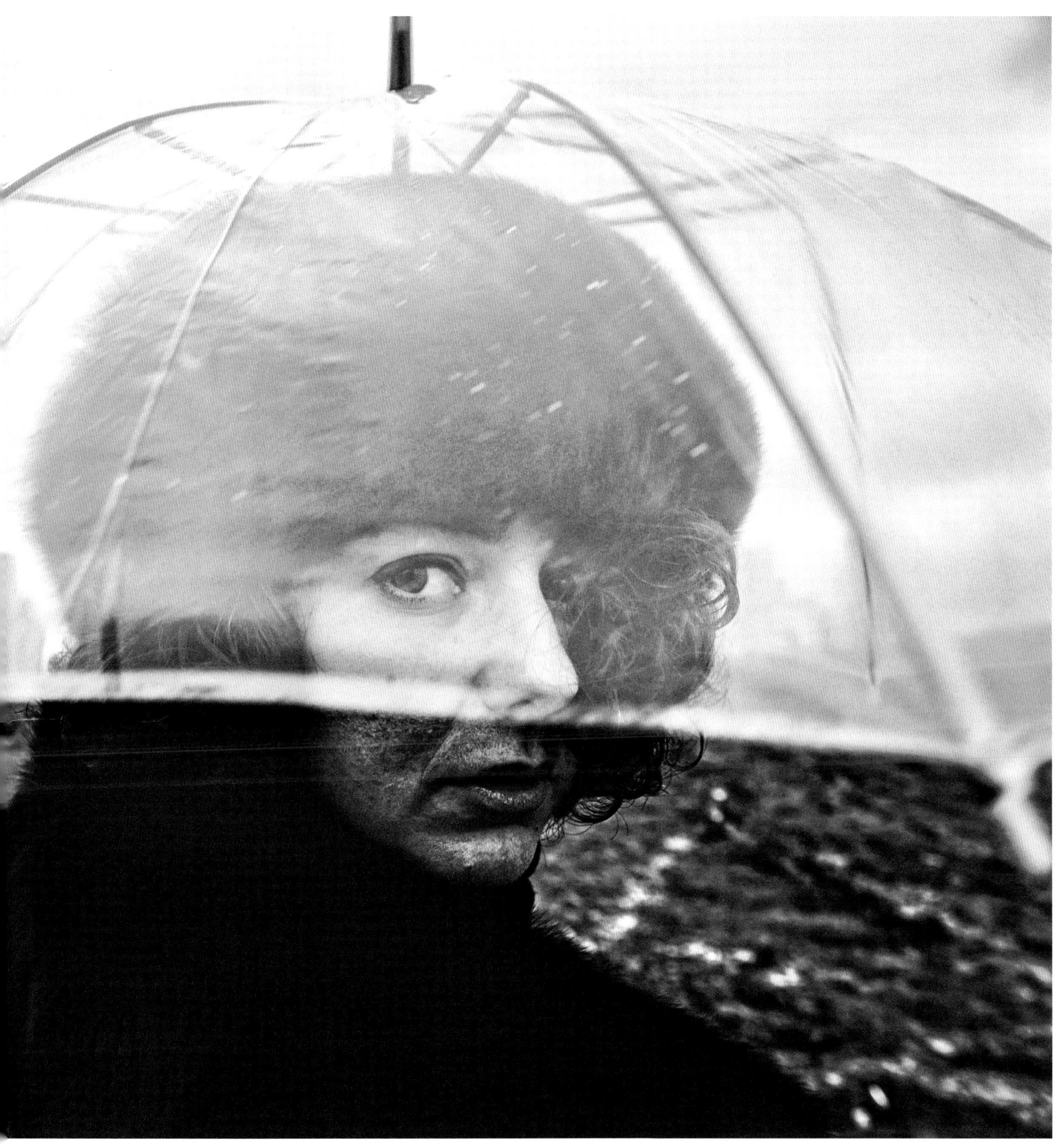

*She*, Istanbul, Turkey, 2018

# 8.

# Nastaran Farjadpezeshk

An elderly woman is crossing an alley in the suburbs. In these areas, the streets are crowded. Old, higher-density buildings still can be found, and even in the summer, flooded pathways catch your eye.

*Nastaran is an electrical engineer who is interested in street photography. She photographs with her mobile phone in the streets of her hometown, Mashhad. Suburban residences and the simple life are her main focus.*

NASTARAN FARJADPEZESHK, Iranian

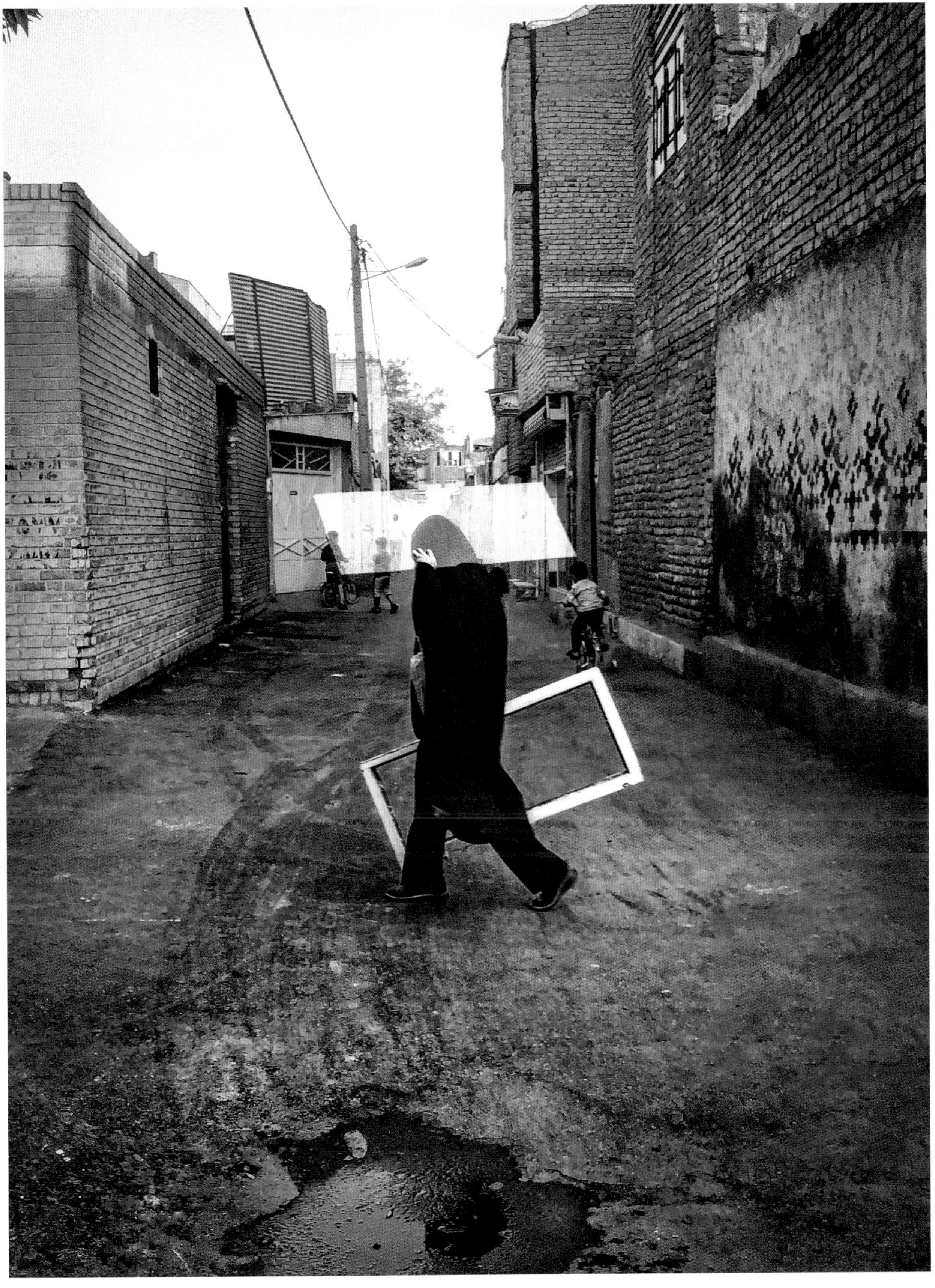

*The Suburban Life*, Mashhad, Iran, 2018

# 9

# Melissa Breyer

One of the side-effects of a being a photographer is observing the world in two dimensions, rather than in the more sensible, three-dimensional way. A similar thing happens when it comes to glass and the tricks of reflection and refraction. Our brain tells us to look right through it, but on the surface of the glass, there is often a strange universe of secret things happening. Such was the case in this photo.

It was taken on a euphoric day in which I found myself in a bistro with my family, sipping a violet mimosa, which added to the Alice in Wonderland mood. I was trying not to be the photographer who is more interested in taking photos than in the people with whom they are spending time. But when this woman behind a glass partition started doubling and twisting before my eyes, I couldn't help but snap a few shots. The beautifully surreal being who emerged made for a photograph that serves as a perfect souvenir of a day that was appropriately swirled with happiness.

*Melissa is a writer and award-winning photographer whose work has been featured in* National Geographic *and the* New York Times.

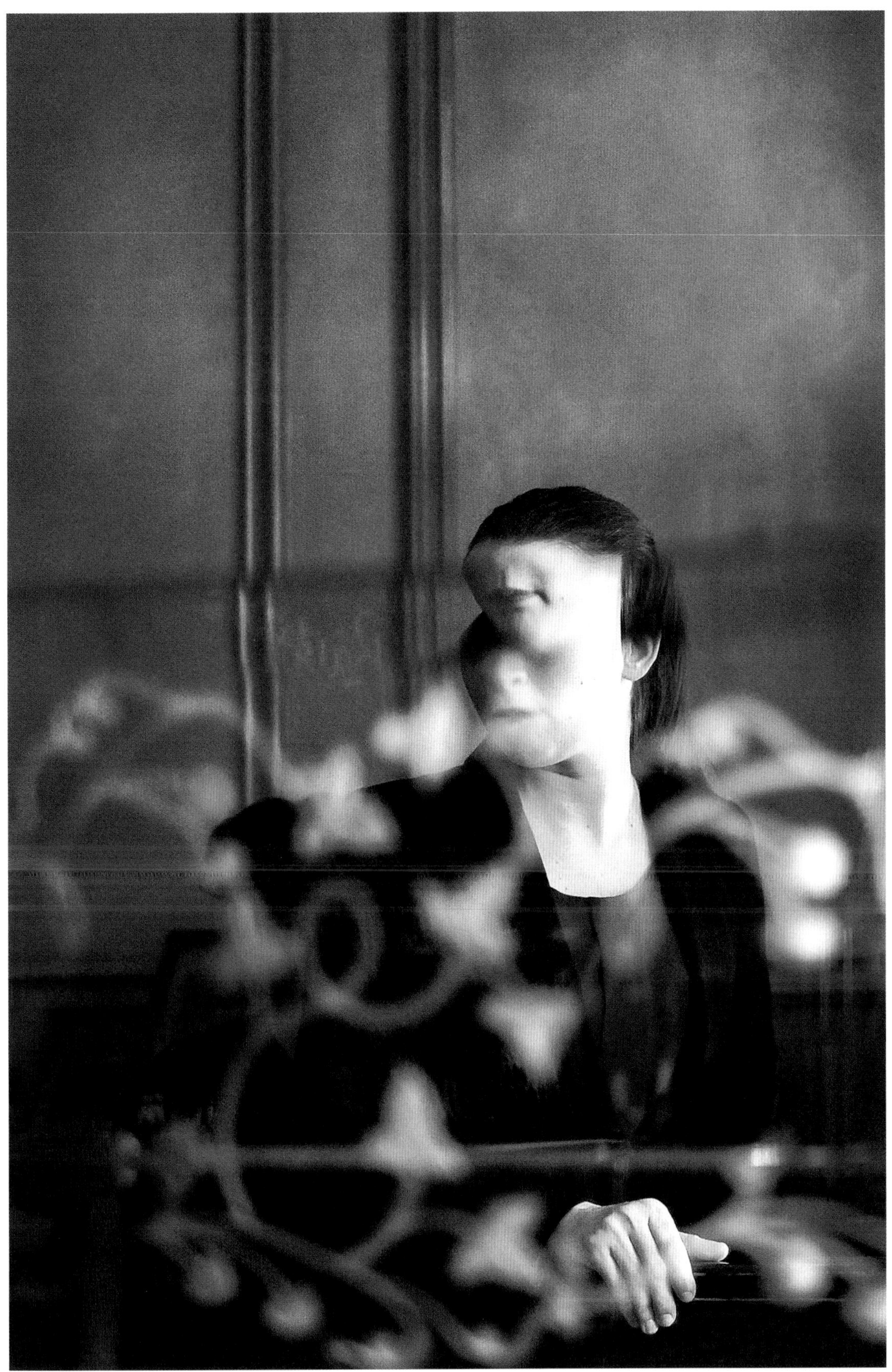

*Untitled*, Yountville, California, USA, 2017

# 10

# Melissa O'Shaughnessy

When I go out to shoot on the streets of New York City, I rarely set out with any plans or preconceived notions about what I might encounter, yet this photograph was taken at a spot on Manhattan's far West Side that I returned to again and again over the course of several weeks. I have dozens of shots of people coming and going through the revolving door, but it was this man, of the perfect height and with the just-right gesture, who gave me the photograph I wanted.

Certainly, with its bright color, architectural geometry, and solitary figure, the image has all the makings of Instagram catnip. But this everyman—a man of average height and build that the architects clearly had in mind when etching that perfect circle in the door—becomes a touch extraordinary in this moment, caught in a yellow capsule of a door in a split-second capsule of time.

*Melissa is a photographer based in New York City. Her first monograph,* Perfect Strangers: New York City Street Photographs, *was published by Aperture in 2020.*

MELISSA O'SHAUGHNESSY, American

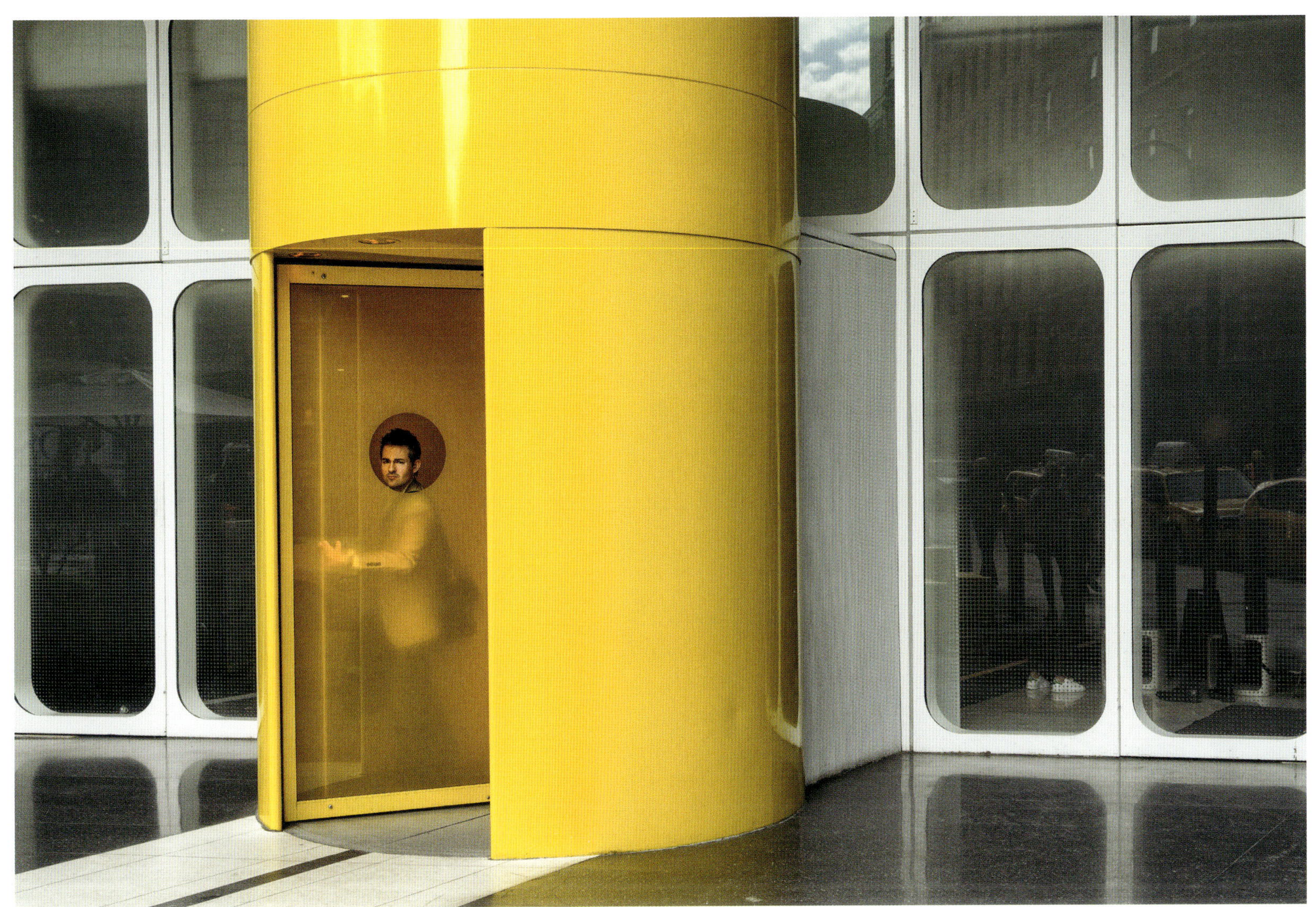

*Washington Street, New York, 2015*, New York City, USA, 2015

# Karolina Trapp

My current hometown is pretty much your typical northern city, so I am strongly attracted to colorful buildings of the warmer regions whenever I have the chance to travel. I saw this underground parking lot entrance on Pershing Square in Los Angeles. It was a sunny day and there were strong contrasts. I was immediately struck by the light, color, and form, and captured a human silhouette almost lost in that vibrant architectural quandary of squares that make a circle.

*Karolina is an award-winning street photographer based in Seattle, USA. She is fascinated by color, form, and movement.*

KAROLINA TRAPP, Polish

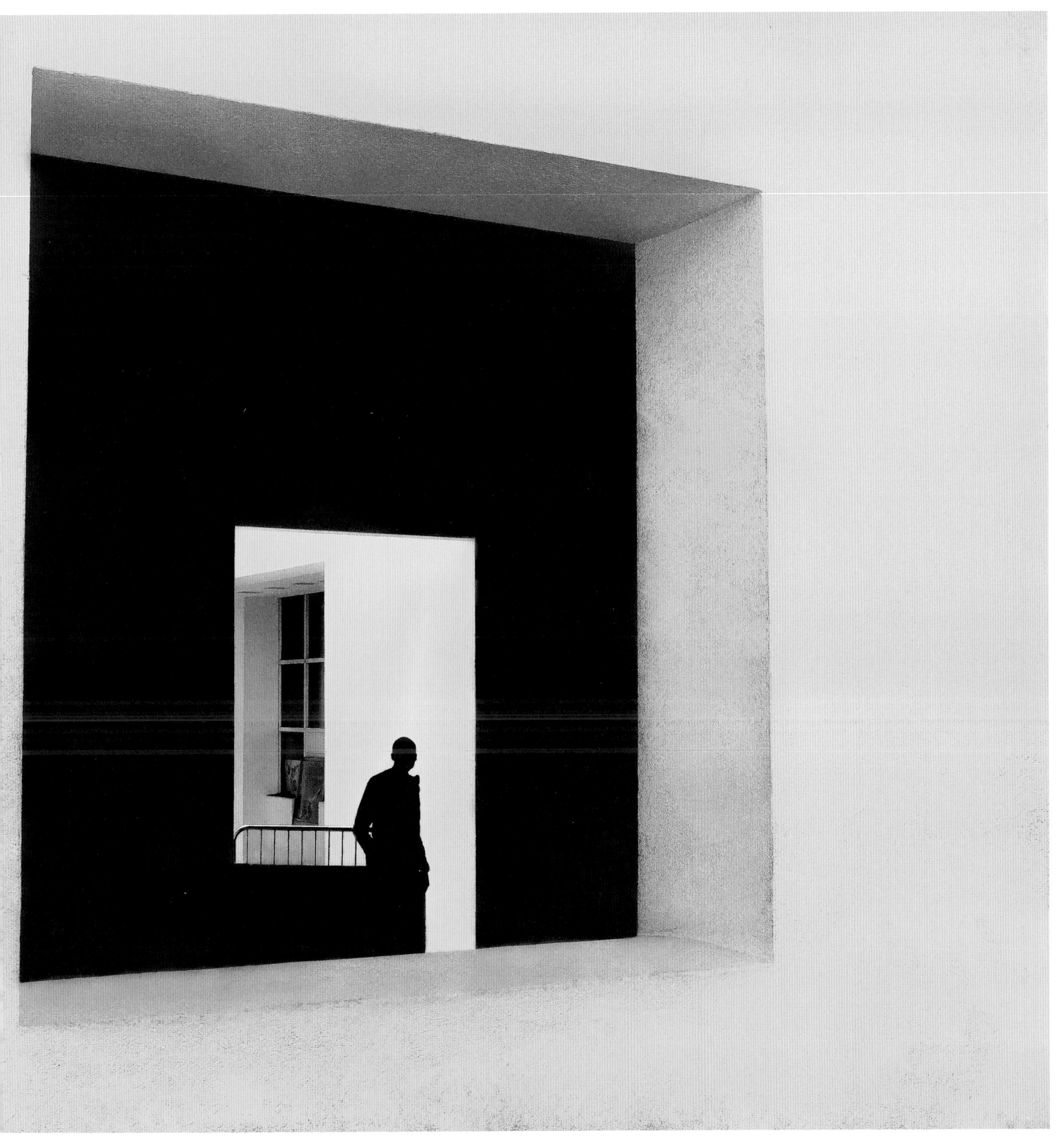

*Squaring the Circle*, Los Angeles, USA, 2017

# Betty Goh

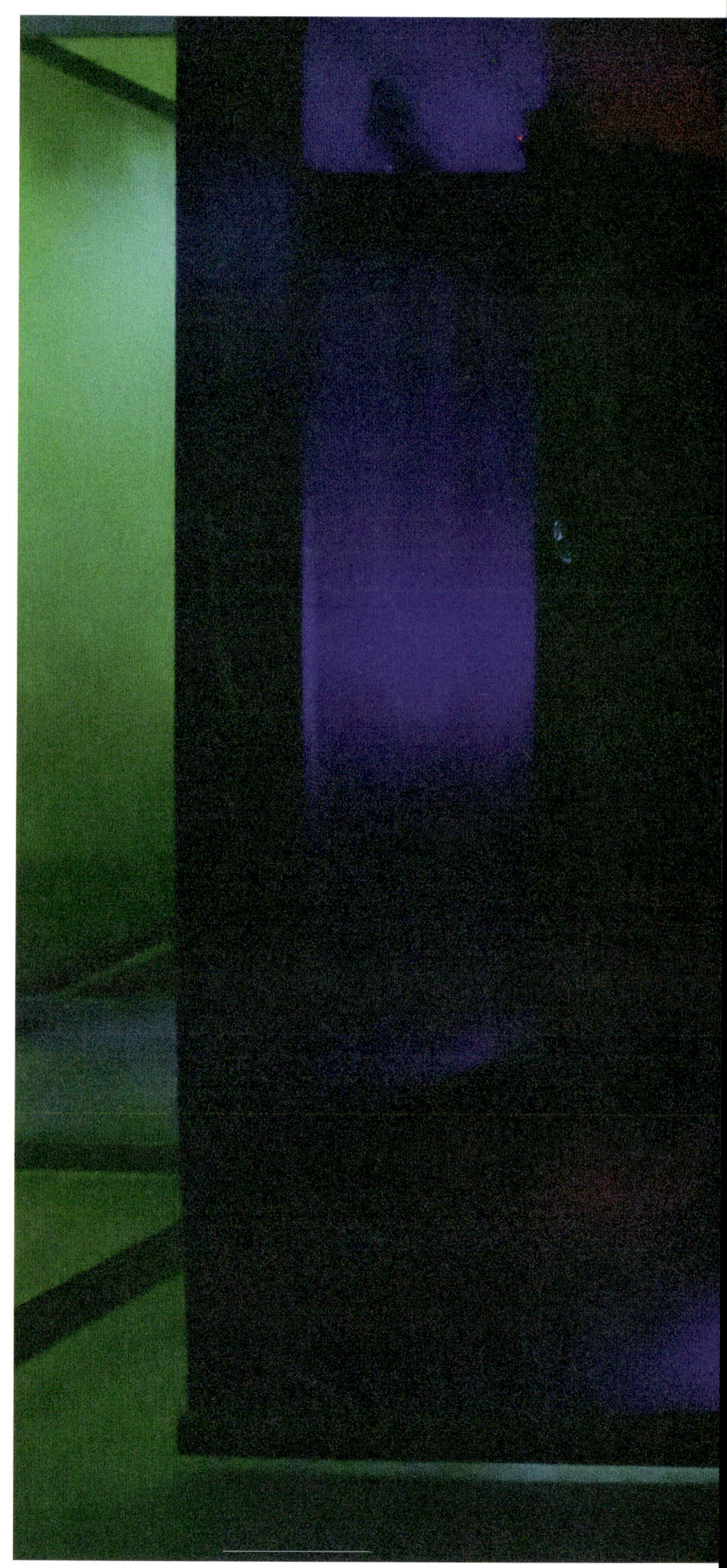

I was at a museum that had a plastic display which looked like a maze. A man was walking through it and I noticed that the reflections were amazing. My favorite parts are the crease lines that fall on the man, and a mysterious reflection of the same man on the left side of the picture.

*Betty's passion is abstract street photography, focusing on urban streets, colors, graphics, reflections, shadows, silhouettes, and lines.*

BETTY GOH, Singaporean

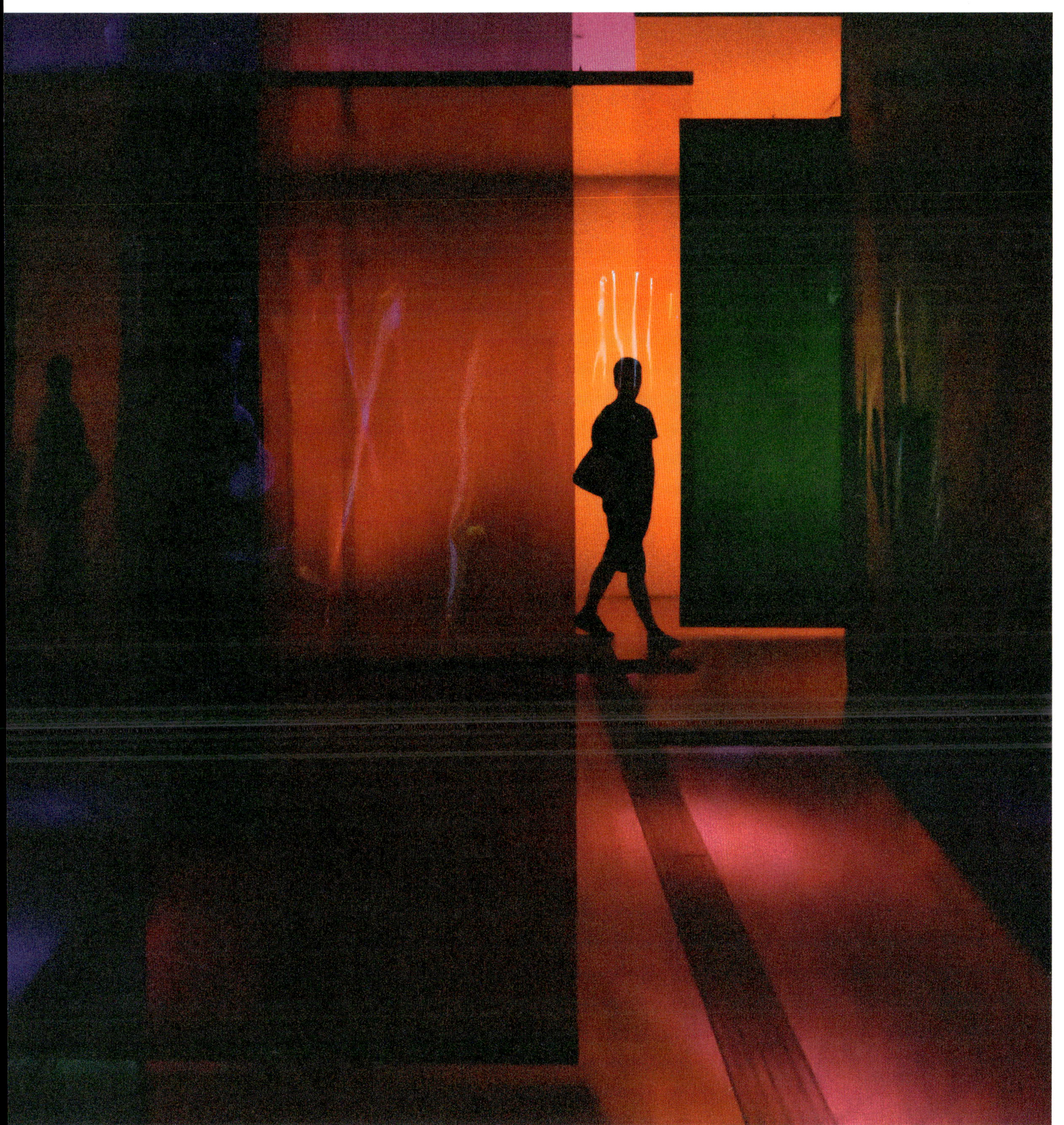

*The Maze*, Singapore, 2018

# 13.

# Kimboid

The humans that surround me on public transport all have their own stories, and I wonder if they realize that the choices that our government makes at every level are shaping their world.

I arrive at a station where I need to change trains. It's busy and people rush in all directions. Rather than be crushed by the impatience, I wait and take photos of the train departing, as it calms my mind. This is my world.

I notice the woman standing near me and move to get a clear shot as the train approaches. The reflection of the passing train lights up her face and casts shadows on those surrounding her. It's all over within a few seconds and I wonder how little these moments are noticed by those around me.

I love this image. It has frozen a moment that I see daily, people seemingly struggling within their own thoughts as they are surrounded by others. They are strangers to each other, yet more alike than they can imagine.

*Kimboid is a Melbourne-based photographer whose work has been exhibited globally. Her images focus on capturing dramatic scenes of commuters.*

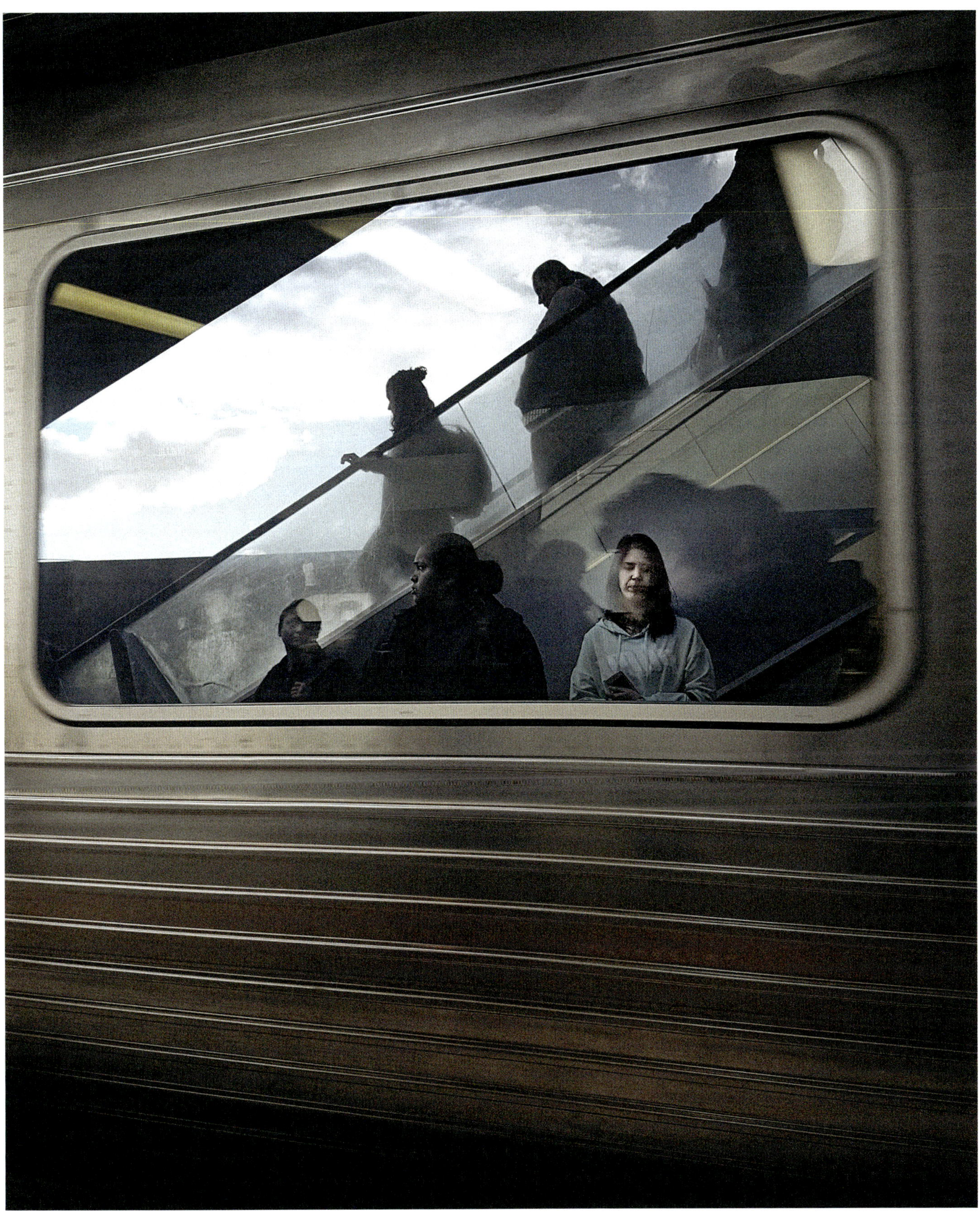

*No One*, Melbourne, Australia, 2019

# 14.

# Farnaz Damnabi

When I was on my way home from work, this scene—women taking naps on public transportation—attracted my attention.

*Farnaz was born in Tehran, Iran. After graduating university in graphic design, she chose to allocate more time to photography. She is a freelance photographer who likes to pay special attention to women's feelings and situations.*

FARNAZ DAMNABI, Iranian

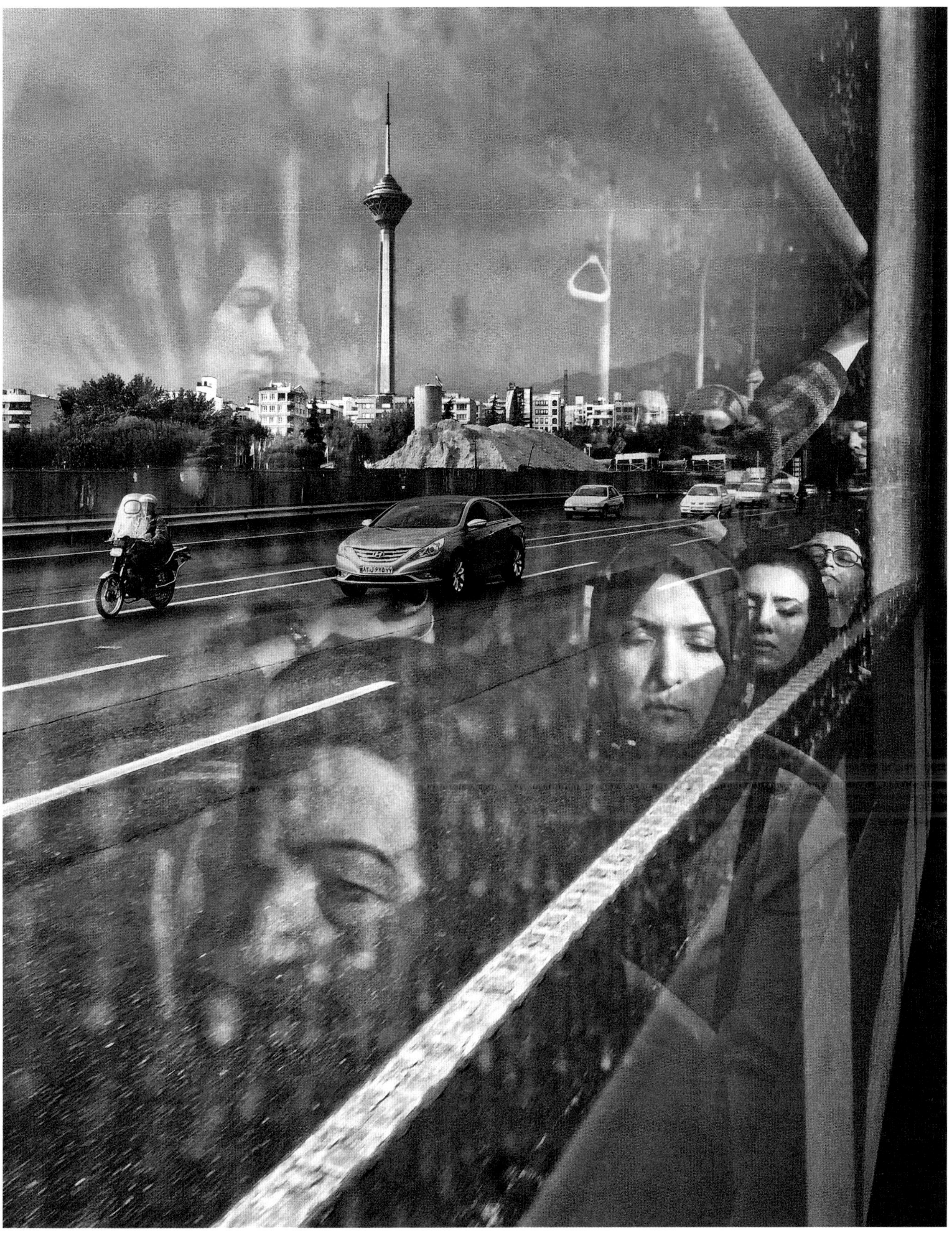

*Loneliness*, Tehran, Iran, 2019

# 15

# Marina Sersale

I was out trying to improve my skills with a DSLR camera and decided to take some photos inside a museum in the EUR neighborhood in Rome. At the cashier's counter this young woman was selling tickets. I started shooting with the camera but then switched to the iPhone as I find it much easier to use. As expected, my best shot was with the iPhone.

*Based in Rome, Marina began taking photographs in 2013, when she bought her first iPhone and started posting on Instagram. Since 2015, her work has been shown in galleries and at photography festivals worldwide.*

MARINA SERSALE, Italian

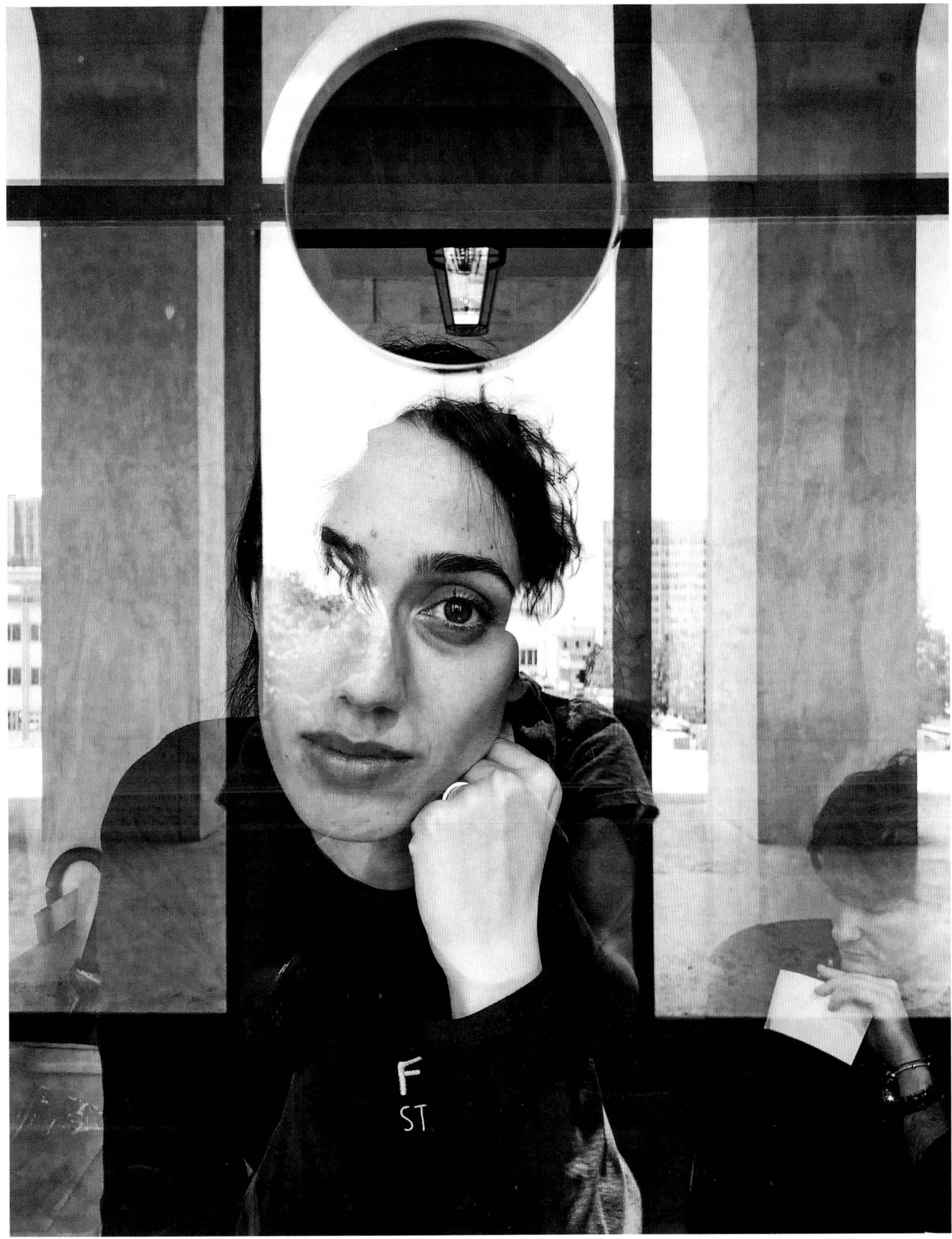

*Untitled*, Rome, Italy, 2018

# 16

# Florence Oliver

Nightfall. The departure is announced.

Those luminous golden lines are about to move and to accelerate. A woman on a nearby train lights me up with a smile.

I like these moments when a small abstraction hides in the reflections and creates a story.

I was a painter at first, then moved on to photography, mainly using my iPhone. As a lover of reflections, I am moved by the abstraction they give to the eye. It is a real joy and a challenge to explore their complexity, their vagueness, until I find the fragile resonance of an emotion.

*Florence started her career as a painter. Now she explores reflections and abstraction with her smartphone. Her work has emerged through Instagram.*

FLORENCE OLIVER, French

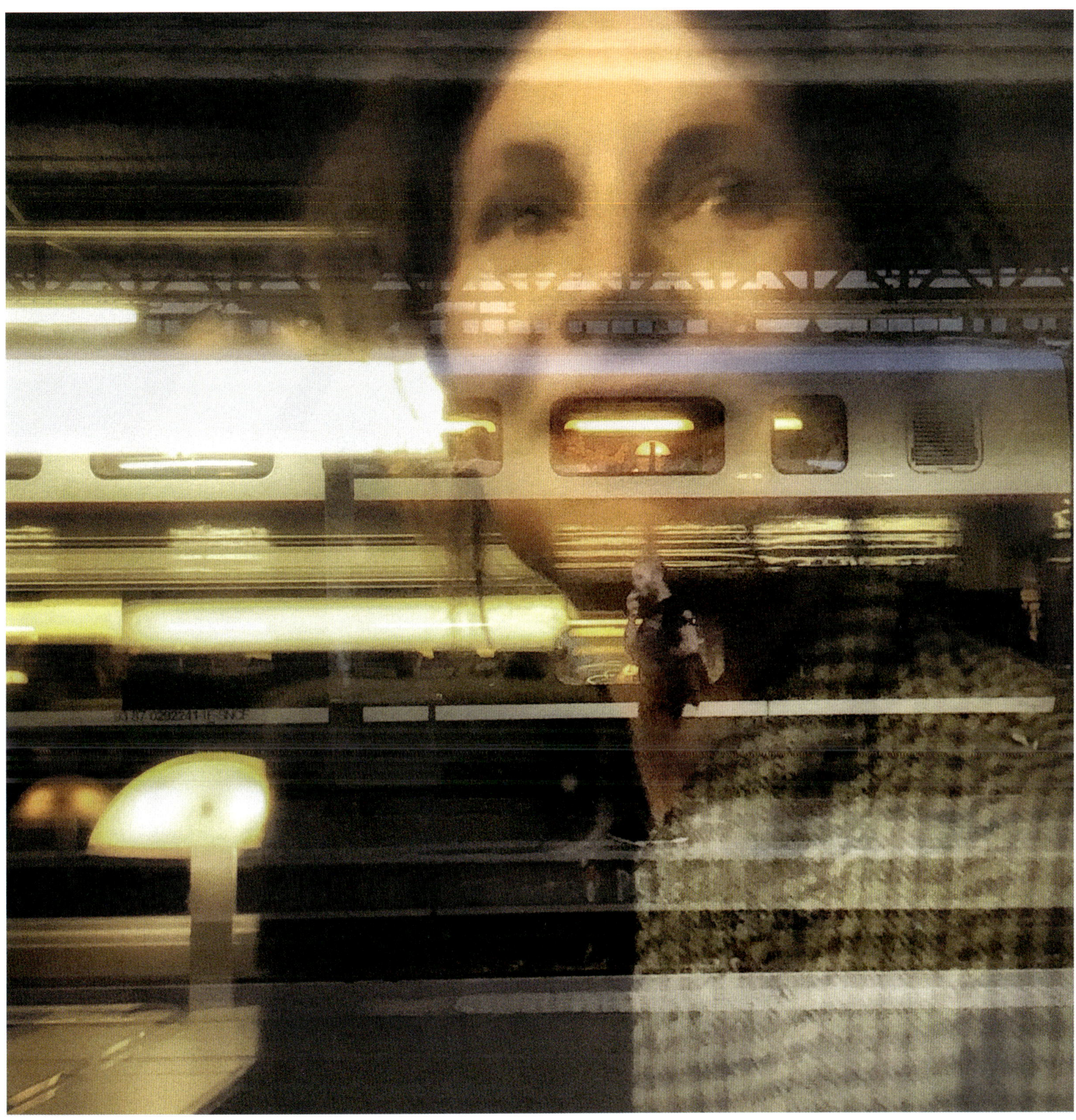

*Gare de Lyon*, Paris, France, 2018

# 17

# Catherine
# Le Scolan-Quéré

This image was taken in 2015 at Sealdah station, Kolkata, in the state of West Bengal, India. Many taxi drivers were parked in front of the station in their yellow Ambassadors. I felt lost in the middle of all these vehicles. The light was not as I would have liked, but the framing suited me, and I locked eye contact with this man. His look told me that I could take the picture, so I did. Then I lost this photograph and found it again two years later. I thought it was one of the strongest images I had taken in this fascinating city.

*Catherine is a doctor based in Rennes. In photography, as in her professional life, it's the human that interests her: human life and emotion in color on the street.*

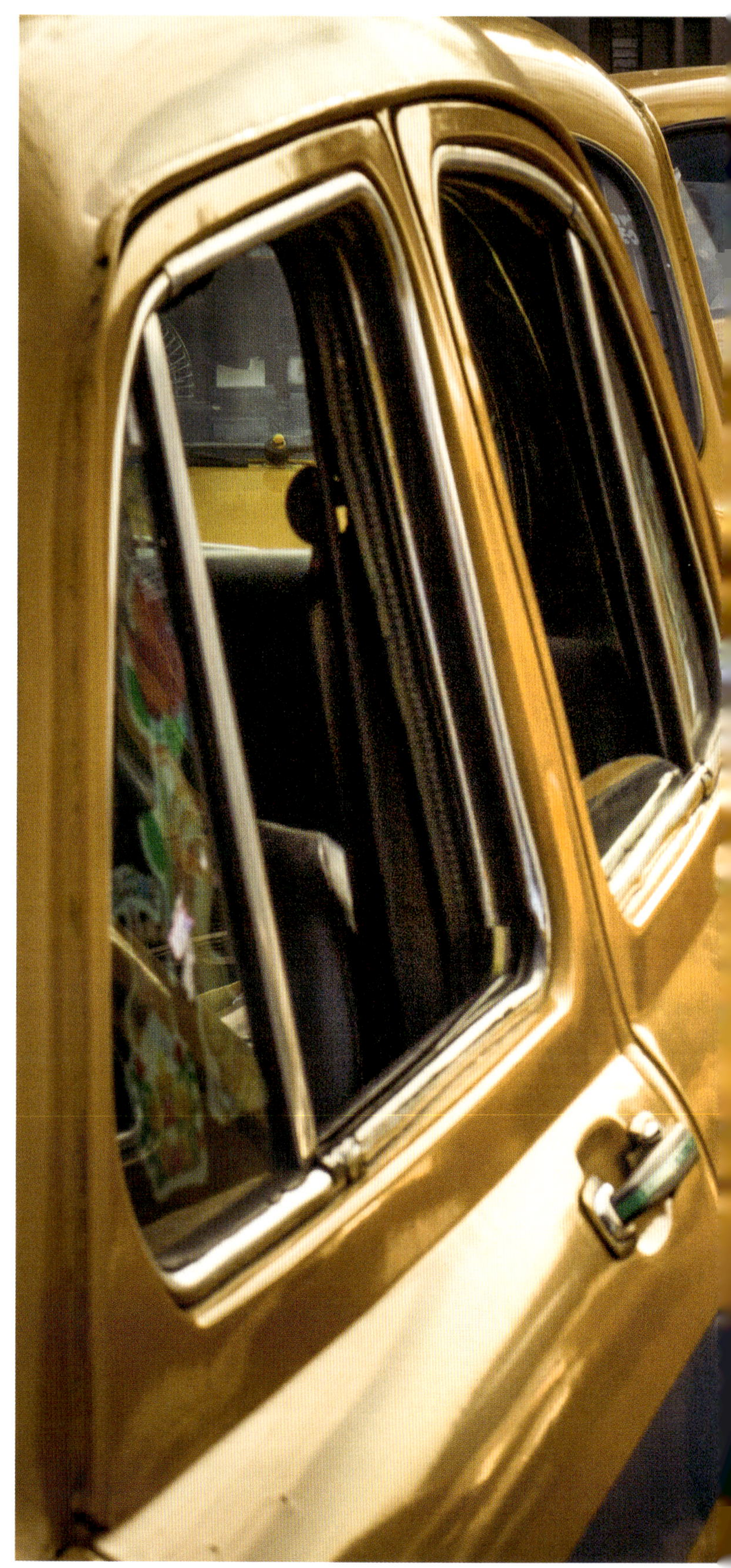

CATHERINE LE SCOLAN-QUÉRÉ, French

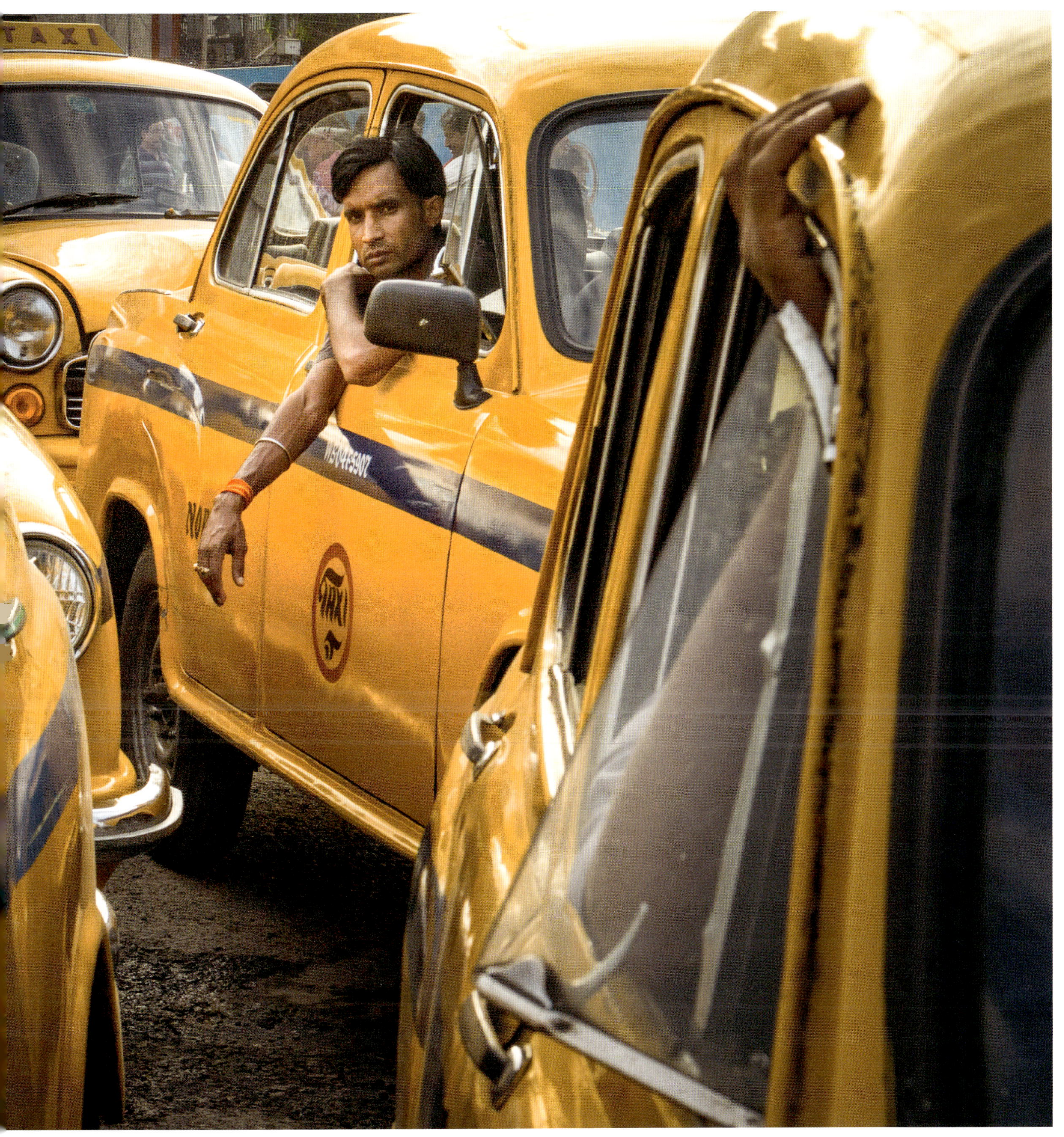

*Taxi Driver, Kolkata*, Kolkata, India, 2015

# 18

# Annu Esko

It was a grey and very rainy day in Vladimir. As I walked through the streets, nothing was happening. Suddenly a yellow bus passed by. A woman sitting on the bus looked at me through the steamy window. The bus was driving very fast and I thought the moment was gone, but then I saw it stopping at some traffic lights. I started to run and reached the bus. The woman wiped steam from the window to see me better and put her hand against the window to say hello. I took the picture, we smiled at each other to say goodbye, the bus set off and she was gone.

That small moment with her meant a lot to me. I felt she was my friend. I will never forget her and our meeting.

*Annu gradually moved into street photography after a long career as a dentist in Helsinki. Her work has been featured at several exhibitions worldwide, in Kuala Lumpur, New York, Paris, Trieste, Brussels, and Sydney, among others.*

ANNU ESKO, Finnish

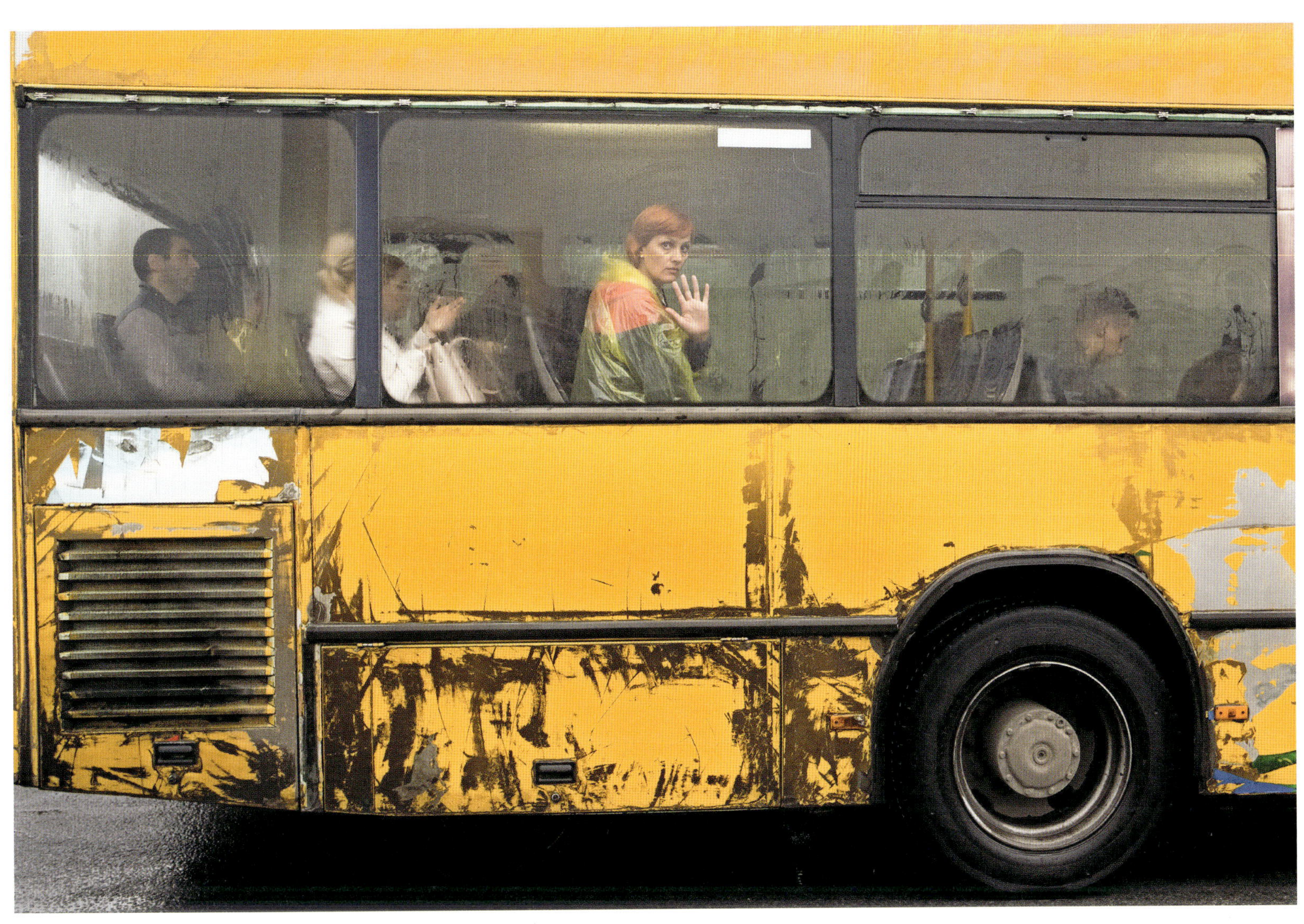

*Untitled*, Vladimir, Russia, 2019

# 19.

# Emily Garthwaite

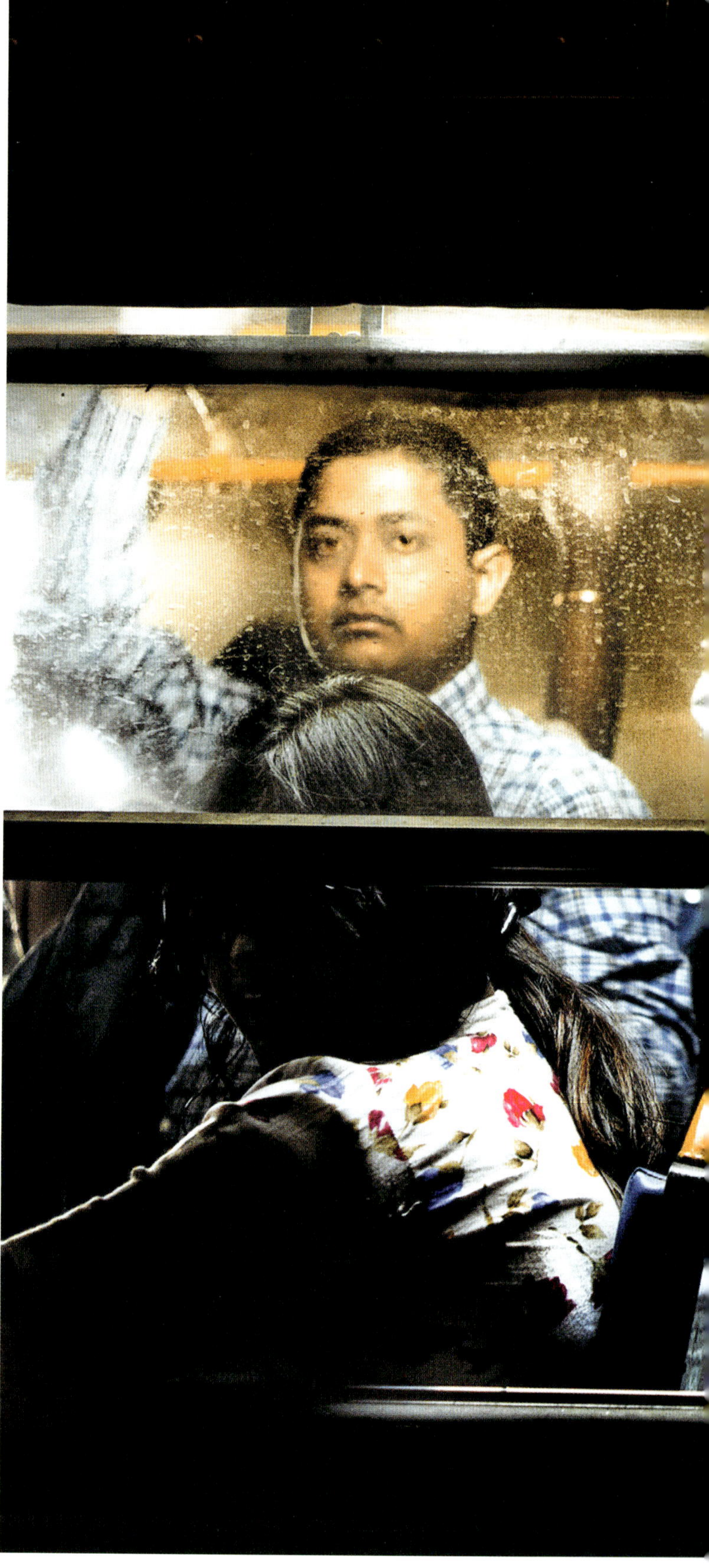

It was almost 7pm and I watched bus after bus filled
with commuters leave the terminal in Kolkata. Some
were happier than others. I must have stayed there
almost an hour waiting for an interesting character,
the right lighting, the right look. This ended up being
the shot.

*Emily is a photojournalist based in Iraq, focusing on
humanitarian and environmental issues.*

EMILY GARTHWAITE, British

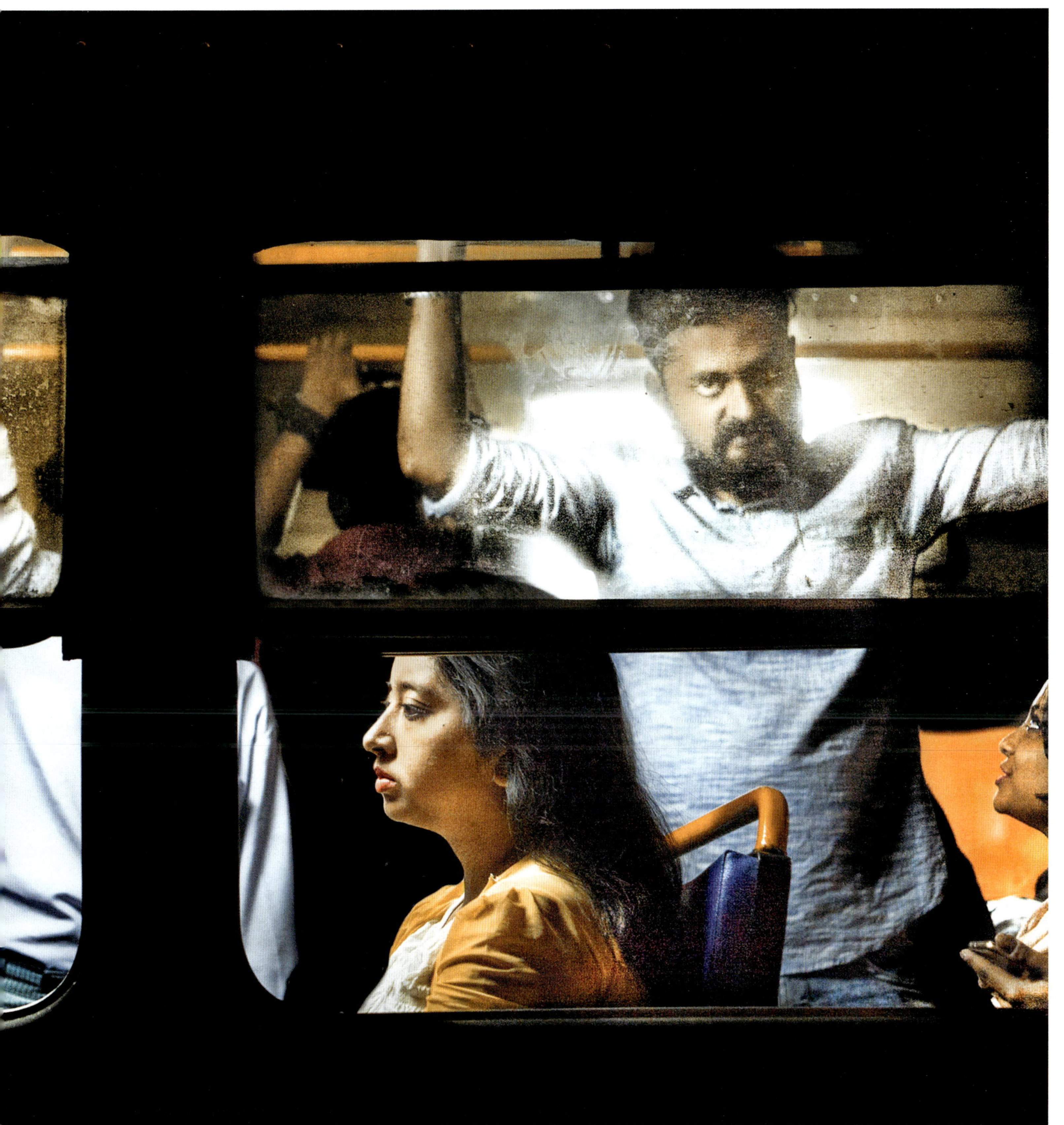

*A Night Bus in Kolkata, India*, Kolkata, India, 2017

# 20

# Elena Alexandra

The night I took this photograph, I felt very sad. My head and heart were full of dark feelings and thoughts. In the gloom, I noticed the girl in red sleeping. Her clothing was so vibrant. Something inside me said very quietly:

"What if you take a picture?"

"I can't. I don't even have the energy to hold my camera."

"Take a picture!"

"If the other passengers notice me, I won't have the energy to explain myself."

"Take a picture!"

Weeks later, this photo became my best known, and gave me the encouragement to push through the tough times. It is a reminder to trust the voice of my real self in my darkest moments. To live authentically and courageously, no matter how lost and powerless I may feel. To know that I am loveable and loved by the universe that gave me this reminder I am now sharing with you.

*Elena's images reflect her experience of deep interconnection with the world surrounding her. Besides her street photography, she works as a researcher and a psychotherapist.*

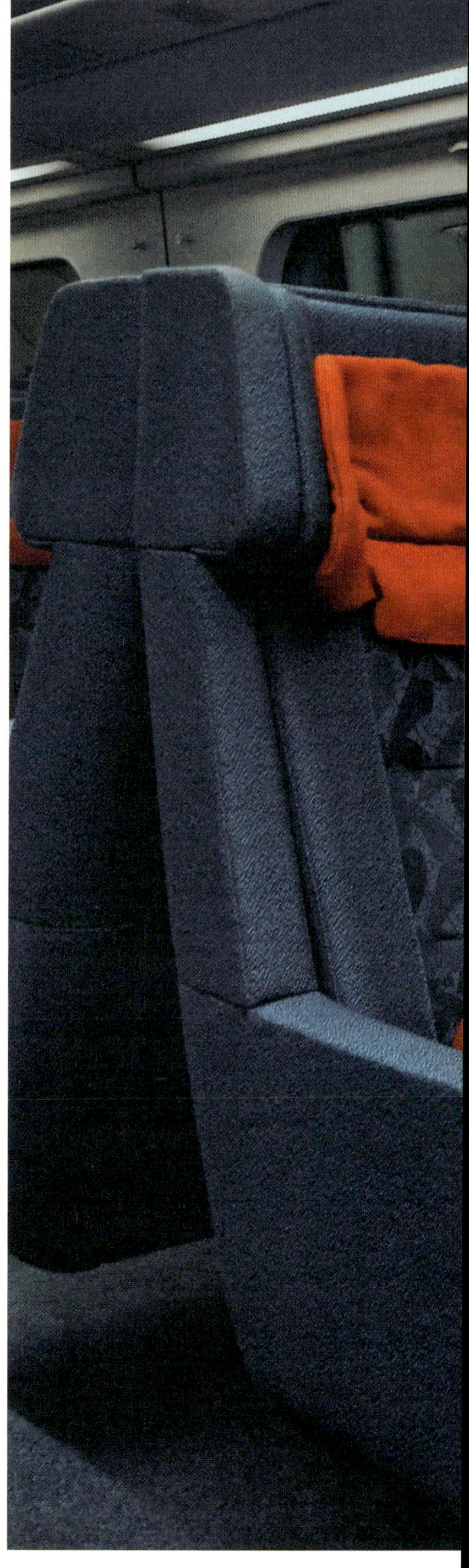

ELENA ALEXANDRA, Russian

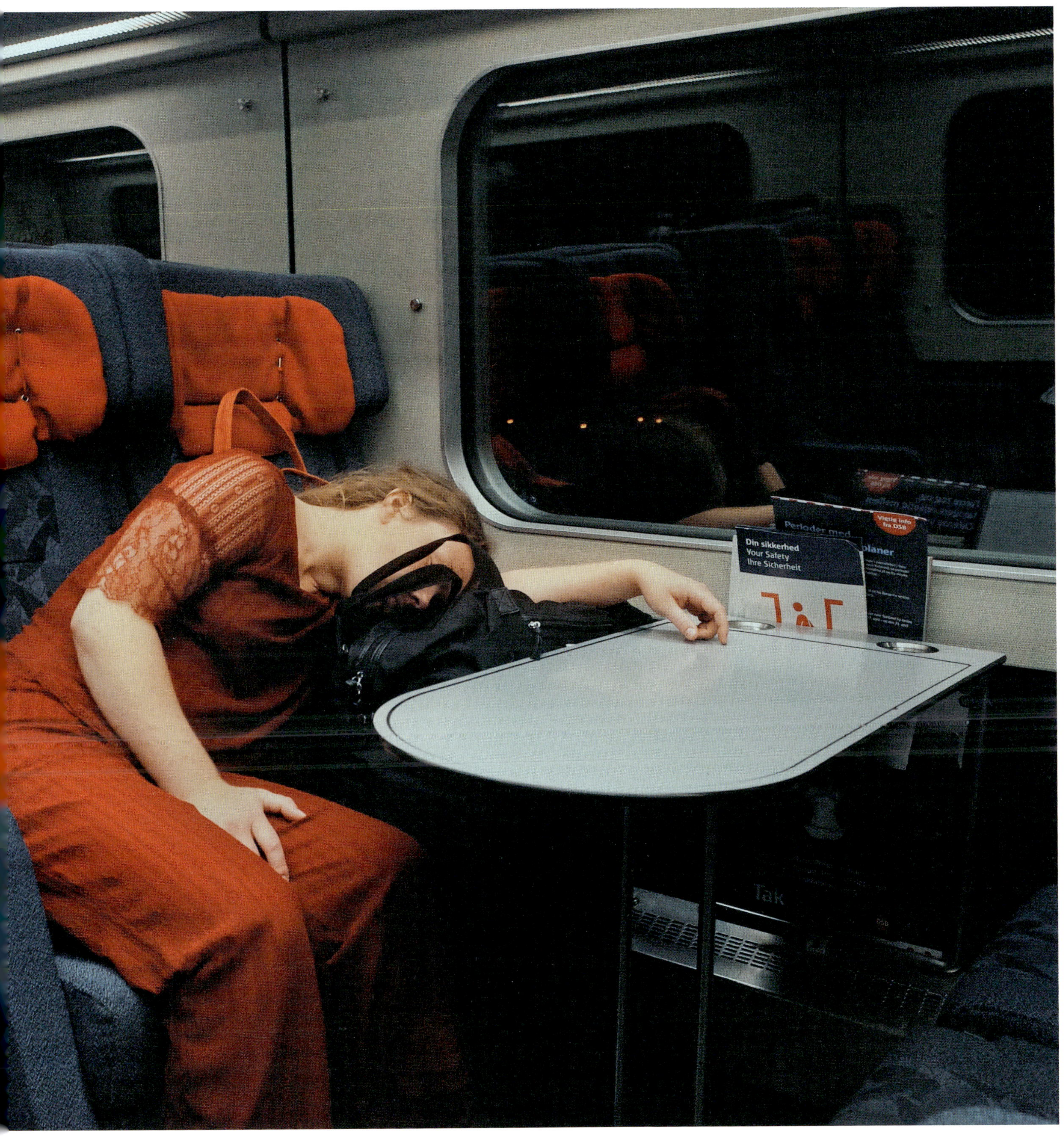

*Sleeping Beauty*, Odense, Denmark, 2019

# Emily Sujay Sanchez

I found this gentleman at the end of the train platform at the Graham Ave. station in Brooklyn, NY.

His expression drew me in because it seemed like the type of sadness we all experience but reserve for our private moments and spaces. To me it was a beautiful public display of vulnerability.

*Documentary and street photographer Emily Sanchez tells emotional stories through her raw and compelling images highlighting life in black and brown communities.*

EMILY SUJAY SANCHEZ, Dominican American

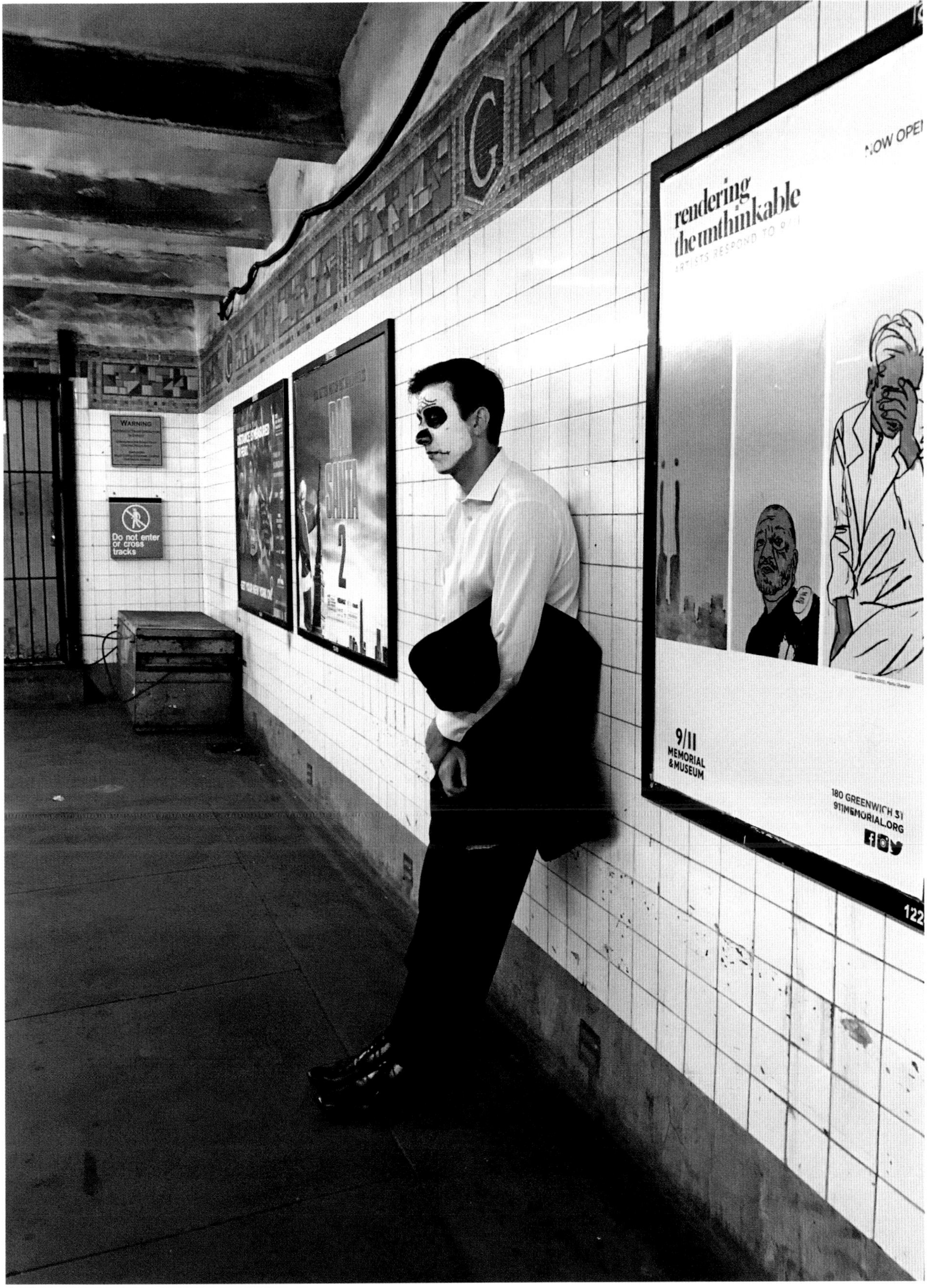


*Untitled*, Brooklyn, New York City, USA, 2016

# Dimpy Bhalotia

I have a natural predilection for capturing unpredictable, larger-than-life moments that lend visual and emotional excitement to my photographs. To me, street photography is my visual lexicon. It doesn't hide behind a smokescreen, but is the truth of what is happening around us. I love capturing these scenes in black-and-white, which is the most decluttered version of my world.

Being present in the moment is a core component of street photography that resonates strongly for me. I strive to make that state of mind contagious, encouraging my viewers to step back from technology to appreciate their lived experience and spread the message of hope, love, energy, and freedom through my photographs. This photograph is one of many I have built out of frames that come from the streets of the world.

*Dimpy is an award-winning fine art street photographer and hodophile based in London. Her work has received much acclaim and won her numerous prestigious awards.*

DIMPY BHALOTIA, Indian

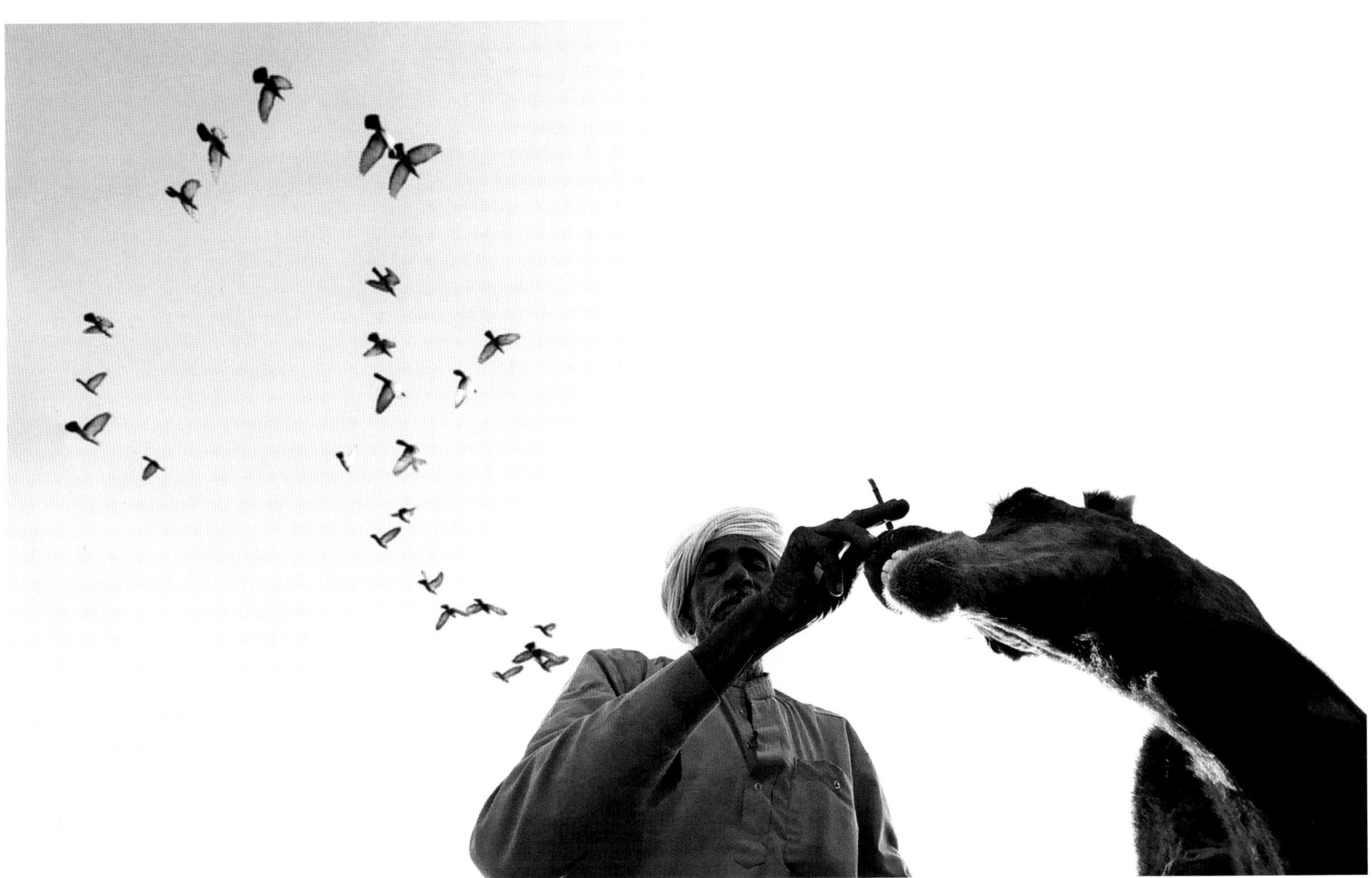

*Shoulder Birds*, Pushkar, India, 2018

# 24

# Polly Rusyn

The procession I had been walking with suddenly stopped and I observed how part of the scene in front of me was in the shade, providing me with more of the silhouettes I'd already been photographing. I noticed the boy on the horse in the sun, and was beginning to feel there was potential for a picture. When I saw the woman in traditional dress I moved behind her to include her in the scene. Things weren't right yet—the silhouettes were overlapping, the horse was looking out of the frame, and the woman was facing forward. I had all the ingredients I needed, but just had to see if they would come together.

I still remember the feeling of excitement in knowing time was limited, along with the anticipation of what might happen. I was fully in the moment. To my amazement the horse turned to look straight at me! I got goosebumps; then at that precise instant the woman looked to the left, and the silhouettes separated. The serendipity of the moment made me hit the shutter, and I knew I had a picture that couldn't be replicated.

*Polly is a professional photographer with a passion for teaching street photography.*

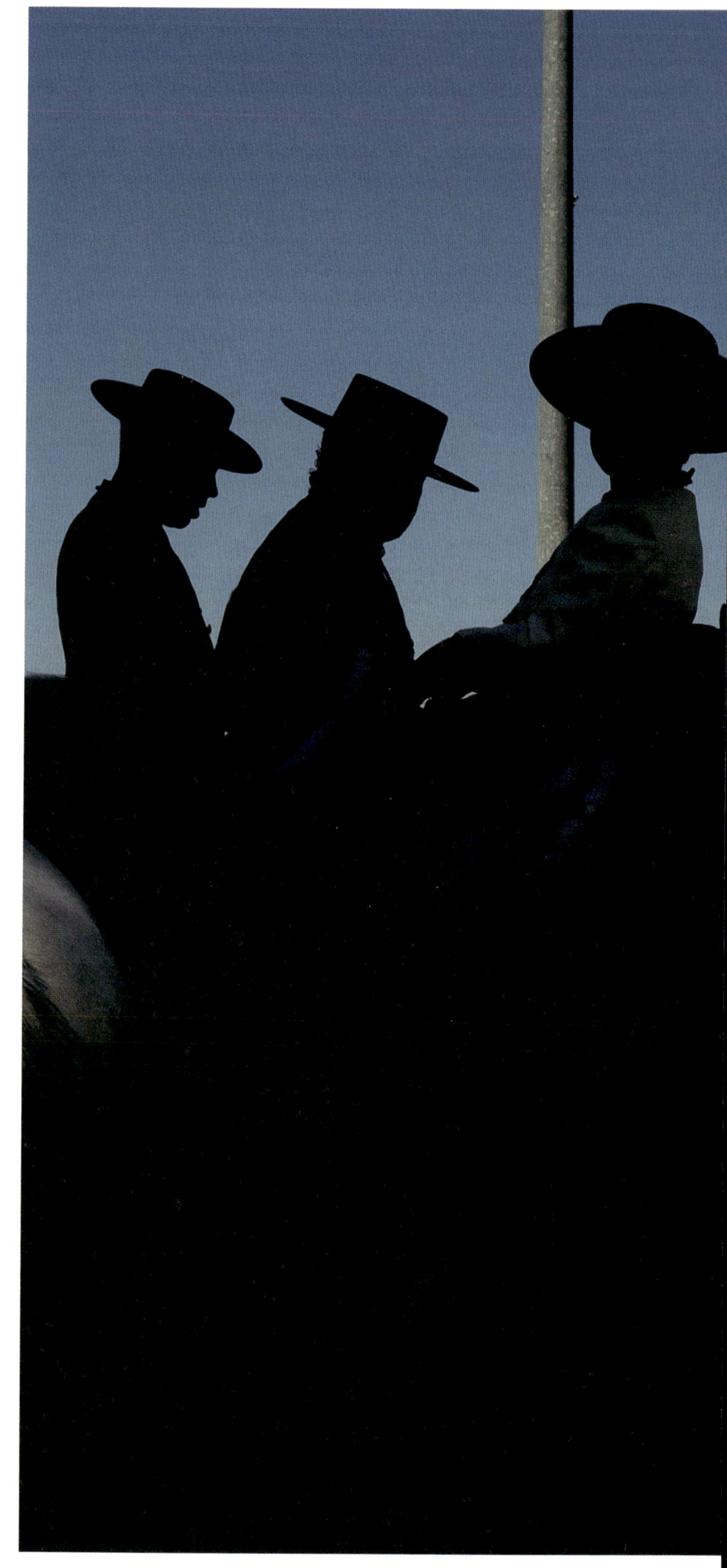

POLLY RUSYN, British

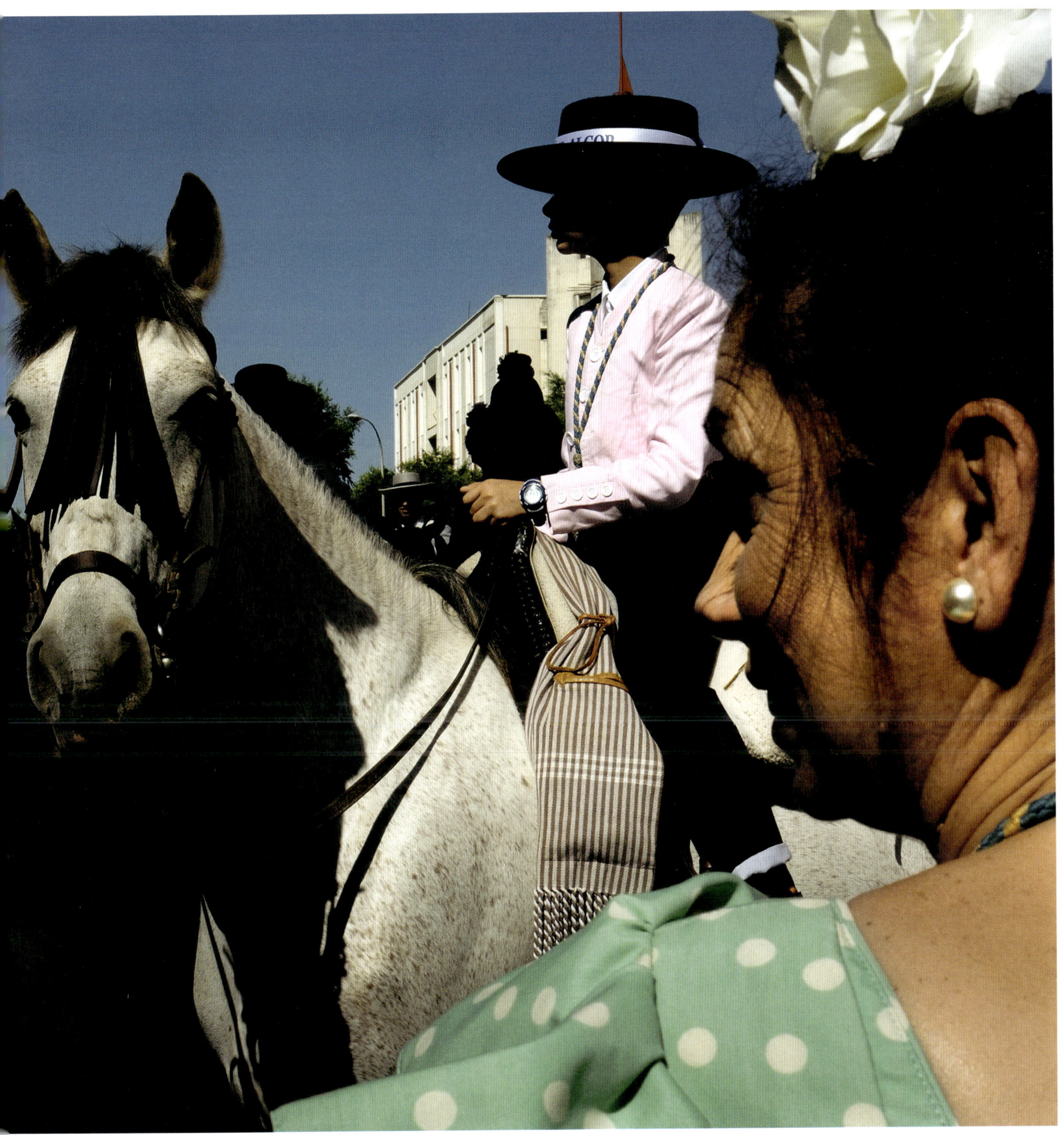

*Seville*, Seville, Spain, 2018

# 25

# Julie Hrudová

I had been walking in Prague for the whole day, looking for situations to capture. As often happens, I didn't find any. When I was almost home, ready to take my shoes off, I saw these two. At that time I was already curating the StreetRepeat Instagram account about repetitions in street photography, and this was definitely one of the potential repeated themes, so I hesitated for a moment. But quickly I decided to make my version of it anyway. Sometimes the hunt for originality holds back creativity. For me, in this case, it was better to think about these things after I shot the image instead of being sorry for not having taken the photo at all.

*Julie is a street photographer and photo editor born in Prague but based in Amsterdam. In her photography she focuses on the strangeness of everyday life. She collects photographic repetitions for her project StreetRepeat.*

JULIE HRUDOVÁ, Czech

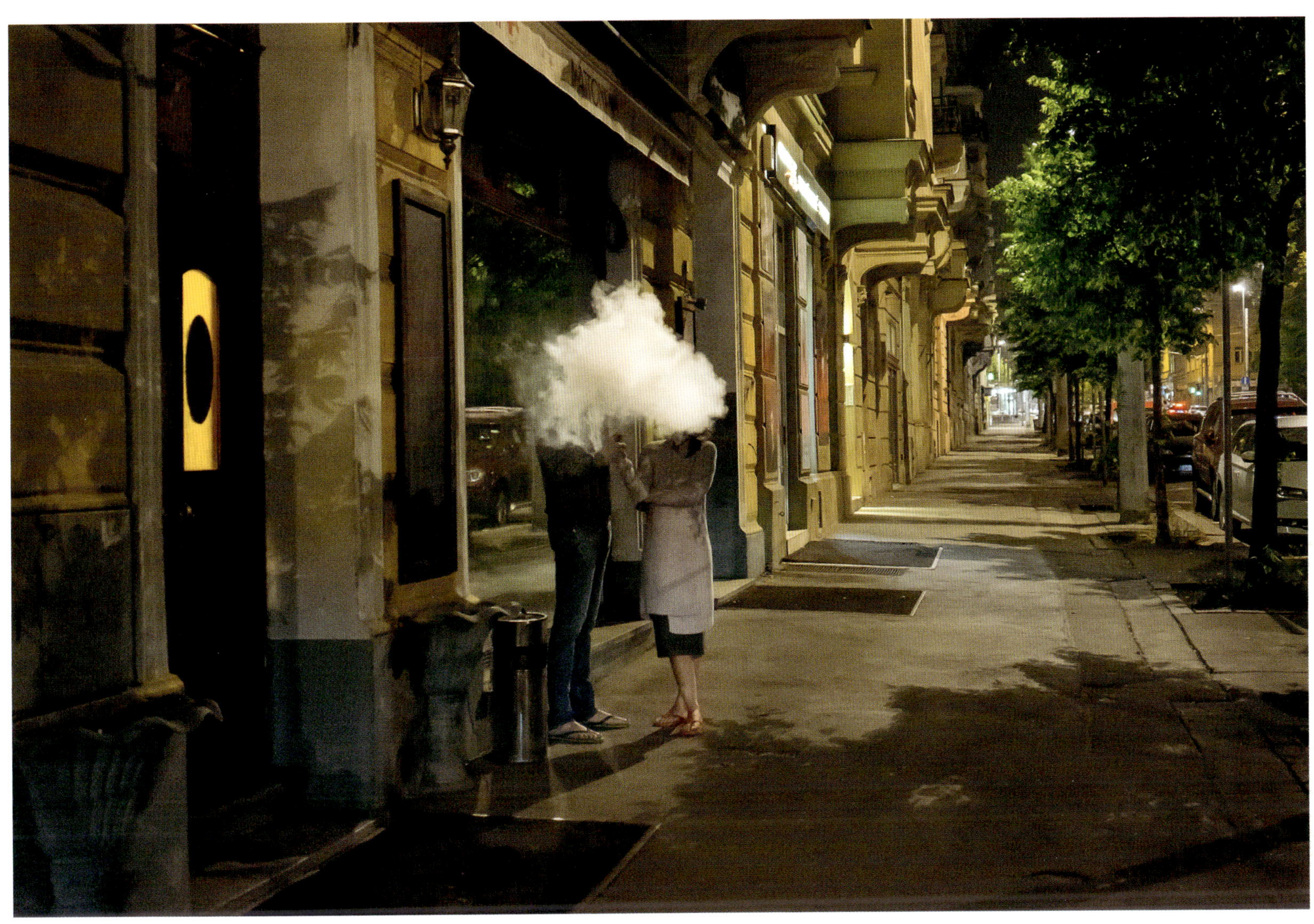

*Prague*, Prague, Czech Republic, 2018

# 26

# Ruti Alon

I am fascinated by the Roma community, maybe because much of it reminds me of the Jews over many centuries. Today, however, there is a distinct difference which contributes to my curiosity. I have visited Roma communities in several European countries. The largest concentration is in Romania, where I came across a very marginalized community outside of Brasov.

I spent a lot of time visiting the village, trying to meet as many of the families as possible and learn about their traditions, habits, social interactions within and outside the family, work skills and education, and living conditions. On one foggy morning, I suddenly saw this amazing scene of the lady with the doll. I assumed it belonged to her daughter, but the way she held it, and the despair in her eyes, caught me unprepared. It was so beautiful, with the turquoise house, while at the same time very sad and hopeless—very much like the lives of so many members of the Roma community across Europe.

*Ruti is a documentary photographer with roots in the USA and Israel. Her work depicts the breadth of life and activity in remote communities around the world.*

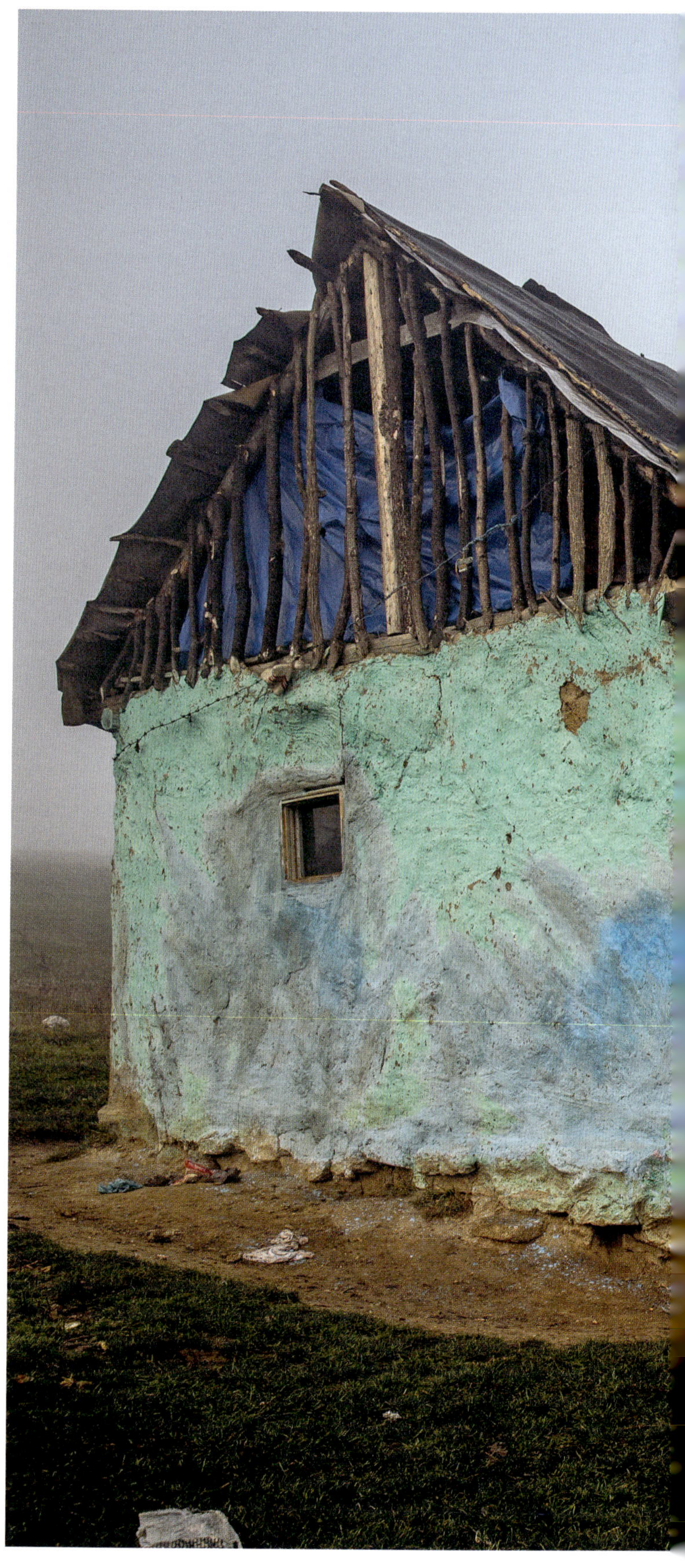

RUTI ALON, Israeli

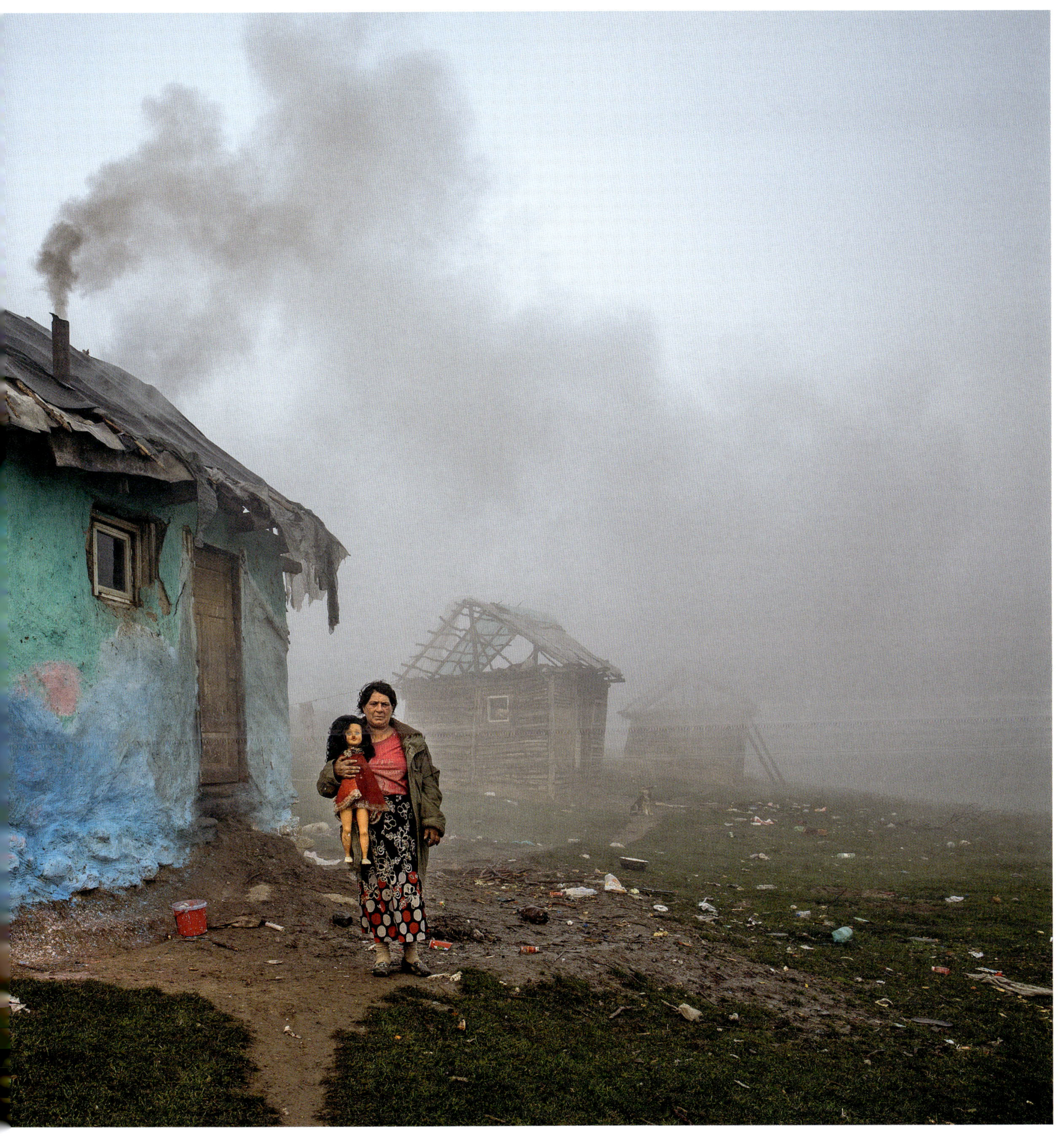

*A Roma Lady with her Doll in a Fog and Mysterious Dawn*, Brasov, Romania, 2013

# 27

# Nina Welch-Kling

Stacks venting steam are unique to New York City and a constant reminder of what lies below the surface—to this day, countless arteries of pipes deliver heat to much of the city. Above the surface, the vapor creates a wonderful filter that allows the photographer to isolate people and create a sense of mystery. This photo was taken in Midtown Manhattan on Madison Avenue in October 2018. On this fall day, the steam was lying heavy and hovering low to the ground due to the humidity in the air, a wonderful backdrop for capturing the motion of everyday life. I photographed a few people crossing the street but the "headless man" was the only one who emerged from the steam with his identity obscured, staying anonymous to the viewer.

*Nina earned a BFA from the School of the Art Institute of Chicago and a Masters in Architecture from UCLA. Since 1995, she has lived in New York City, where she continues to explore creative outlets for her ideas and her passion for photography.*

NINA WELCH-KLING, German

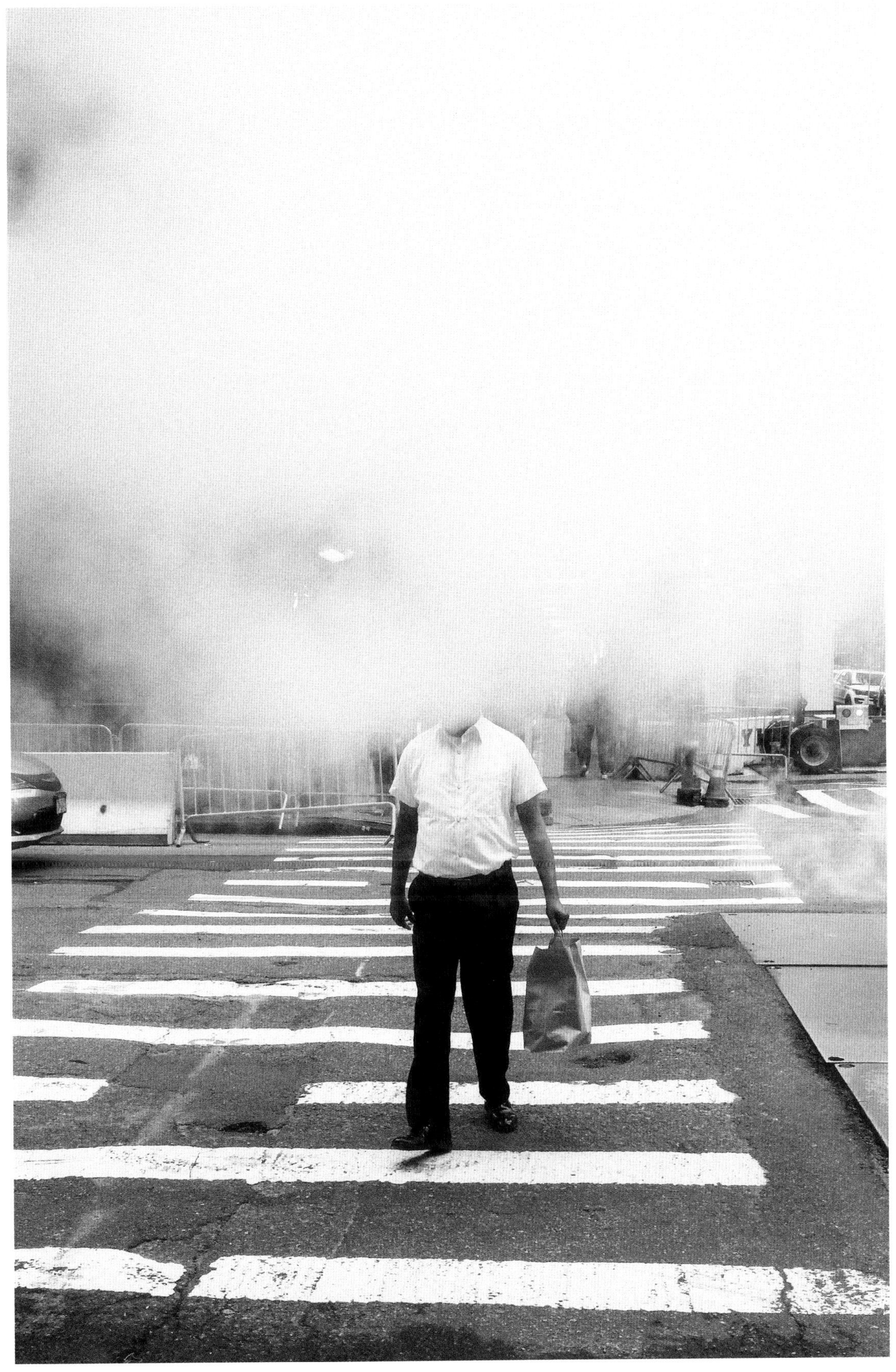

*Untitled*, New York City, USA, 2018

# 28

# Gisele Duprez

I was walking on the boardwalk at Coney Island, which is one of my favorite places to shoot. I noticed two cute dogs being pushed by their owner in a baby stroller. Getting down low into my usual position, I took a shot or two. Then I noticed the man with the white beard staring at the dogs with amusement and curiosity. Feeling like something interesting was about to happen, I waited for him to enter the frame and took the shot.

*Gisele's long-term projects focus on Coney Island, NY, and Cuba. Her work has been featured in publications including* Rolling Stone, *and has been exhibited internationally.*

GISELE DUPREZ, American

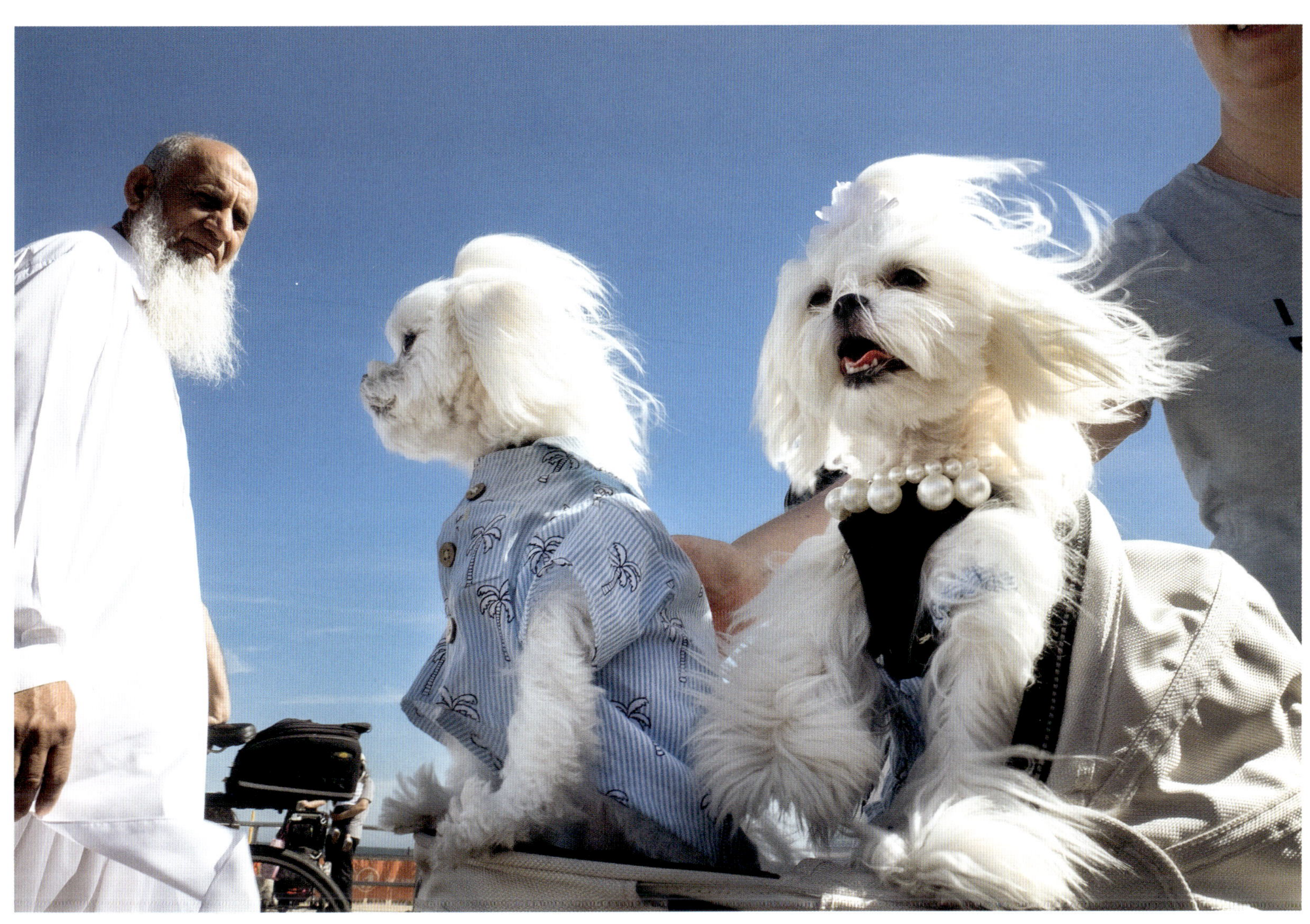

*Good Hair Day*, Brooklyn, New York City, USA, 2019

# 29

# Eva Erdmann

One morning, just inland from the ghats of Varanasi, I was walking and shooting in the amazing maze of narrow streets when suddenly I found myself facing this goat perched on the sill of a closed window. I had to shoot before she moved. I took my first shot so as not to miss this epic scene. Quickly, I leaned on the opposite wall and waited for the walking man to appear in my viewfinder. I got the shot!

*Eva is a French-born photographer. Her work is a personal interpretation of the world with a focus on India. She chooses what to photograph by looking for a feeling.*

EVA ERDMANN, French

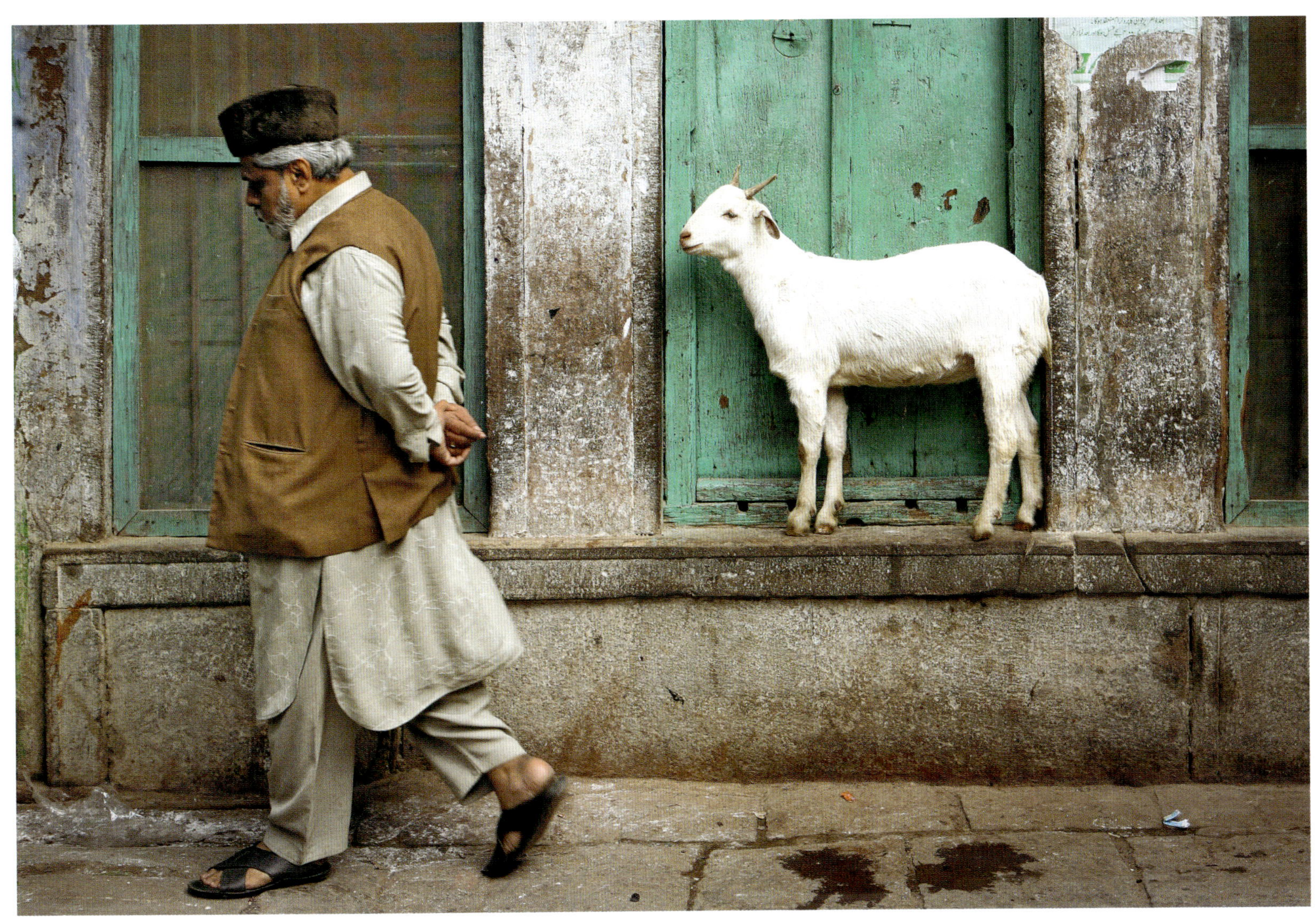

*Perching Goat*, Varanasi, India, 2014

# 30

# Ania Kłosek

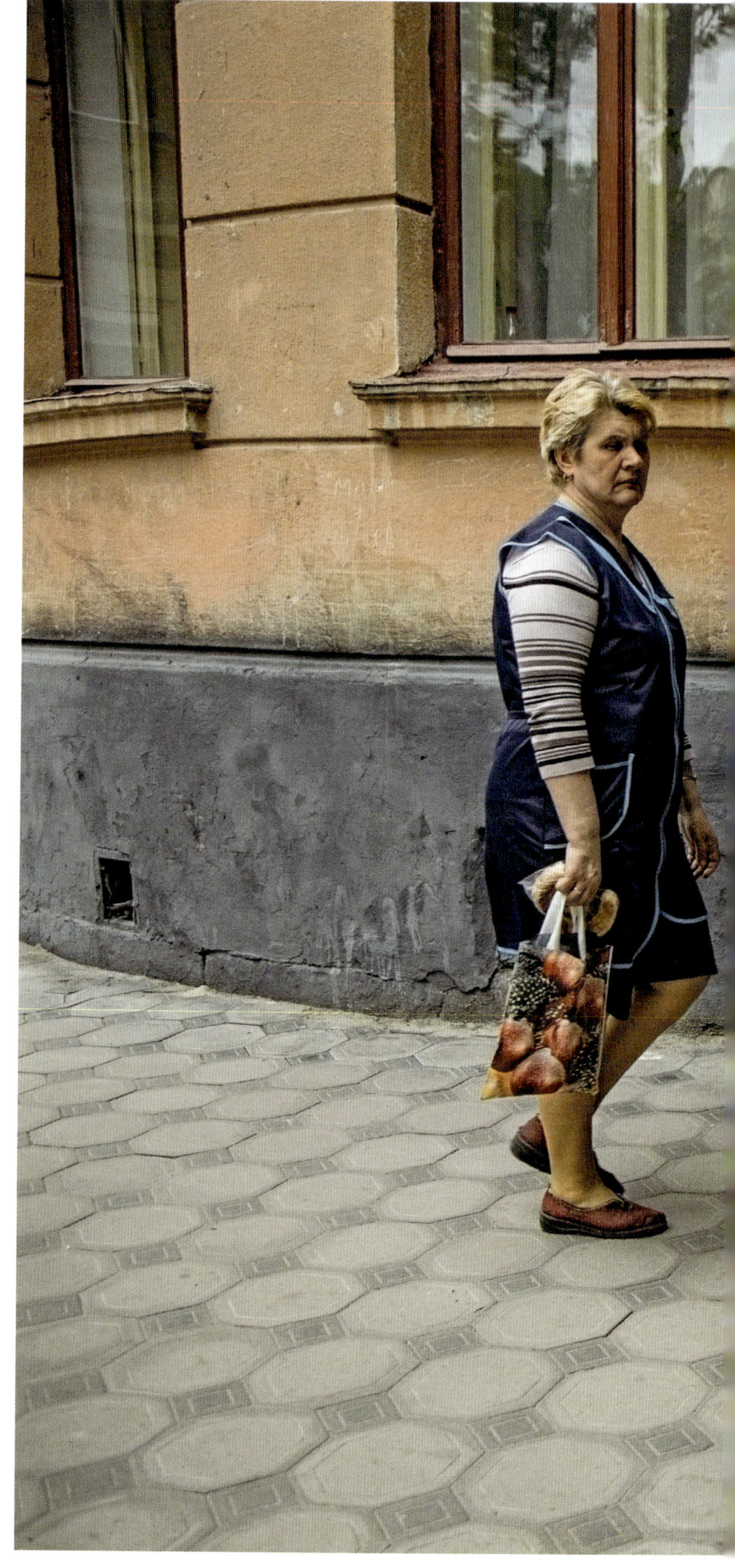

This photo was taken during one of my trips to Ukraine. A group of children were playing after the Mother's Day assembly at school. I focused on this beautiful little dancer who had immediately caught my attention. I took a couple of shots and when the lady with the apron appeared in the frame I knew it was the moment. I like the contrast here between childhood and adulthood, dreams and reality.

*Ania is well known for her documentary and street photography, for which she has received prestigious awards. Post-Soviet life is one of her favorite subjects.*

ANIA KŁOSEK, Polish

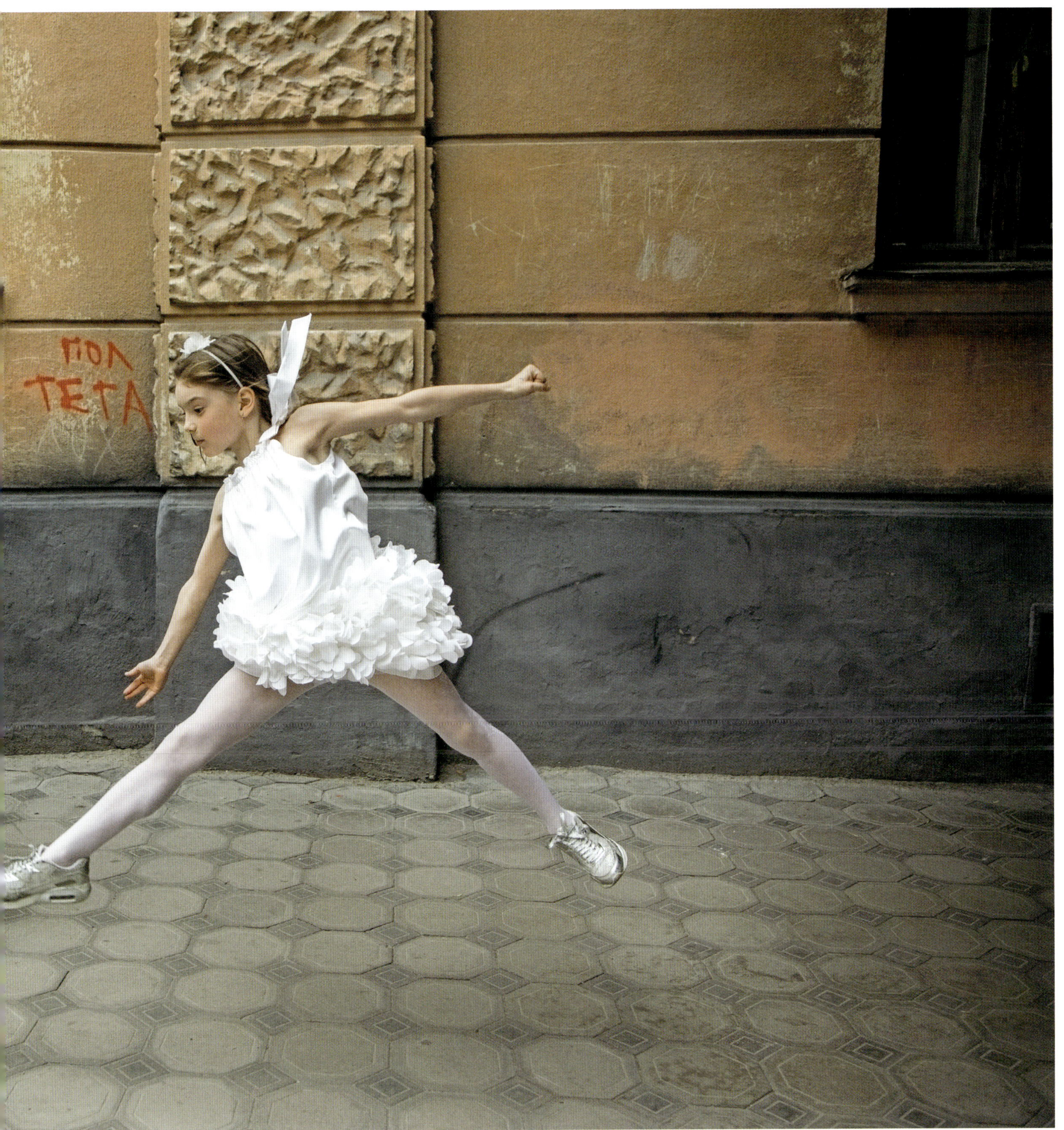



*Untitled*, Lviv, Ukraine, 2017

# 31.

# Rebecca Norris Webb

For fifteen years, I photographed menageries that I'd discovered all over Cuba—from tiny zoos to pigeon societies to quirky personal collections of animals. By far the most common creature I found was the bird—from roosters to cockatiels, pigeons, and parrots. I love the complex questions this raises: Of all the creatures, why are birds the most popular animal in Cuban menageries? Does this hint at some kind of longing for flight in a country where few people are allowed to travel? Does it suggest something about Cubans and their relationship to the natural world of their "violet isle"—a little-known nickname for Cuba inspired by the color of its soil?

And why, years later, does this image continue to be a favorite of mine? Perhaps it's because it brings to mind Paul Valéry's advice: "One should be light like a bird, and not like a feather."

*Originally a poet, Rebecca often interweaves her words and photographs in her eight books, many of which explore people's relationship with the natural world.*

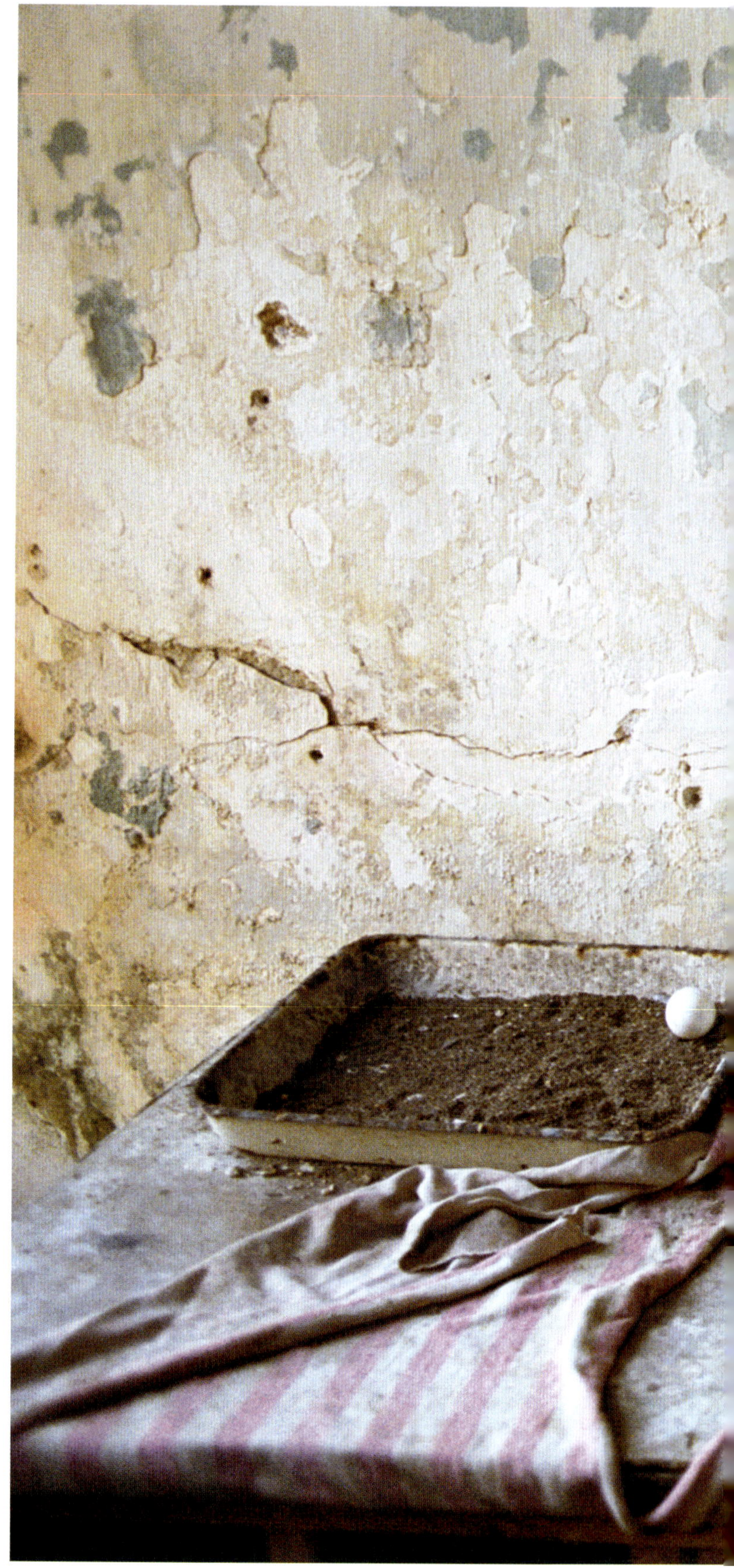

REBECCA NORRIS WEBB, American

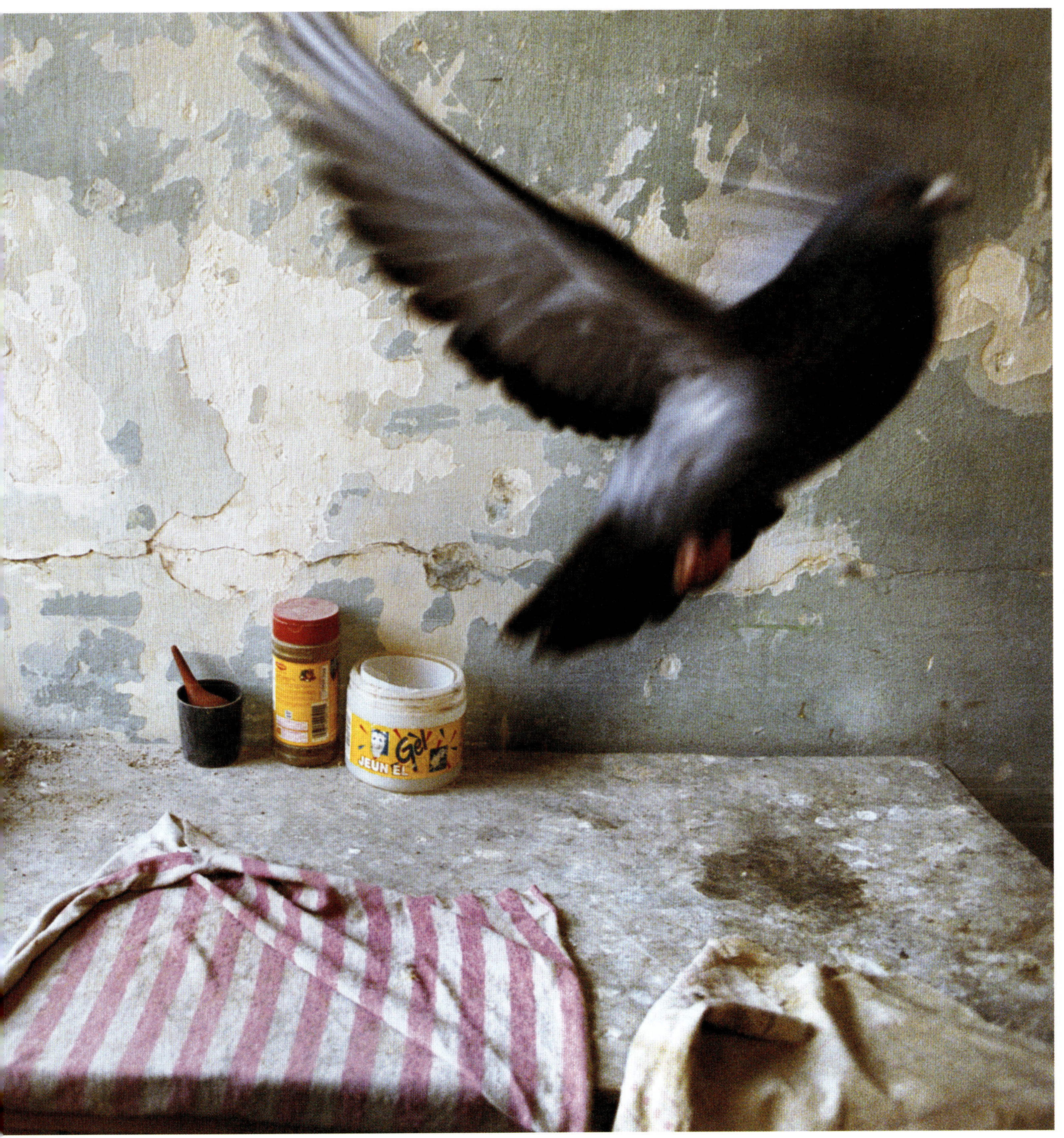

*Light Like a Bird*, Havana, Cuba, 2007

# 32

# Neta Gov

I love to take photos of birds. This man is hiding his face, not from the birds, but because I am a woman. According to his religion, he is not permitted to look at me.

*Neta is an artist, painter, textile designer, and photographer based in Tel Aviv, Israel. She never studied photography, and uses a very small and simple camera.*

NETA GOV, Israeli

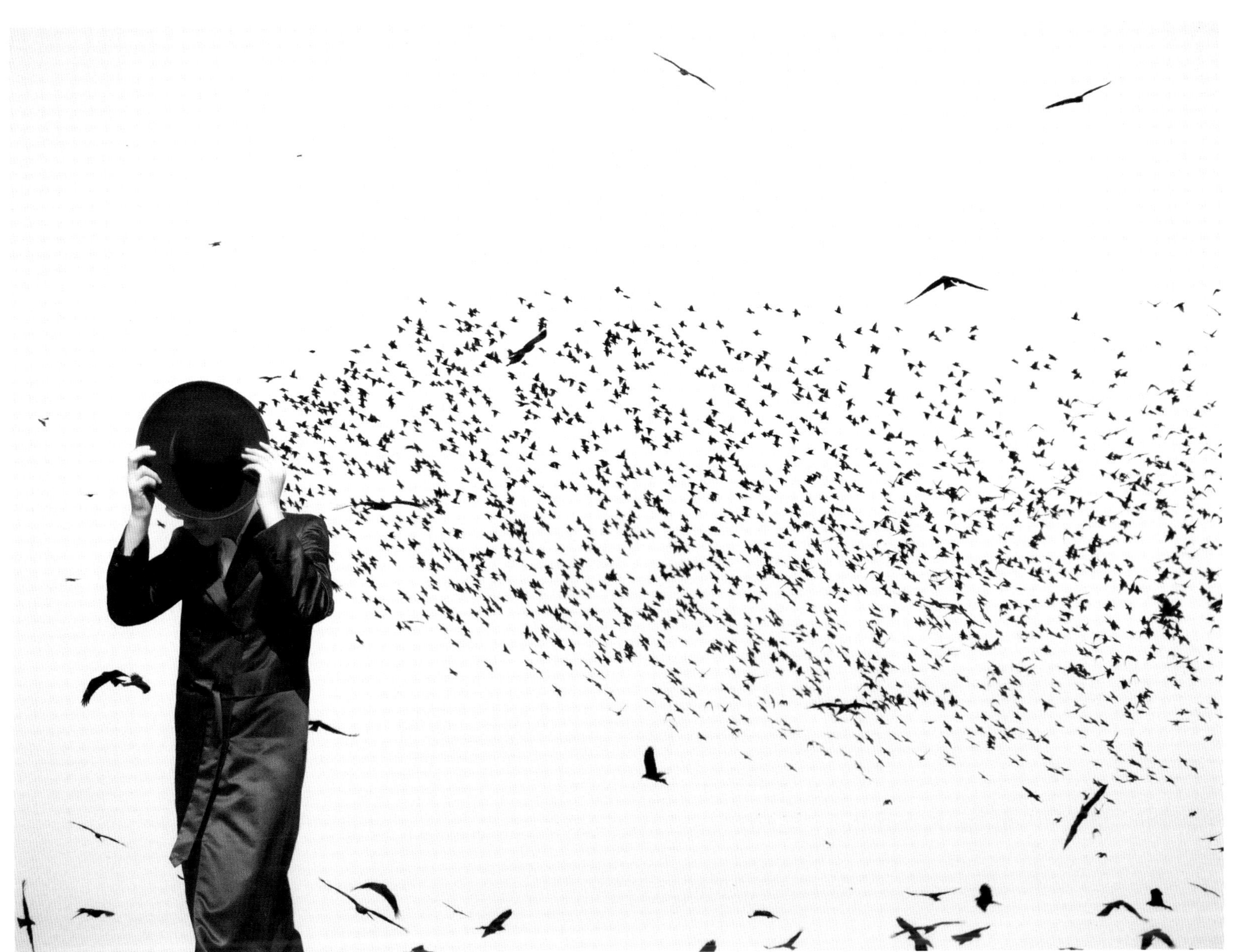

*Birds*, Tel Aviv, Israel, 2018

# 33

# Eléonore Simon

In the midst of a snowstorm in February 2017, I headed to
Coney Island, hoping to capture another side of a beach
I had photographed many times before. I feel at home in
the restlessness of a big city like New York, but often find
myself seeking quiet, eerie moments.

As I had imagined, Coney Island was deserted with
the exception of a handful of curious souls and a few
locals going about their lives as usual, despite the freezing
cold and gusts of wind. Walking back from the pier, I saw
this man in the distance and came closer just in time to
capture this image. I love the way the slight curve of his
body is framed, simultaneously isolating him and turning
him into an organic part of the graphic metal structure.
In a twist on Muscle Beach photography, he looks almost
frail in this sea of snow, lines, and geometric shapes.

*Eléonore is a Valparaíso-based photographer whose work
has been featured in numerous international exhibitions
and festivals. She is a member of the international
collective, UP Photographers.*

ELÉONORE SIMON, French

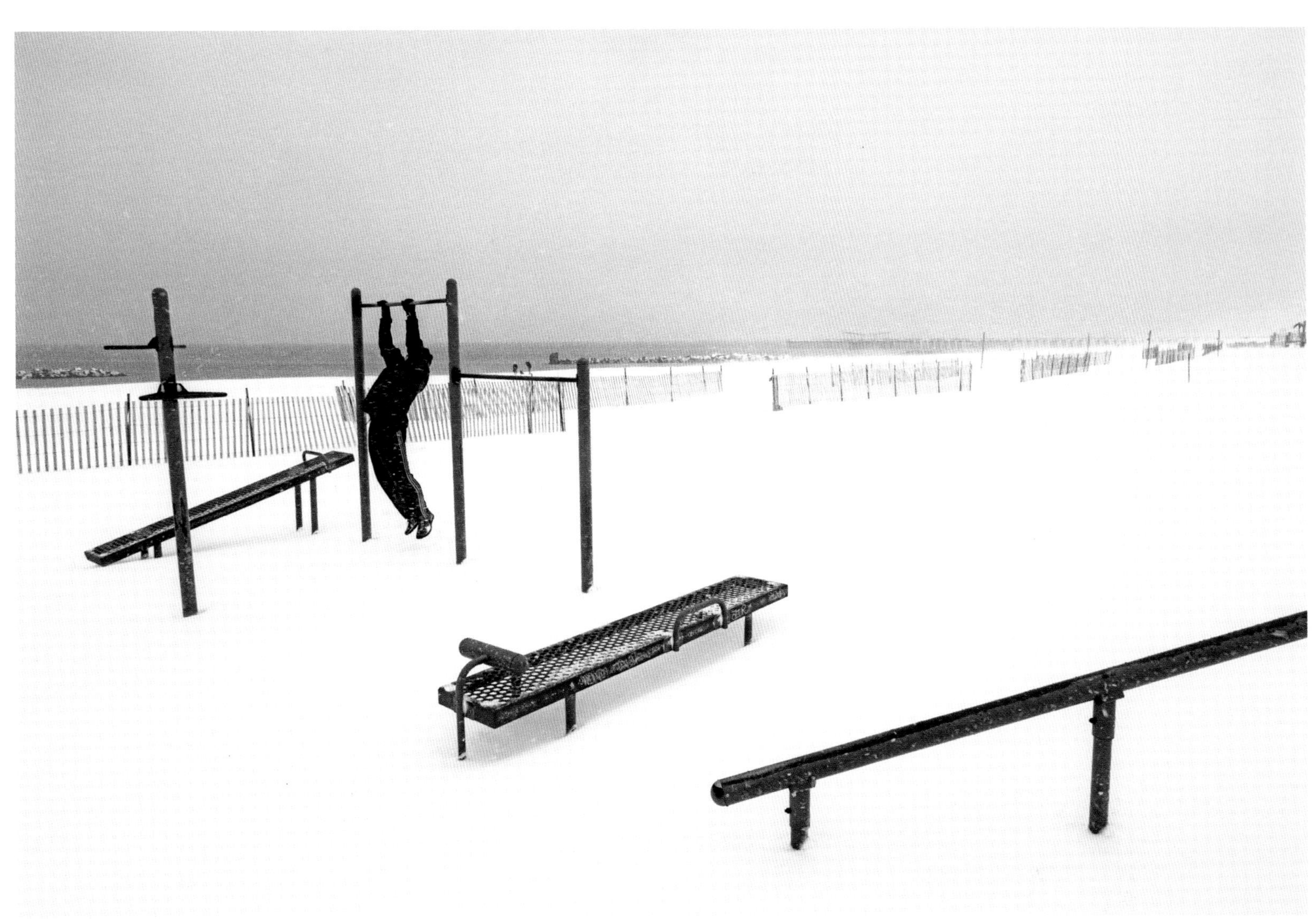

*Winter Shapes, Coney Island*, New York City, USA, 2017

# 34

# Victoria Orlova

I observed everything in India; I was captivated by every detail. It seemed to be so normal to see young guys frolicking in the sea, they do that every day, but if you give yourself a chance to look closer, you'll see that they interact with the water as they would with a partner or a friend, or just someone whom they respect and are a little afraid of ... This connection is deep and mature, like many other things in India.

*Victoria is a video editor and photographer. She focuses on "daily images" that capture her own ambiguity.*

VICTORIA ORLOVA, Belarusian

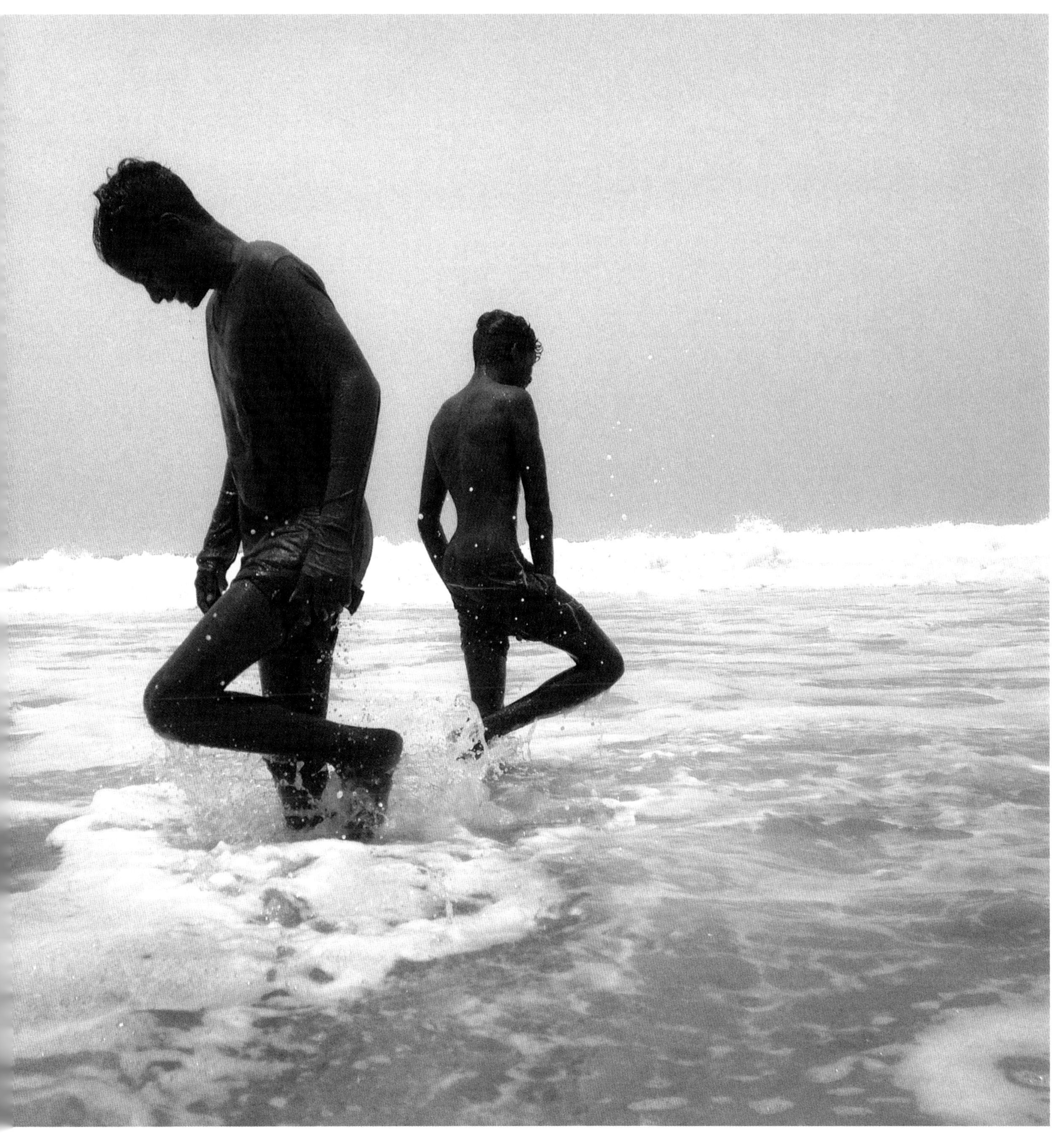

*A Connection*, Varkala, Kerala, India, 2018

# 35

# Marina Volskaya-Nikitina

At night, when all the fuss and crowds are gone, many unnecessary details of the day dissolve in the dark. The synthetic light of the night is like a movie set for the most mundane objects. The people you meet at night seem truer: thoughtful, lonely, sad, or in love. At night it is easier to be in the moment, and be inspired. It is rare luck to be in the right place and with the right light, and there is always a good reason to take the camera and wander.

I am deeply in love with cinema and my passion for movies plays a key part in my projects. I love it when life directs a scene, with me just assisting.

I have spent many evenings at this bus stop near my house, filming passengers for my *On the Way* project. The traffic signal provided a very satisfying backlight, uniting two strangers for a second. It turned out to be an interesting metaphor. The night light brought a cinematic feel to the whole scene.

*Marina is from Nizhny Novgorod. She works in color, candidly photographing everyday life in the night city. In 2020, she began her studies at the School of Contemporary Photography, St Petersburg.*

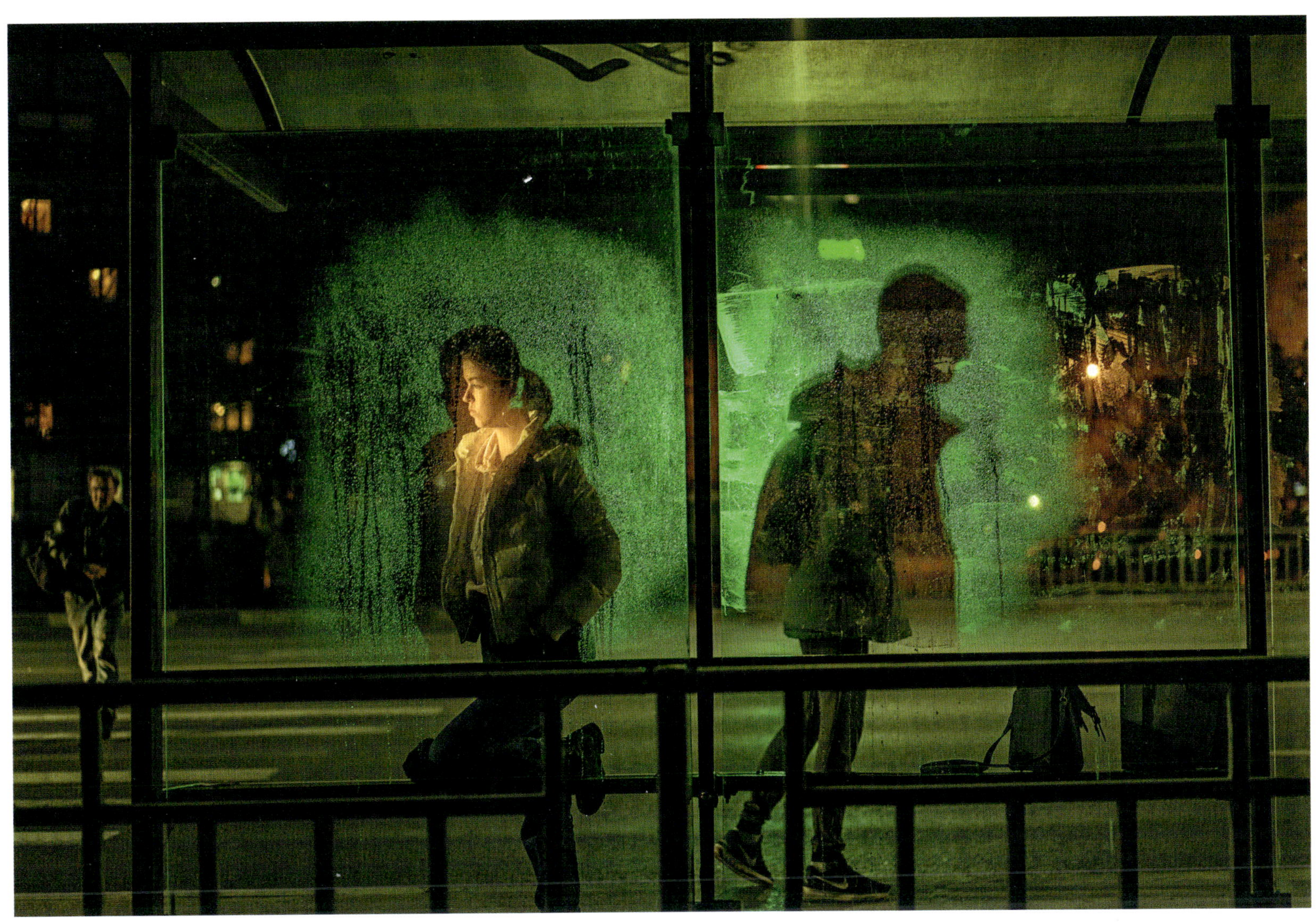

*Breakup*, Nizhny Novgorod, Russia, 2018

# 36

# Andrea Torrei

They say you have to be in the right place at the right time and I think this photograph is a case in point. In one of the many small, colorful alleys of Harar, you may come across girls going home from school in their beautiful uniforms, playing on the streets and sharing their joy with you.

*Andrea is an Italy-based photographer interested in documentary and street photography. Her work, in black-and-white and color, focuses mainly on gender and social issues.*

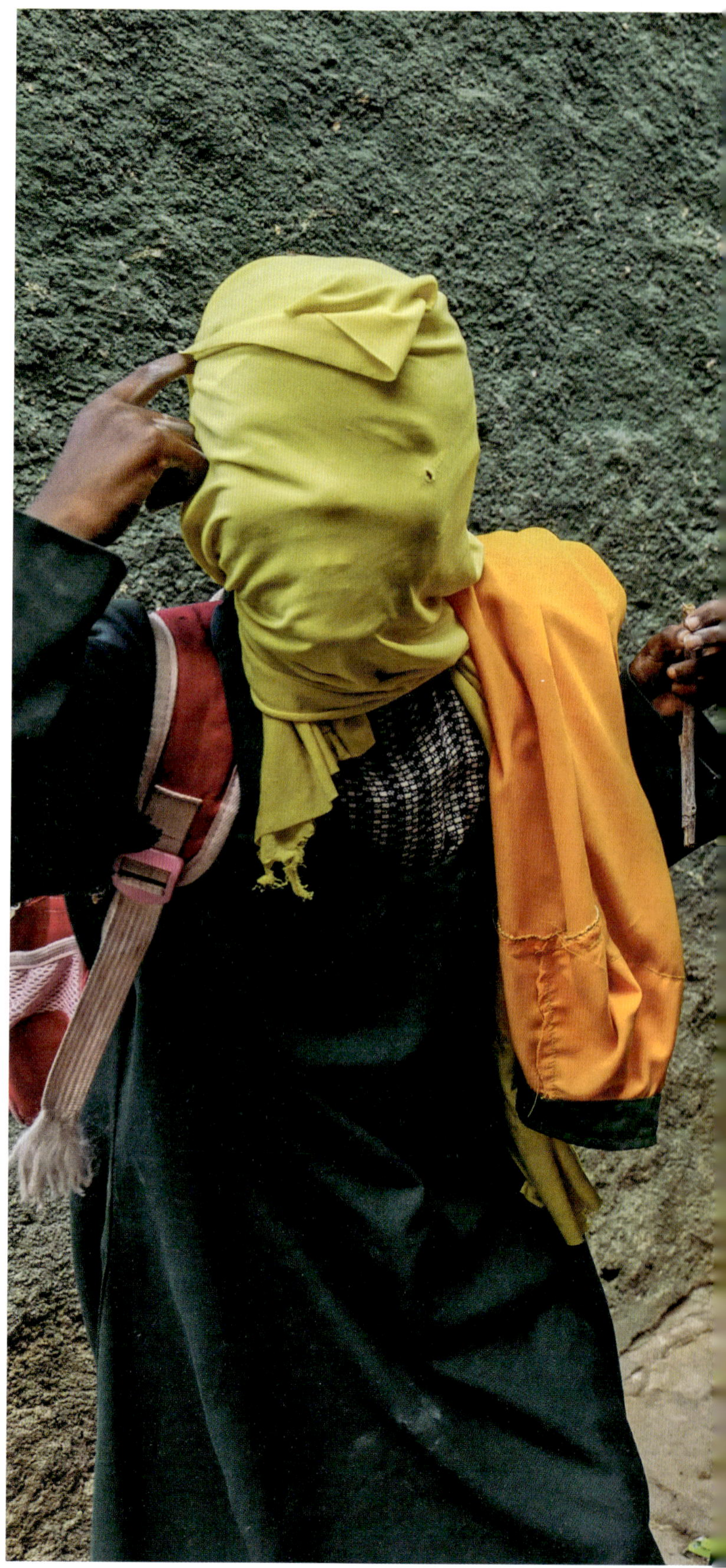

ANDREA TORREI, Italian

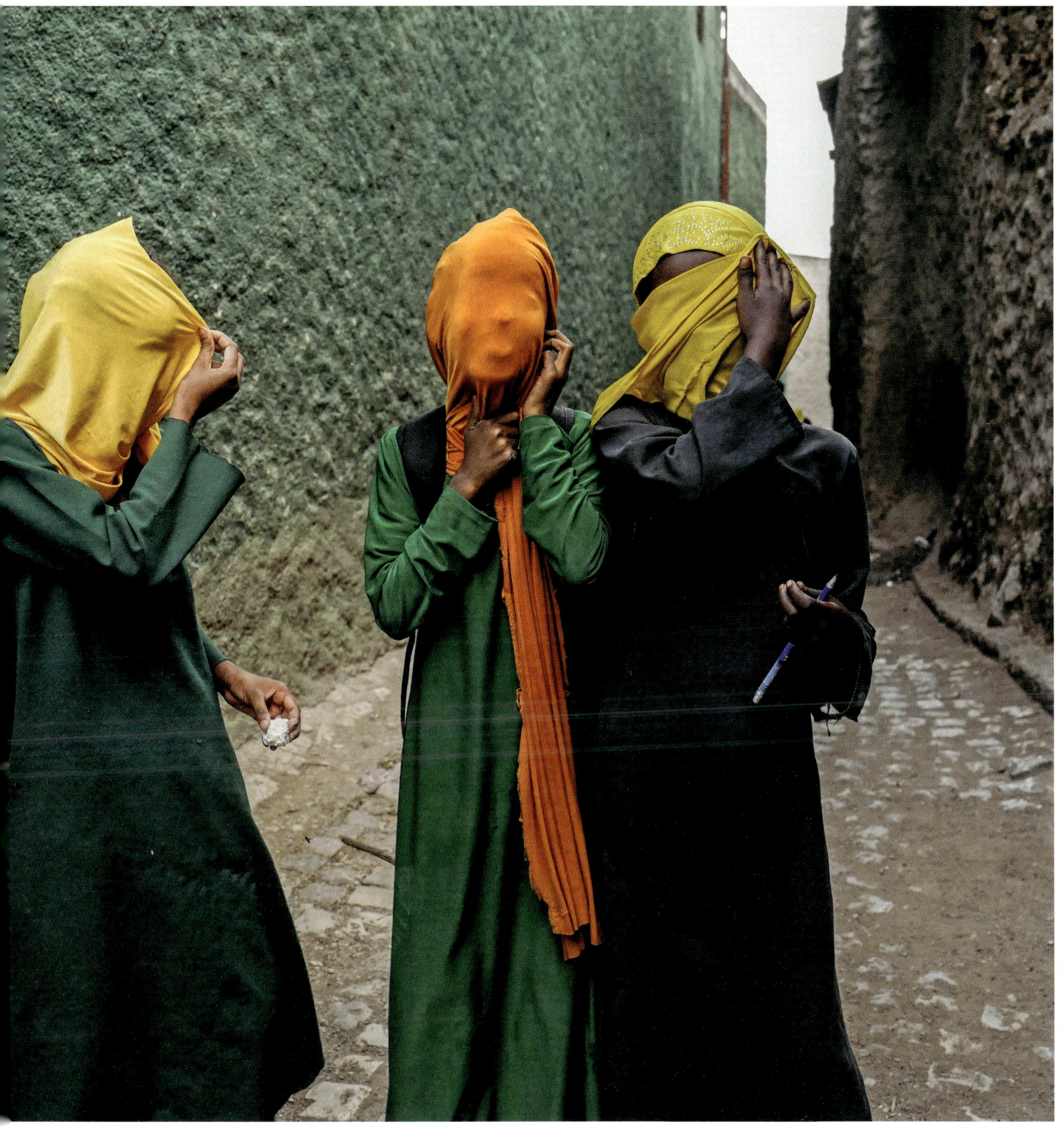

*Untitled*, Harar, Ethiopia, 2019

# 37

# Francesca Chiacchio

After two years of shooting on the street, looking for the "right moment" to catch, I felt the need to look for something more compelling, something that told a story.

This is how I heard about an event happening on the Italian Adriatic Coast called "Summer Jamboree," in which people from all over the world gather to dress and dance as if they were in America in the 1940s and '50s. As soon as I got there, I was fascinated by the atmosphere.

Everybody in town was dressed and styled as they would have been in those days. My impression was that they weren't dressing just for the occasion but that behind their style they identified with the philosophy of life. Like these women, who were the first I met on the way to an evening event. Their beautiful red hats really captured my attention.

*Francesca is an architect who decided to abandon her profession to follow her dream: photography. She has been rewarded with several exhibitions and publications.*

FRANCESCA CHIACCHIO, Italian

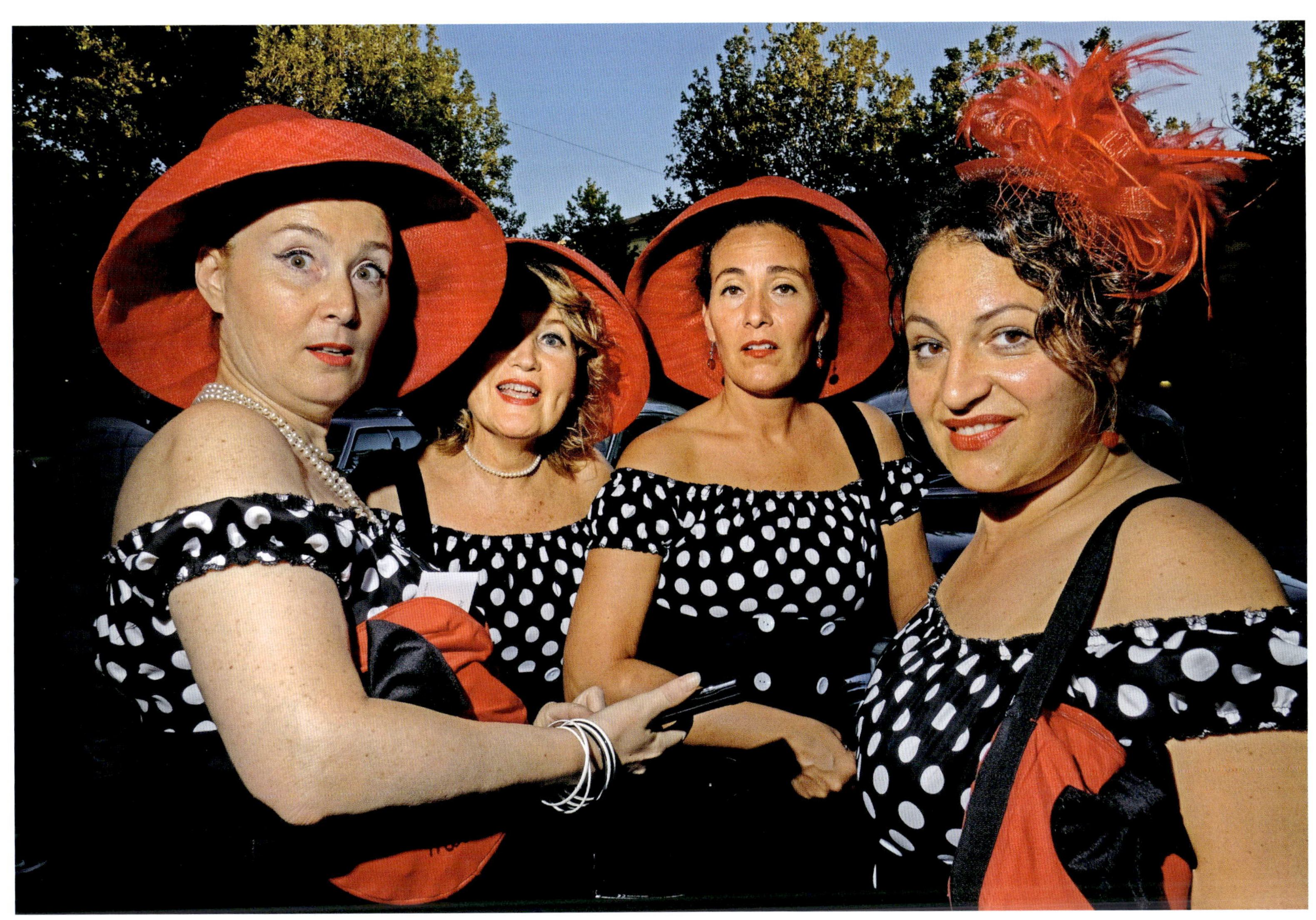

*Red Hat Girls*, Senigallia, Italy, 2019

# 38

# Natela Grigalashvili

This is a photo from my series *Women with Headscarves.* This square, black, transparent fabric will one day turn into headscarves for these girls. It is truly thin and practical; it isn't slippery and can easily be attached to hair. The women from this region mostly start wearing them after marriage. They are a tradition, a symbol, and an inseparable part of their lives. From childhood, they are used to working, having respect for their elders, and caring for each other. They share and preserve traditions.

In the mountainous Adjara region, they say that everything slowly changes as time goes by. The people of the mountains are moving downhill and those who stay recount how fast the environment is changing; what used to exist yesterday has already disappeared and even the things from today will be gone tomorrow. This is why I wanted to photograph the black headscarf with these women and girls, as today it is the symbol of their femininity, loyalty, simplicity, and inner peace.

*Natela is a Georgian documentary photographer who has been capturing the lives of Georgian people since the 1980s.*

NATELA GRIGALASHVILI, Georgian

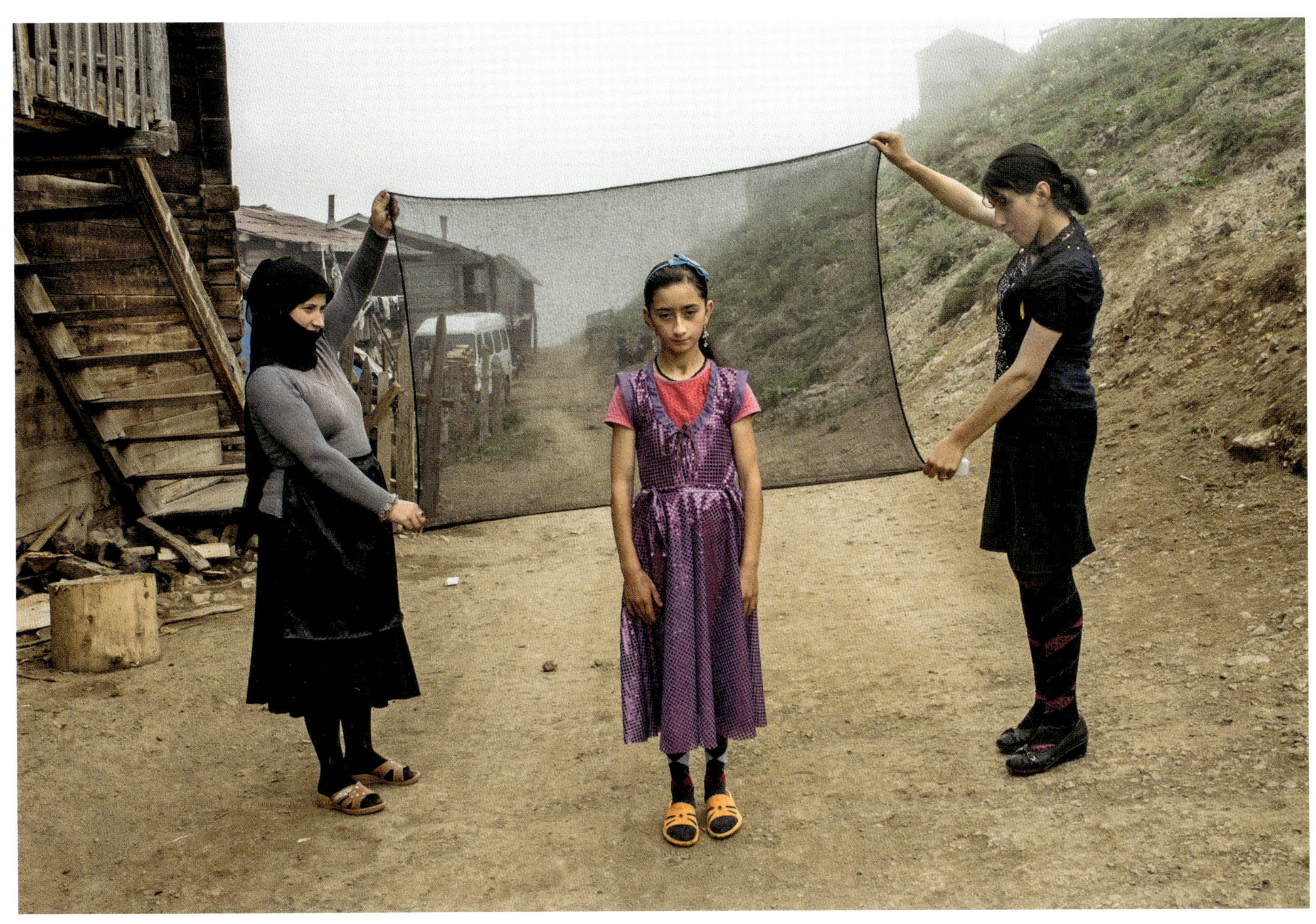

*Untitled*, Adjara, Georgia, 2014

# Fatteme Pezeshki Moghadam

These children were playing, one with a stick in his hands and the other with a rug-like piece of fabric.

Suddenly, when the boy on the left shook his stick, there was a gust of wind and the carpet flew into the sky as if he had a magic wand and the carpet was a bird.

*Fatteme is a teacher, writer, and photographer based in Tehran, Iran, and a member of the National Iranian Photographers' Society. Photography gives her the chance to encounter people who show hidden layers in different moments.*

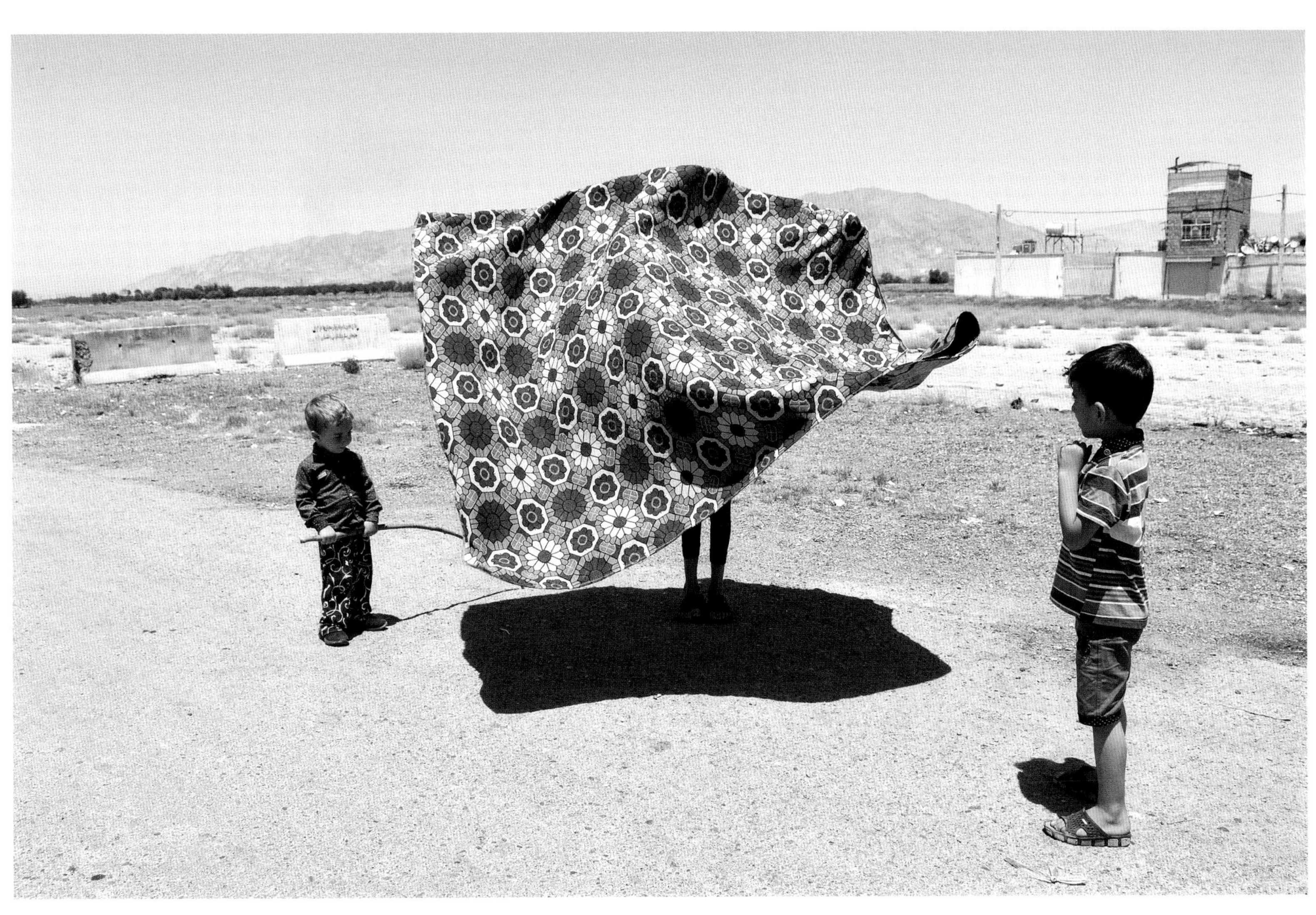

*Flying Carpet*, Shahre Rey, Iran, 2018

# 40

# Cristina Garlesteanu

The beauty of street photography comes from never knowing what you will find right around the corner. A little walk downtown with some photographer friends brought me in front of the scene. Pure luck, one click … and that was it. Sometimes, it takes lots of patience, waiting, anticipating … But that day it took only luck.

*Cristina is a Bucharest-based photographer. She focuses mainly on candid street scenes and loves black-and-white photography.*

CRISTINA GARLESTEANU, Romanian

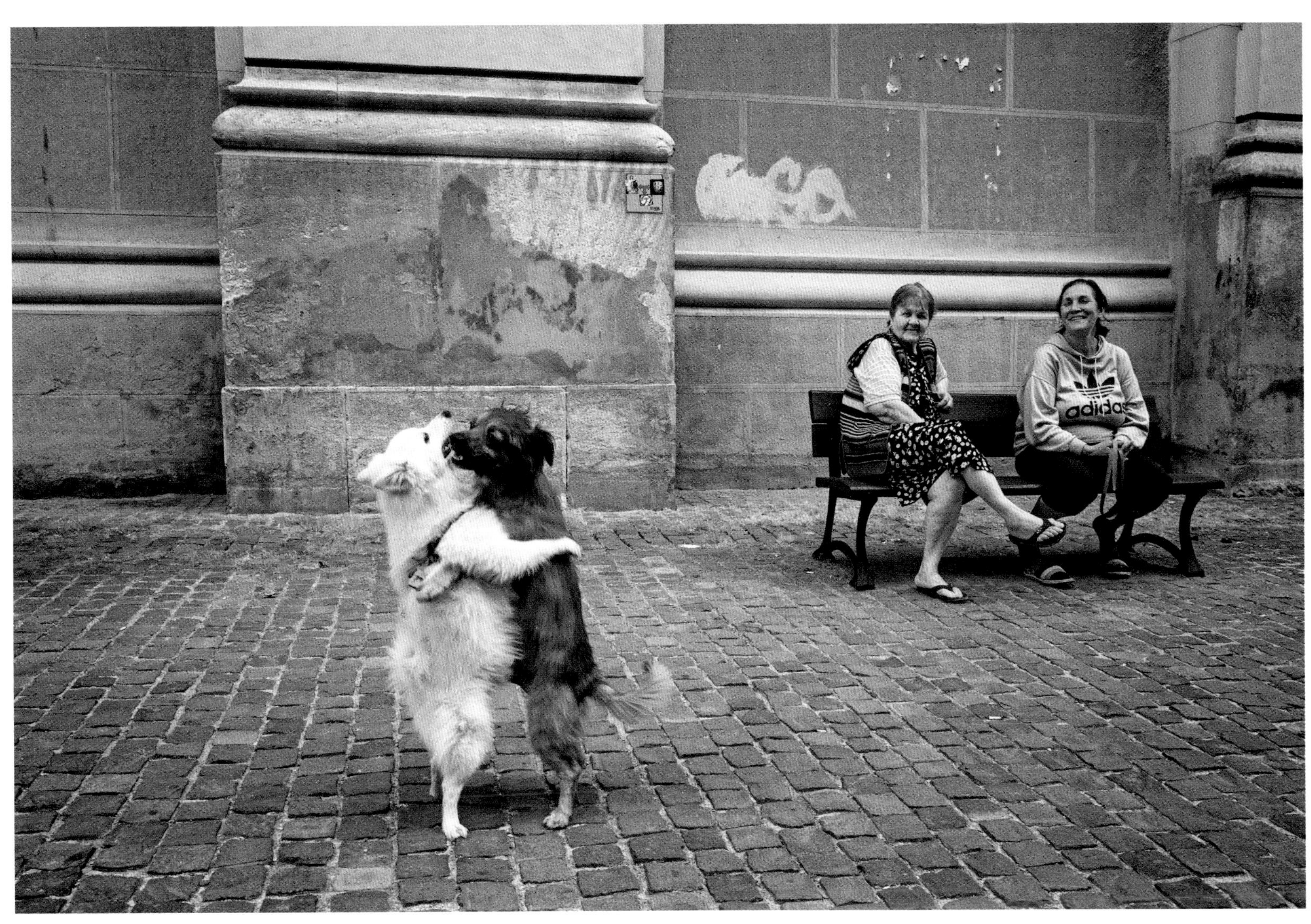

*Untitled*, Bucharest, Romania, 2017

# 41

# Diana Maria

I was walking over one of the bridges across the Danube in Belgrade when I saw this scene: a young man was encouraging his dog to come out of the water. I was impressed by the dog's fight. In the end it managed to get to its owner, and that's what made me capture the scene.

*Diana lives in Bucharest, Romania. She looks at the world with curiosity and joy, trying to discover meanings and nuances that might go unnoticed with a mere glance.*

DIANA MARIA, Romanian

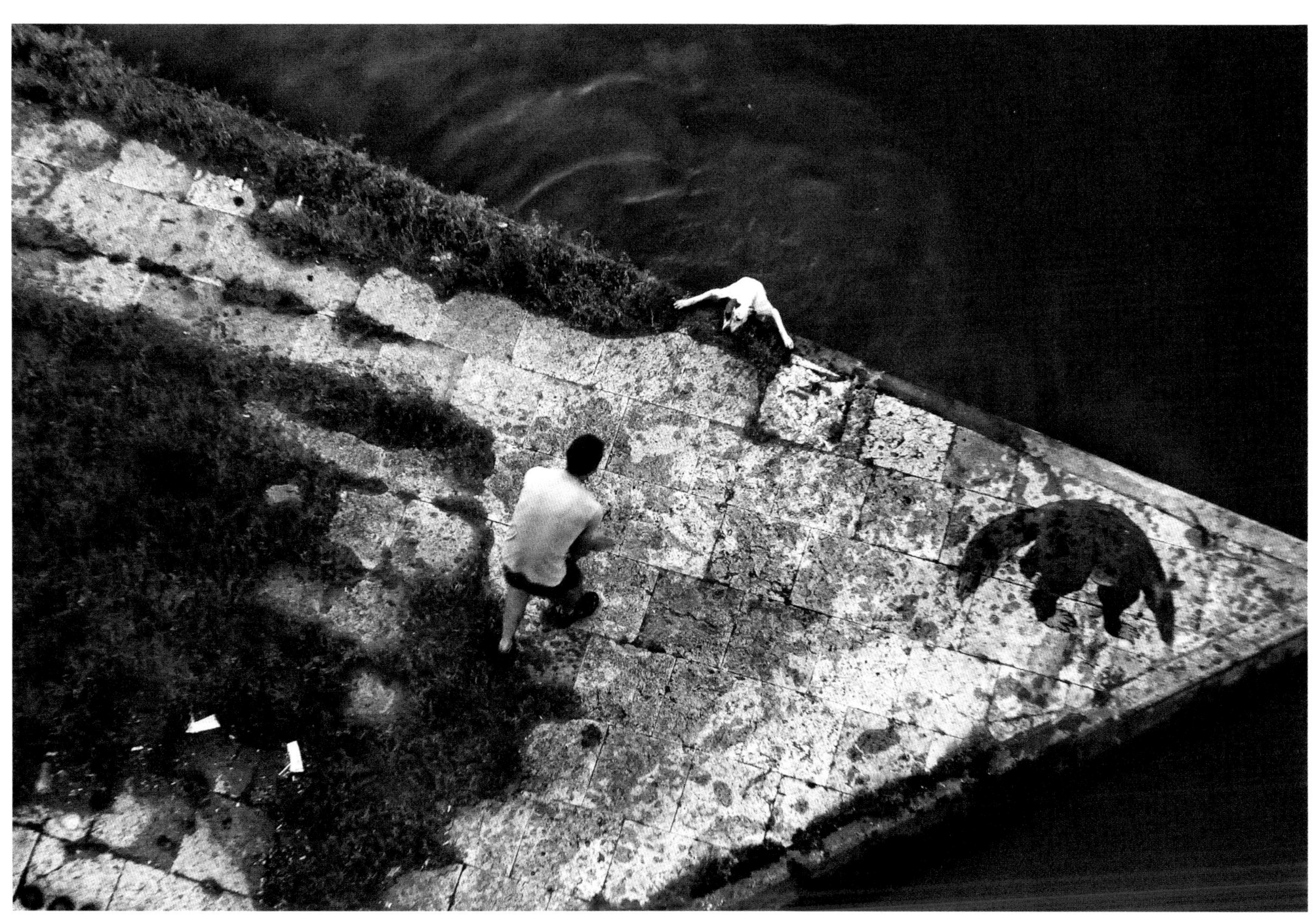

*Untitled*, Belgrade, Serbia, 2013

# 42

# Sandrine Duval

One morning in March 2018, I arrived by bus in the small town of Sighnaghi (located in the wine region of Kakhetia) in Georgia. There was a thick fog and I couldn't see further than a hundred yards.

Just as I arrived and left my bag, I decided to go and explore the city. The atmosphere was ghostly; it was captivating and melancholic, but very photogenic.

I felt as if there was something to capture but couldn't quite figure out what yet, as if time had stopped. I was feeling lonely. I took my camera out and walked through the few deserted streets to the main square, where I saw this lady emerging from nowhere out of the mist, next to an old car. The dog in the foreground created the only animation.

I had to capture it, inspired by this suspended moment of movement.

*Sandrine is a self-taught photographer based in Paris. On the lookout for unusual, mysterious, graphic subjects, she was led to photography, from film (slides) to digital, by her taste for travel.*

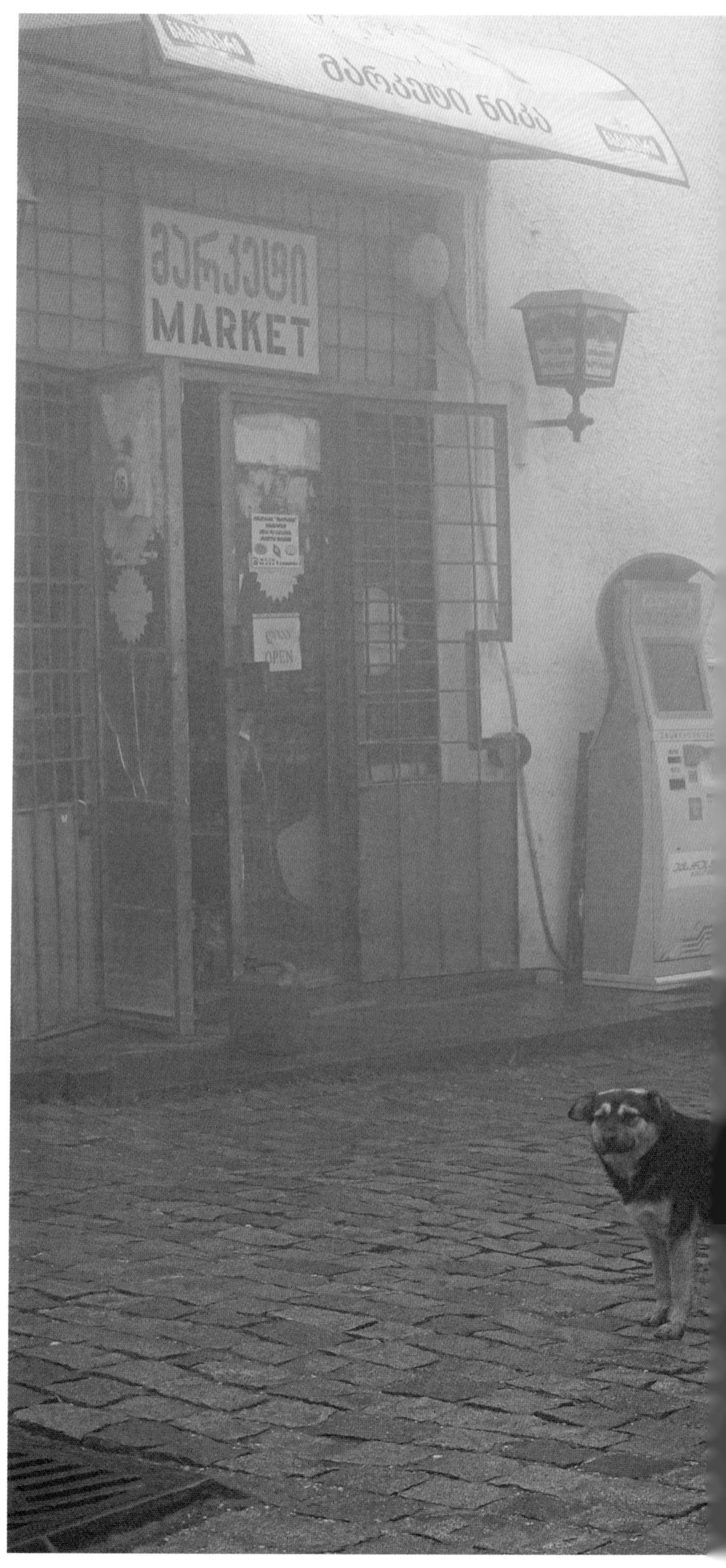


SANDRINE DUVAL, French

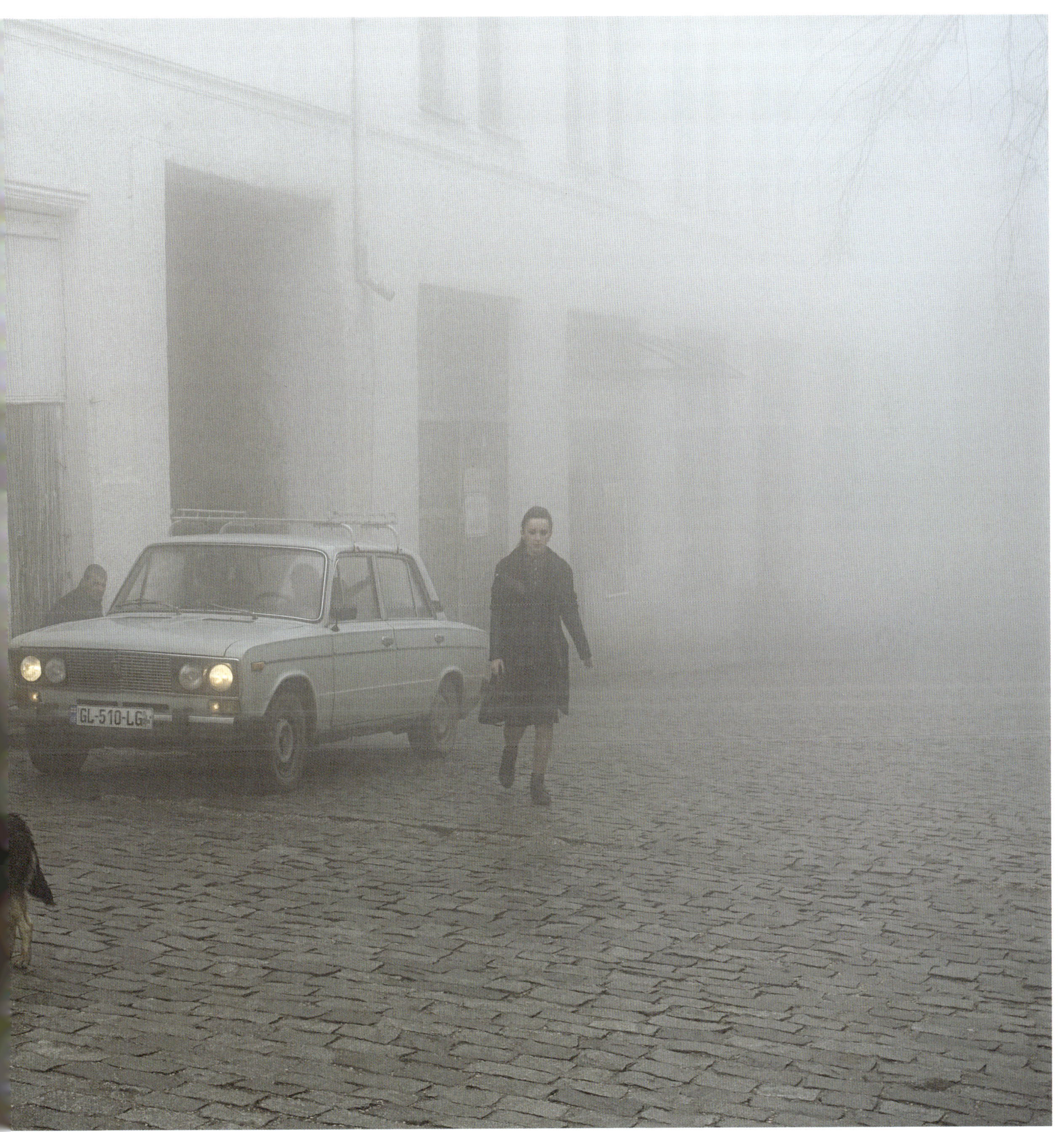

*In the Mood*, Sighnaghi, Georgia, 2018

# 43

# Patti Fogarty

Harlem, New York City. The city huddled down for the big blizzard where the weather takes control of the streets. The view is one thing, the feel is something else entirely. Life goes on.

*Patti (1958–2019) was based in Manhattan, where she focused on street photography. Her main places of interest were Union Square (where she photographed people), the Bronx and Queens (where her subject was the melancholic grittiness of old industrial landscapes and how people adapted to them).*

PATTI FOGARTY, American

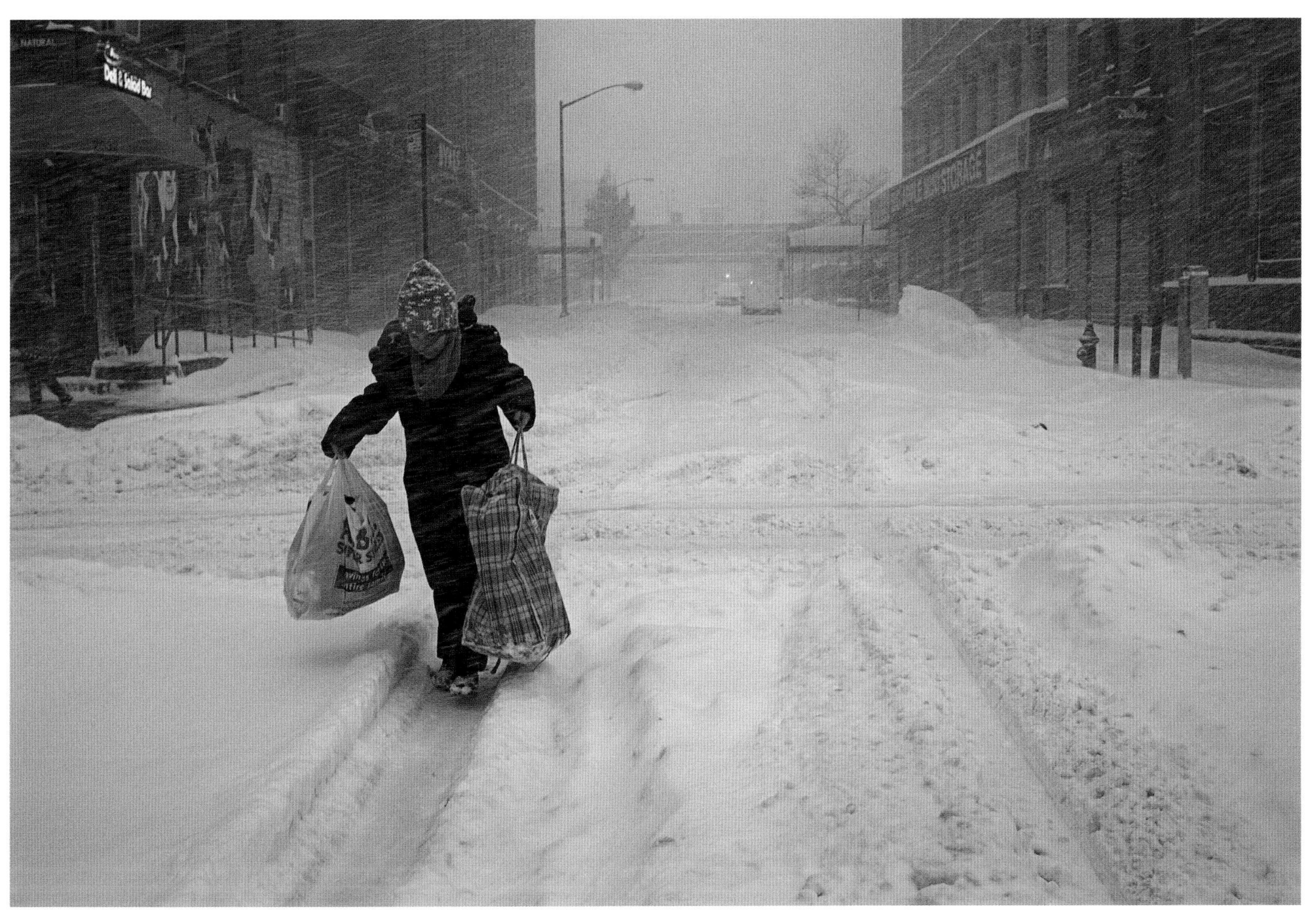

*Stepping Out*, New York City, USA, 2016

# 44

# Magda Chudzik

It was a misty autumn morning near the Vistula River in Krakow, Poland. I had decided to set off for work early with the intention of taking photographs on the way. Strolling on the banks of the river, I suddenly spotted a group of rowers heading toward the Bernatek Footbridge. Instantly, I realized I had a split second to take a symmetrical photograph of them—the rowboat was moving rapidly. I was thrilled; it was a quick shot of adrenaline. I rushed under the footbridge and pressed the shutter button. Had I hesitated for a moment, I would have missed this perfect opportunity.

*Magda is a graphic designer, webmaster, and photographer. She works with light and clear forms, vesting her photos with a dose of nostalgia.*

MAGDA CHUDZIK, Polish

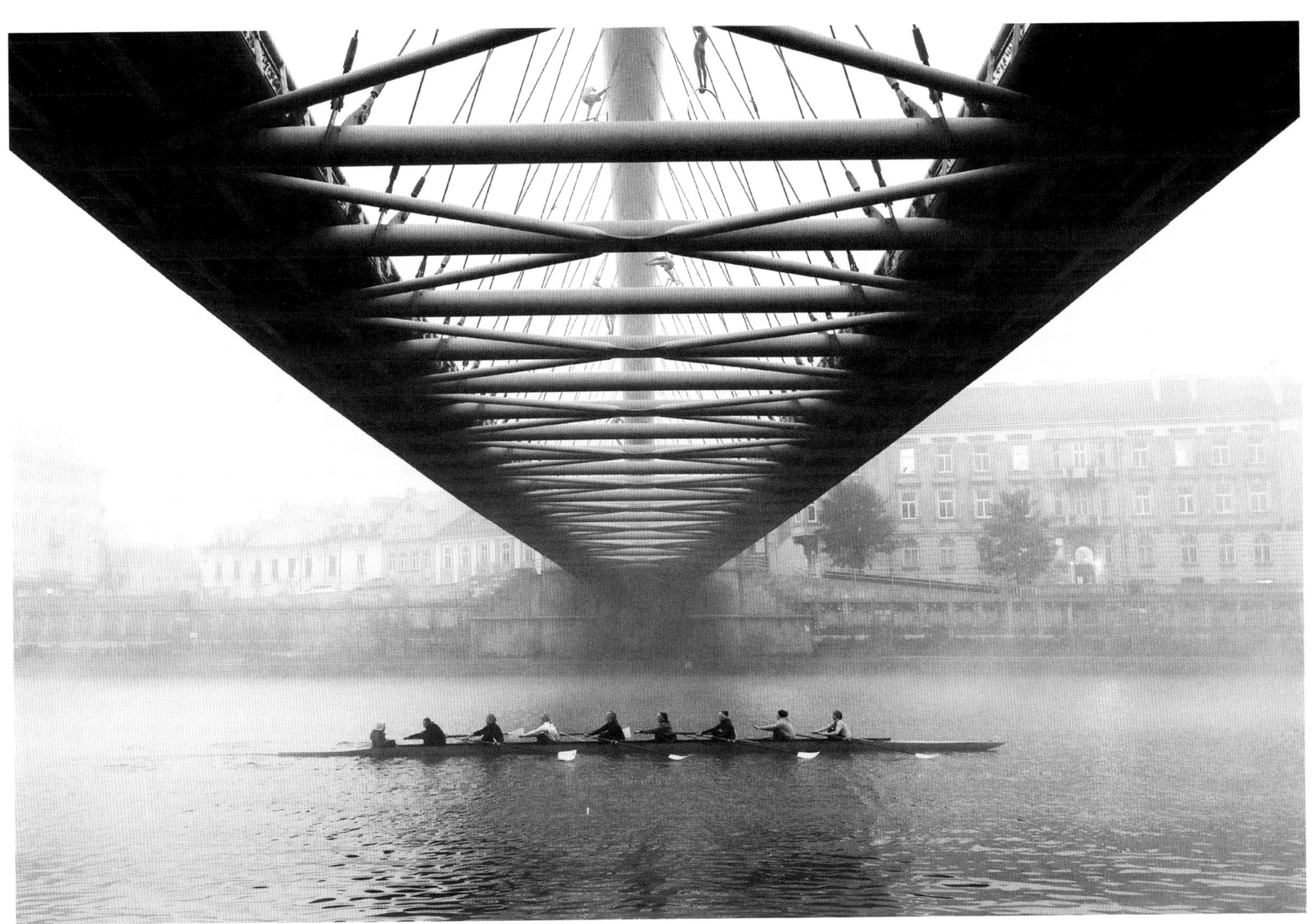

*Symmetry*, Krakow, Poland, 2018

# 45

# Danielle L. Goldstein

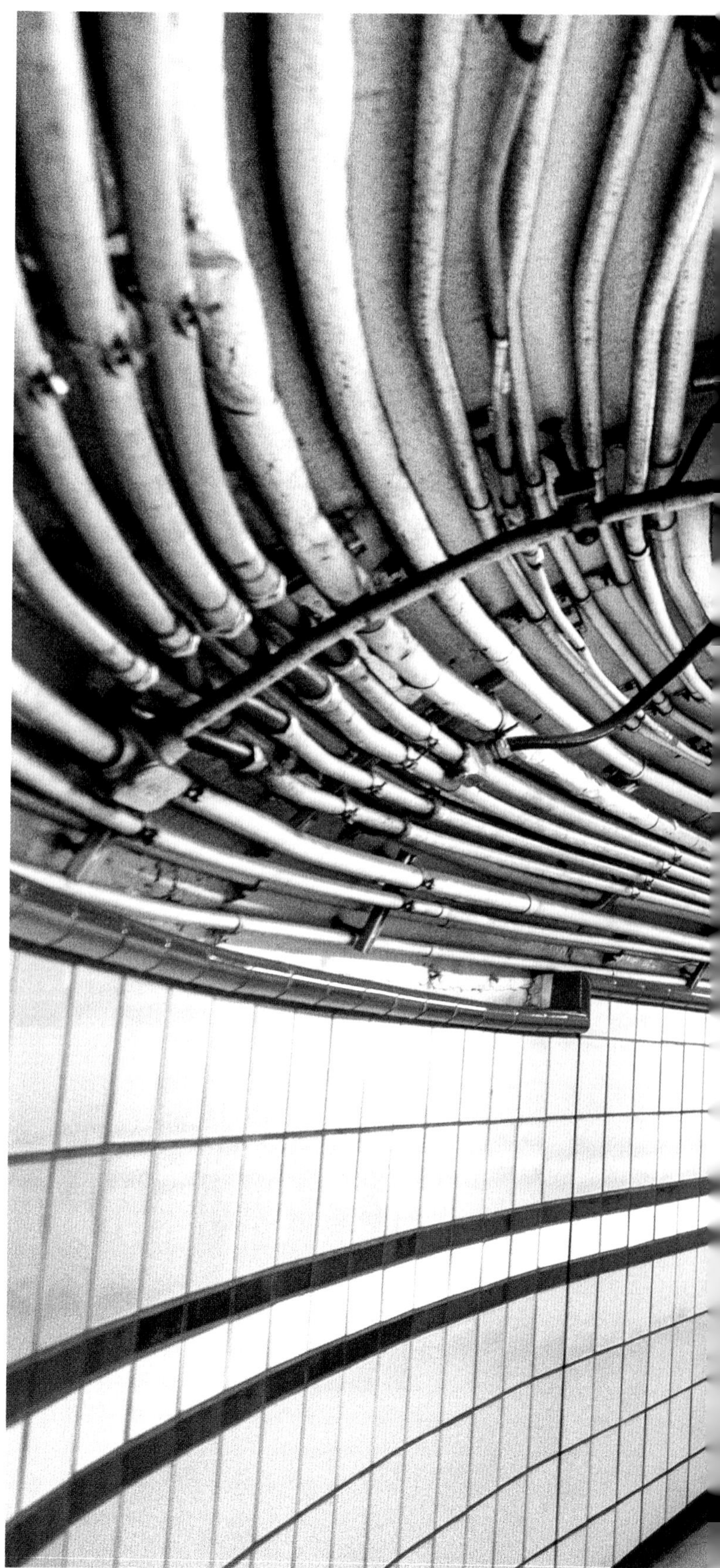

New York City is vast, in its architecture, infrastructure, and commerce, as well as in its sensory onslaught and constant supply of humanity. That is what makes it both fascinating and overwhelming. It's easy to get lost here. But we often forget that this dense urban forest is, in reality, a collection of individual trees.

I aim to highlight these individuals and their relationship to the structures of the city. Bringing awareness to the city's small moments is an act of devotion to the individuals who reside here and to the beauty of their surroundings. I sought out this location for its graphic architecture and complex lines. It's industrial and gritty, representative of New York's unusual charm. It was quite empty on that day, and I waited patiently for someone to enter my frame. When she did, with her confident saunter, the connection between the industrial and the human was complete.

*Danielle is based in New York City. Her work has been exhibited internationally and is part of the permanent collection of the Museum of the City of New York.*

DANIELLE L. GOLDSTEIN, American

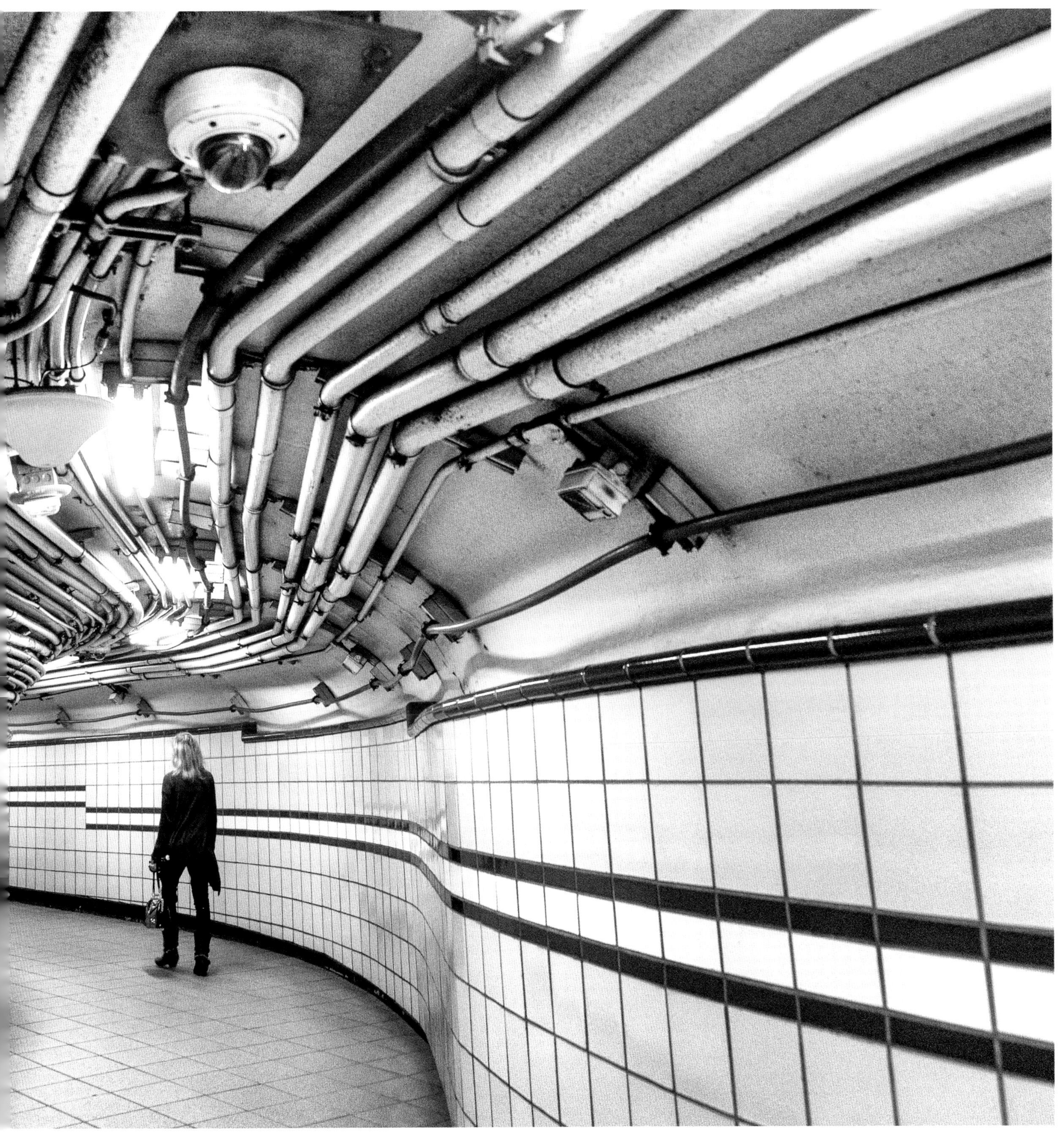

*Alone*, New York City, USA, 2019

# 46

# Ushi Grant

This image was taken in Munich, Germany, during a trip there in 2018. I was drawn to the lines and of course the play of light and shadows when suddenly a woman appeared on the side of the street. I was happy when she decided to cross the road and I managed to capture her seemingly mimicking, with her legs, the triangle of lines that she had stepped into.

*Ushi is an Australia-based photographer drawn to capturing the theater of life as it is played out on the street, both at home and during her travels.*

USHI GRANT, Australian

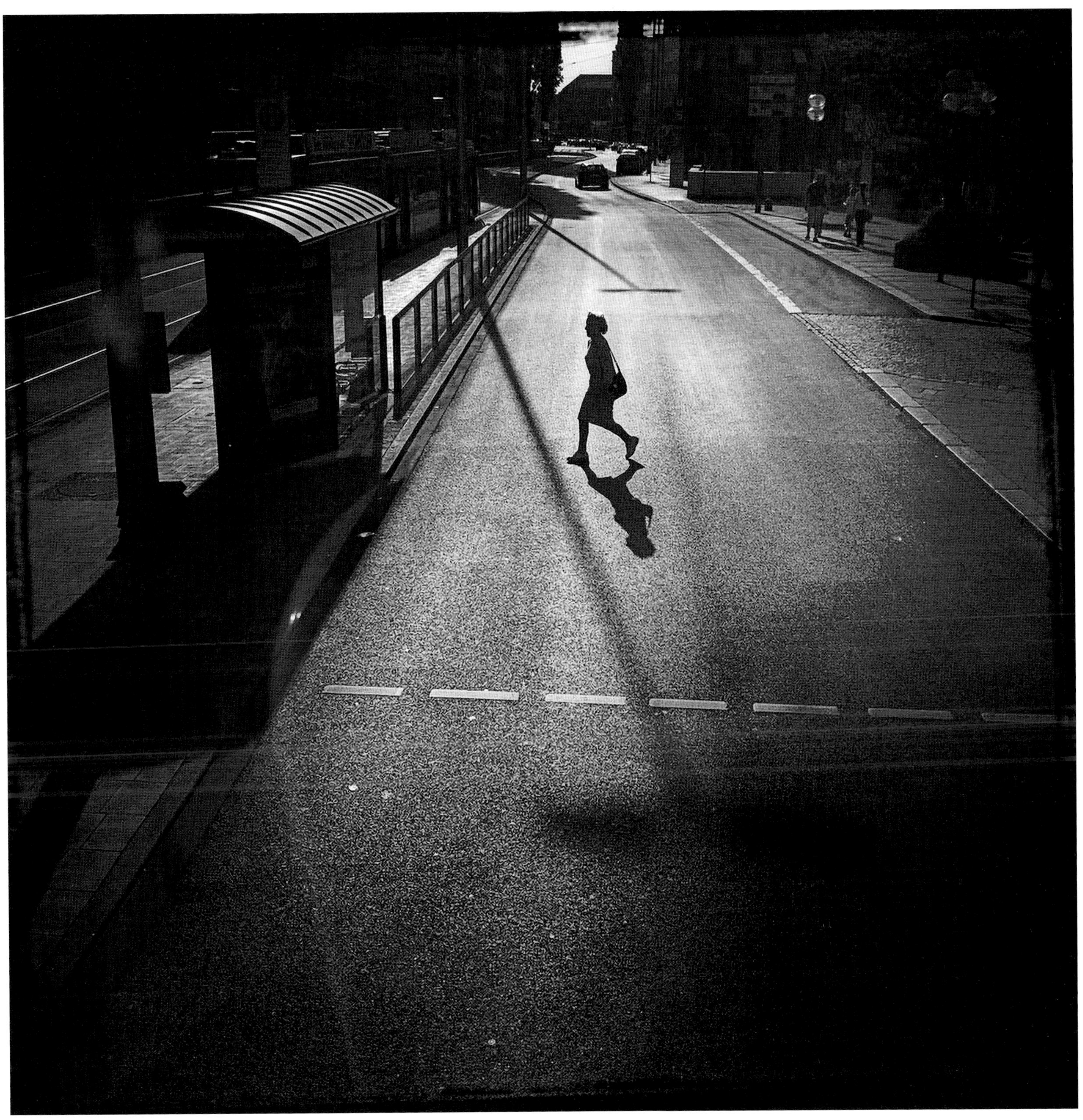

*Cross the Line*, Munich, Germany, 2018

# 47

# Selnur Okudan

When I focused on the green tent, this man appeared with his shining hair in the middle of the darkness, so I captured him.

*Selnur began in travel photography and then came to explore the surprises and special moments that happen on city streets. Now she follows the soul of those critical moments, which allows her to live in a dimension very different from the real world.*

SELNUR OKUDAN, Turkish

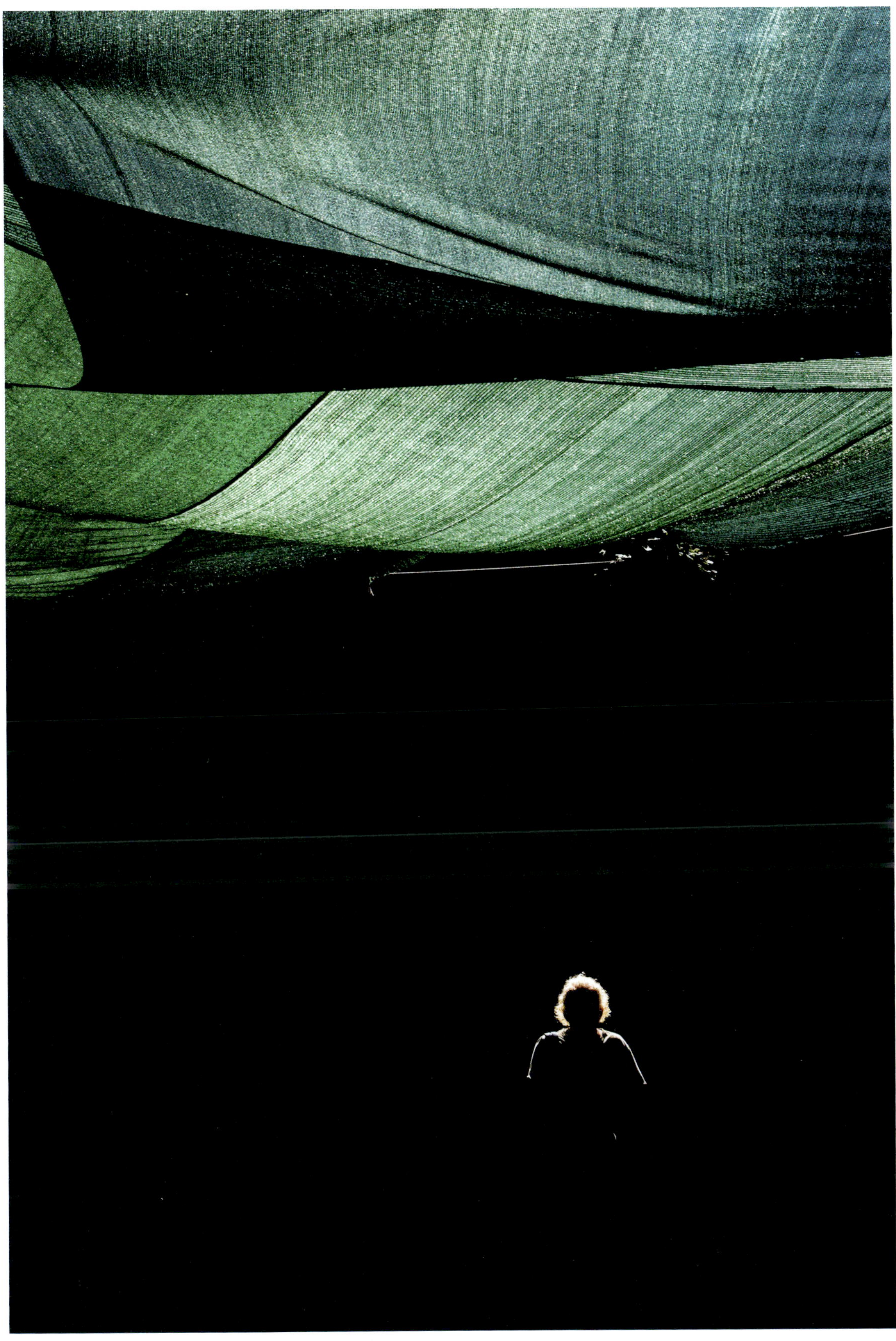

*Light Hair*, Antalya, Turkey, 2018

# 48.

# Valérie SIX

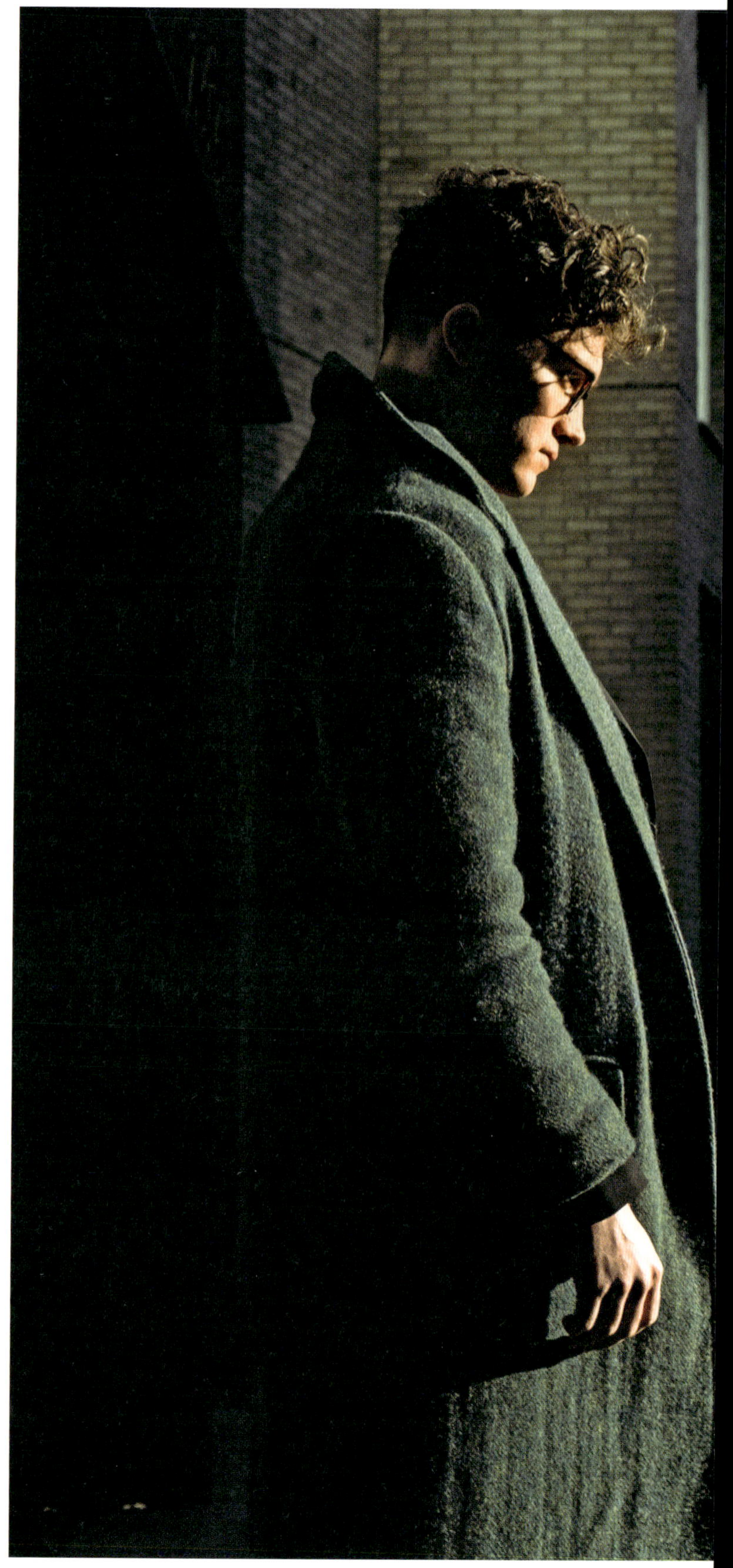

Shoreditch, a vibrant district in the East End of London, is one of my favorite places for street photography in the city. It's steeped in history, and its architecture, narrow lanes, eclectic shops, and bars are the perfect stage for the kind of theatrical pictures I like to take. Spotting this man from afar, I immediately thought that his attitude, his large green coat, and the way his face was lit by natural light would make him a good subject. By chance, the man didn't move an inch, keeping his position and sullen expression during the several shots I took of him, leaving me wondering about his thoughts. Knowing that Shoreditch was also the place where Shakespeare performed his early plays, at the Curtain Theatre, makes this image even more dramatic in my eyes.

This image is part of the series *Shades of Thoughts*.

*Winner of the Women Street Photographers Artist Residency 2019 in NYC, Valérie uses the streets as a setting in which to compose enigmatic scenes, projections of her amused or questioning eye on our world.*

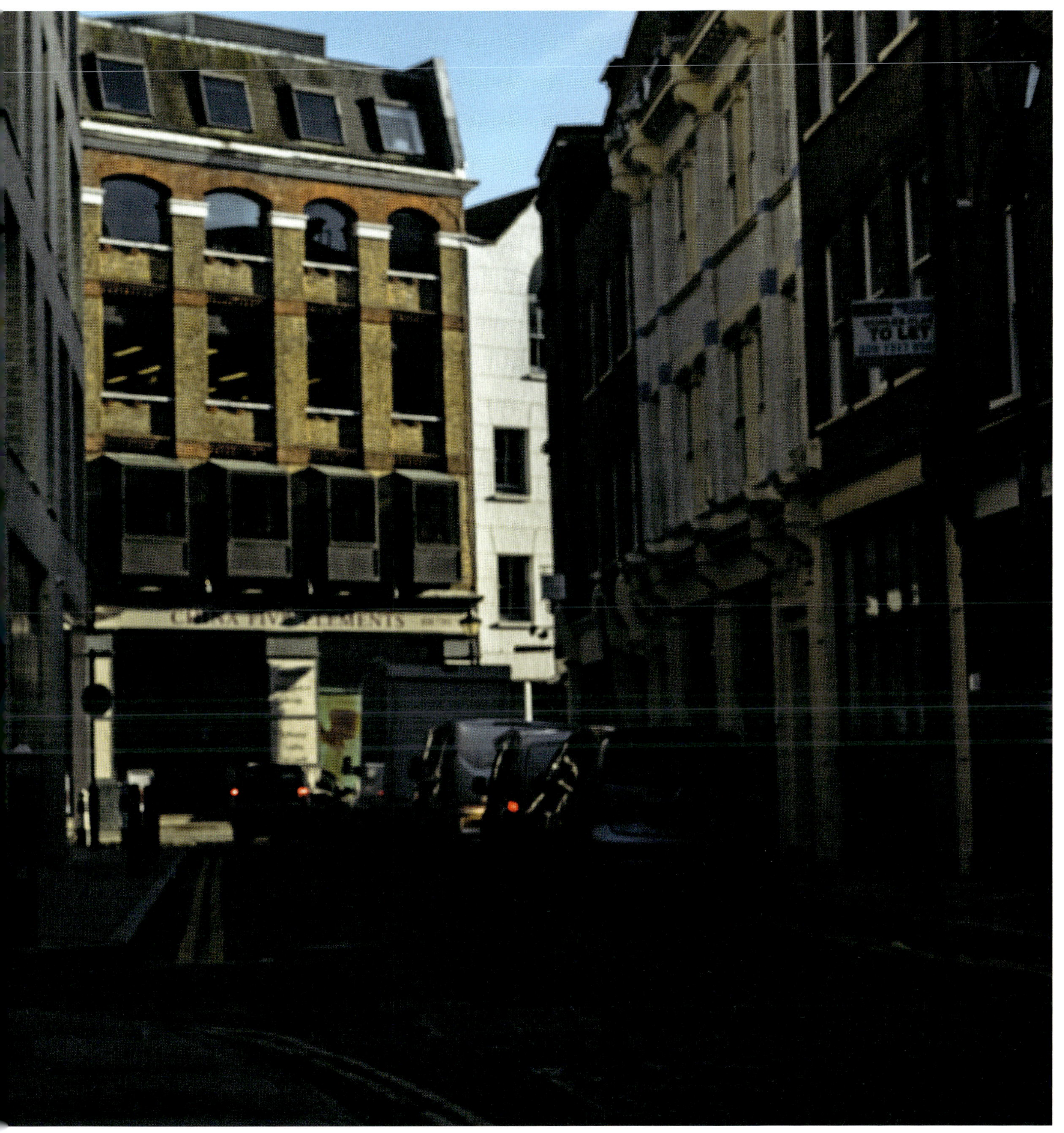


*Curtain on a Thought*, London, UK, 2018

# 49

# Suzanne Stein

Melissa lives with DJ on the street in the East Village, NYC. The power of a scene or portrait is dependent on a spark of energy that's hard to define, an intangible force that compels me to take a picture. Sometimes it only lasts for a second, as in this image. Melissa is thinking about turning herself in to the police to serve a sentence in jail because of several outstanding warrants for her arrest. To do so she will have to leave her partner DJ.

When I'm out on the street and see a scene that has that electric feeling, I can't move on until I take a picture. I remain calm as I work to photograph a moment, but in my mind I'm frantic, sometimes maniacally chastising myself as I work and try desperately not to fumble lens caps, stumble backward, or make some compositional error that will render the scene meaningless.

It's an intense joy when I'm able to succeed in making a picture that tells the story of what I'm seeing and feeling in front of me.

*Suzanne is a New York-based photographer. Her work is characterized by an artistic, narrative approach to social realism.*

SUZANNE STEIN, American

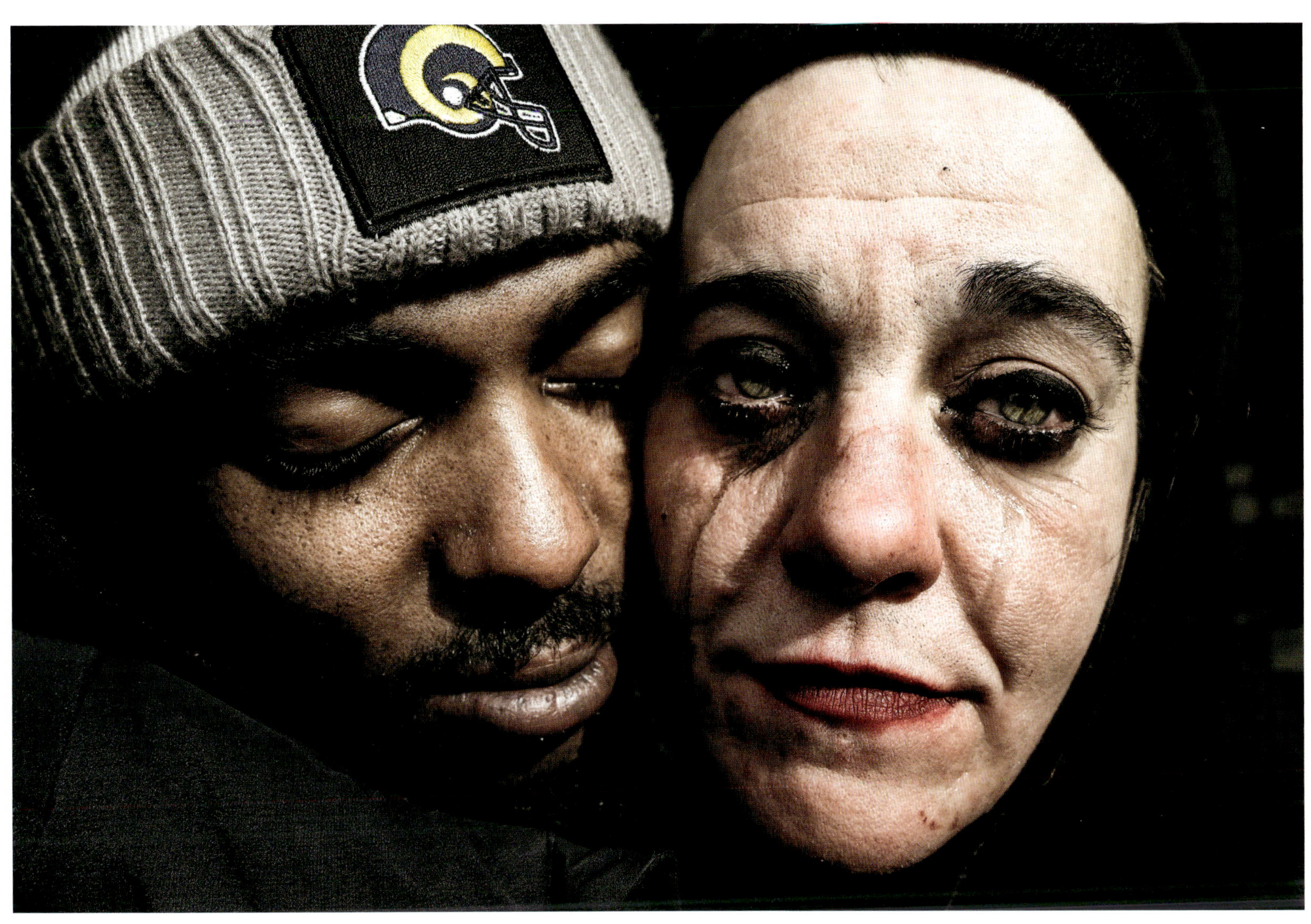

*Melissa and DJ*, New York City, USA, 2019

# 50.

# Vanessa Pallotta

I was in the car when I saw a poster of this famous
woman on a bus in front of me. I immediately decided to
put the windshield wipers on, so as to be able to use a
soap-and-water filter, a way of creating something totally
different and very personal.

*Vanessa is a photographer based in Rome. Her work has
been published in major magazines such as* Vanity Fair,
Vogue, *and* L'Officiel.

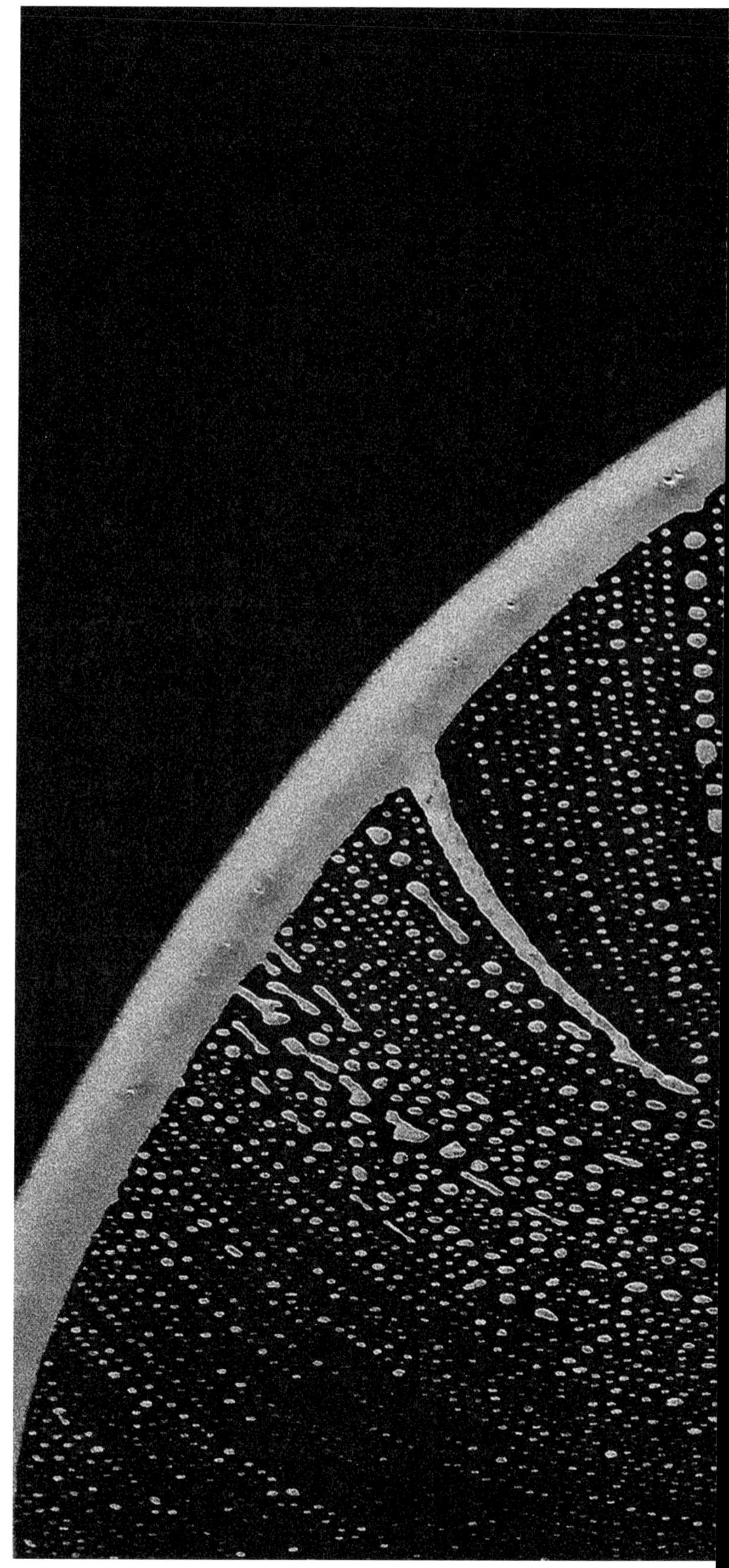

VANESSA PALLOTTA, Italian

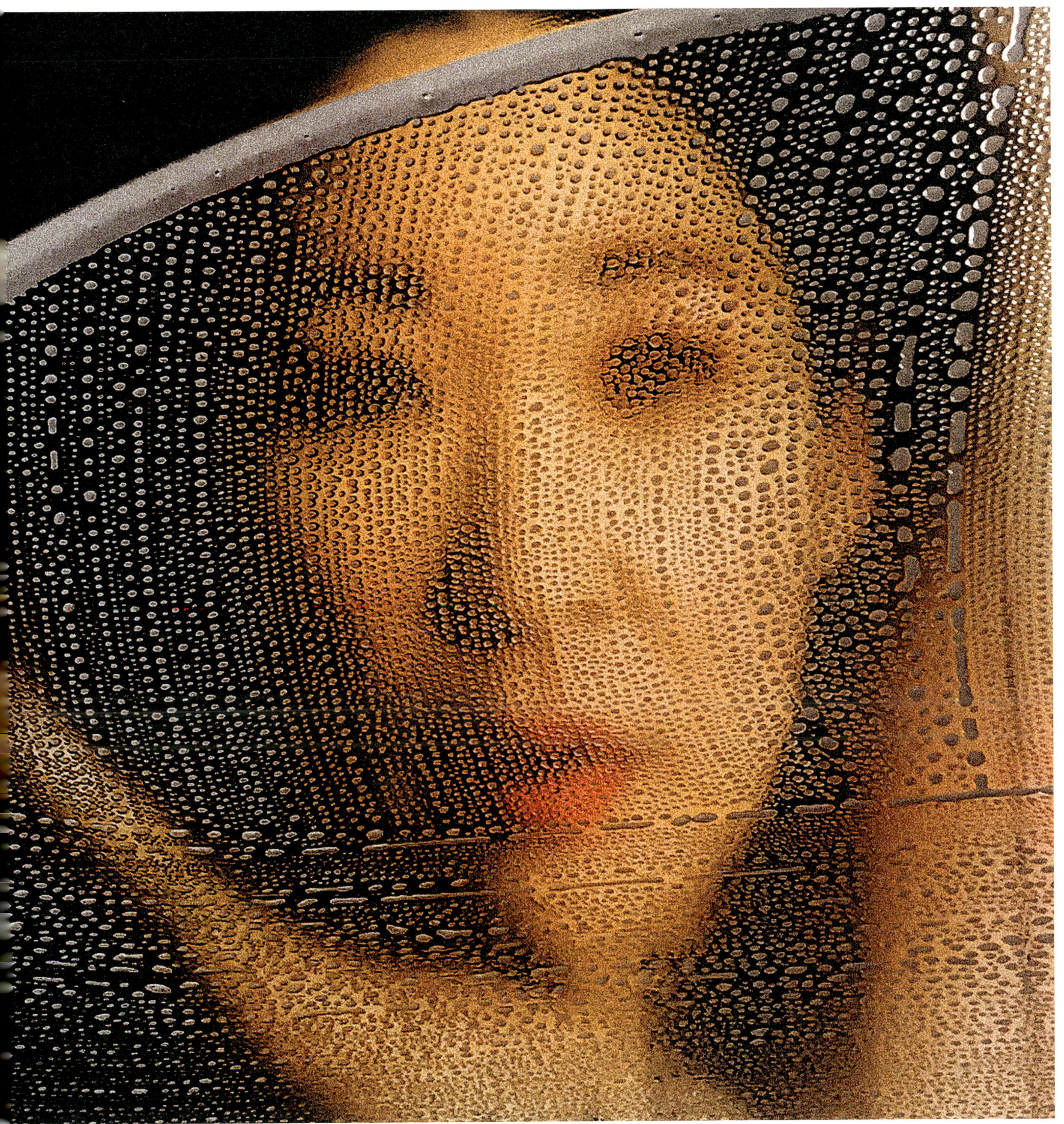

*Oh*, Rome, Italy, 2018

# 51.

# Anna Biret

I live for the spontaneous encounters that can only happen in the streets; the gazes, compositions, and colors lead me to create portraits through human contact and empathy. A woman covering her eyes from the sun, a shadow pouring over the edges of a fruit stand, a scarf that is stolen by a sudden gust of wind: These ordinary scenes become the extraordinary fragments that compose my photographs.

*Anna discovered street photography in Mandalay in 2018. The ordinary scenes of the people whom she crosses paths with become the extraordinary fragments that compose her photographs.*

ANNA BIRET, French

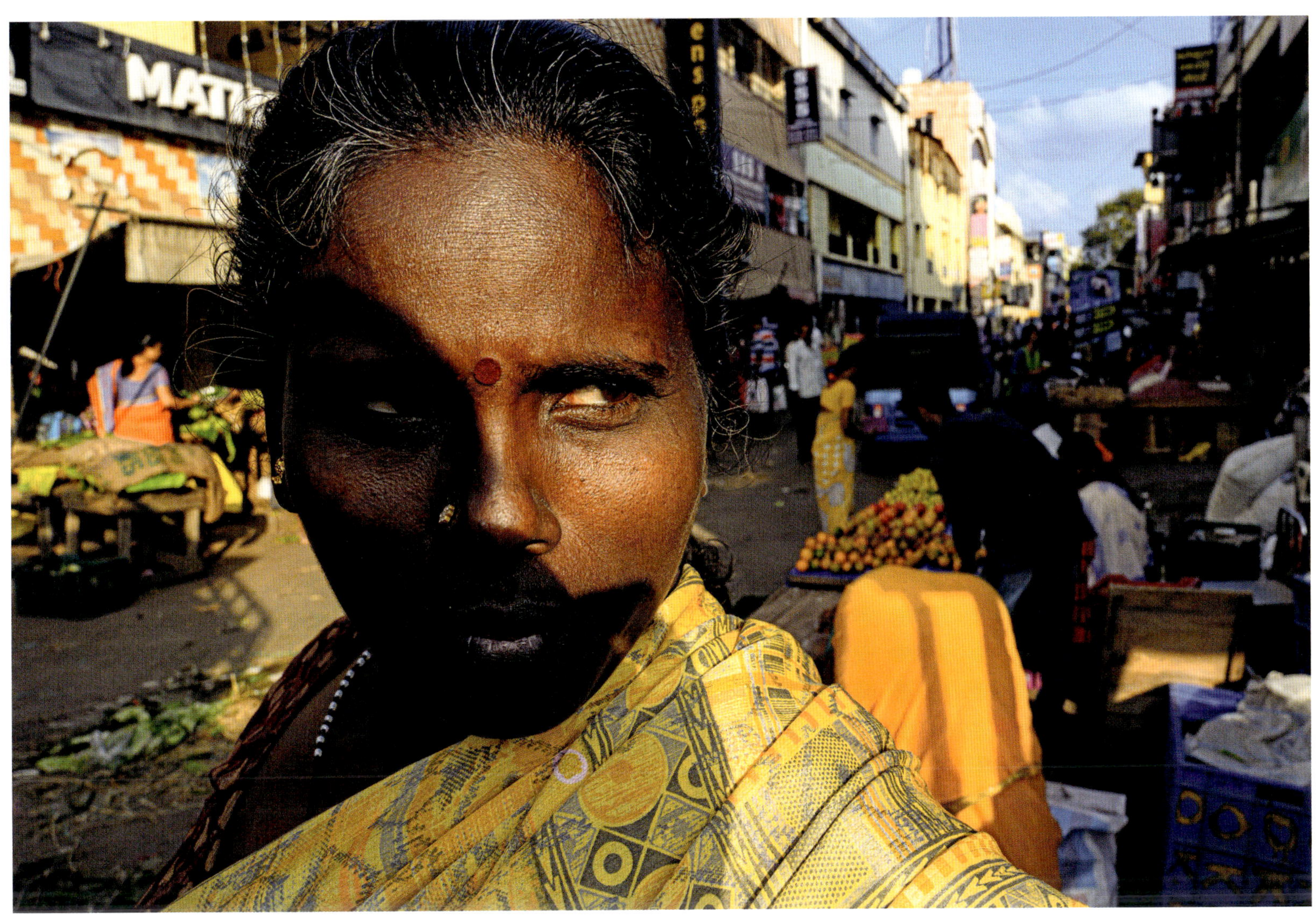

*Mysterious Woman*, Chennai, India, 2020

# 52

# Michelle Groskopf

Hollywood can definitely break your heart on any given day. I saw this man smoking something a little rough on Vine Street. I usually walk on by but the striking simplicity of his shirt and hand against the sidewalk made me stop and ask. The tones of it all. Got a nod and quickly took the shot. It exemplifies many things I love about photography, pared down and direct, but you can't separate the beauty from the man's life. You can't ever forget about the man.

*Michelle is an LA-based photographer specializing in editorial, commercial, and street photography. Her street photography is represented by PARISTEXASLA gallery.*

MICHELLE GROSKOPF, American/Canadian

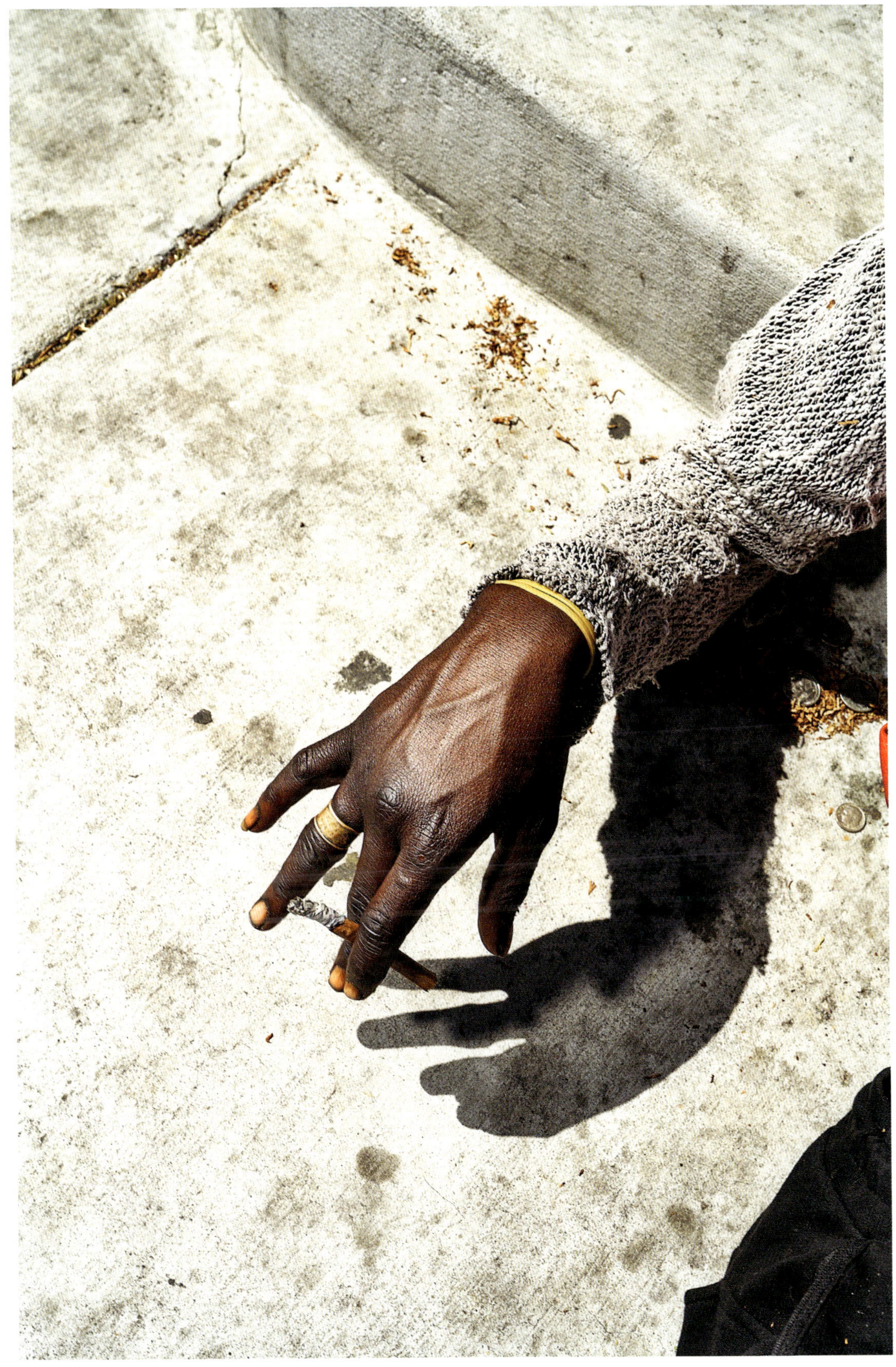

*Untitled*, Los Angeles, USA, 2019

# 53

# Ioana Marinca

On my way home from assisting on a photoshoot, my camera was around my neck. I saw this couple and had to take a picture—even if it meant standing on the left side of the escalator (for Londoners this is a cardinal sin). I think I took three frames; her hand was only resting on his shoulder for one of them. It's this kind of fleeting gesture I love noticing, whether in London or elsewhere.

*Ioana is a Transilvanian-born freelance photographer. Now based in East London, she enjoys exploring the concepts of home and belonging.*

IOANA MARINCA, Romanian

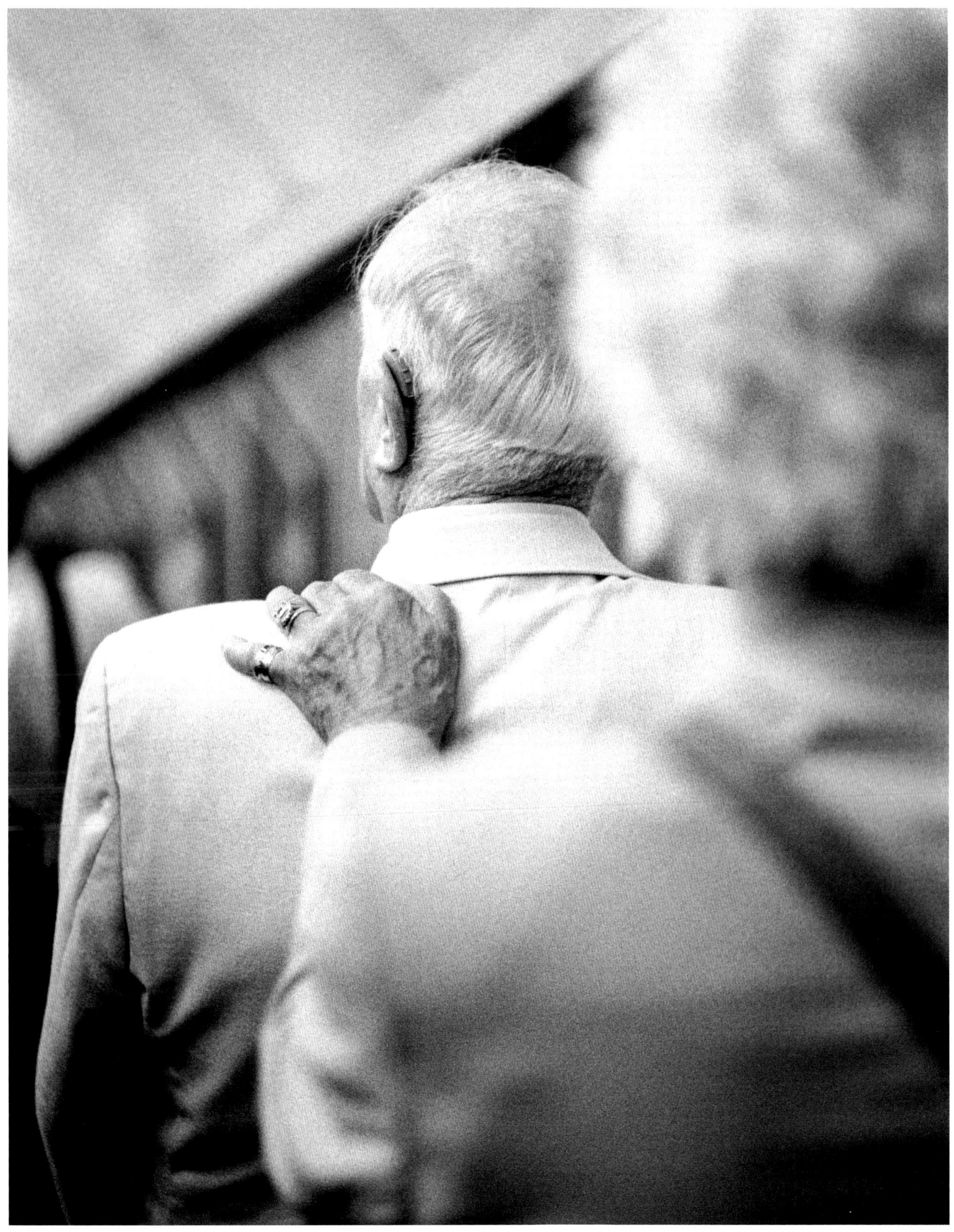

*London Underground*, London, UK, 2019

# 54.

# Libby Lolmsen

When visiting a new place I always challenge myself to create unexpected images, different from those taken by photographers before me.

The ancient port town of Hội An is a bustling, chaotic place celebrated for its color. In contrast I created a series of black-and-white, minimalist images using shadows and solitary figures. I believe that these best capture the essence of the local people.

The title *Nón lá* is derived from the name of the traditional Vietnamese conical hat.

*Libby is a street photographer from Perth in Western Australia. She is inspired by travel, contrast, color, and the beauty in everyday moments.*

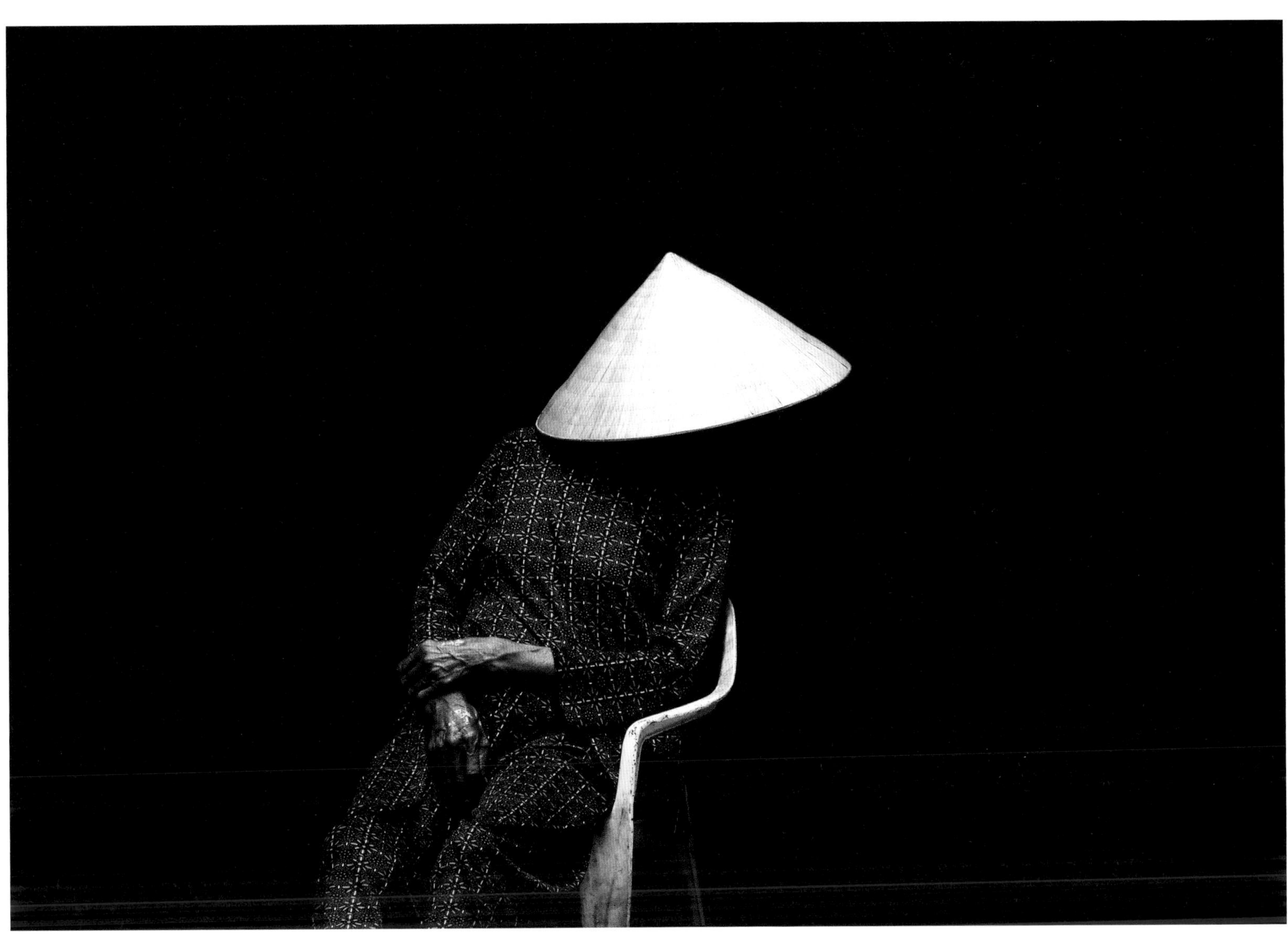

*Nón lá*, Hội An, Vietnam, 2015

# 55

# Patty Jansen

This photo was taken in Paris in August 2018. It was an exceptionally hot day, and many people were wearing straw hats to protect themselves from the burning sun. I was testing the required exposure settings on my camera when this man passed by. I shot without thinking or having expectations, but it turned out the relative underexposure made his hat seem to float above his sand-colored suit against a deep dark background. Sometimes photography is all about experimenting and the joy of the unexpected. I remember the intense smile it left on my face.

*Patty is a medical doctor with a passion for photographing the harmony between humans and their context by focusing on colors, geometry, and composition. Her work has emerged through Instagram.*

PATTY JANSEN, Dutch

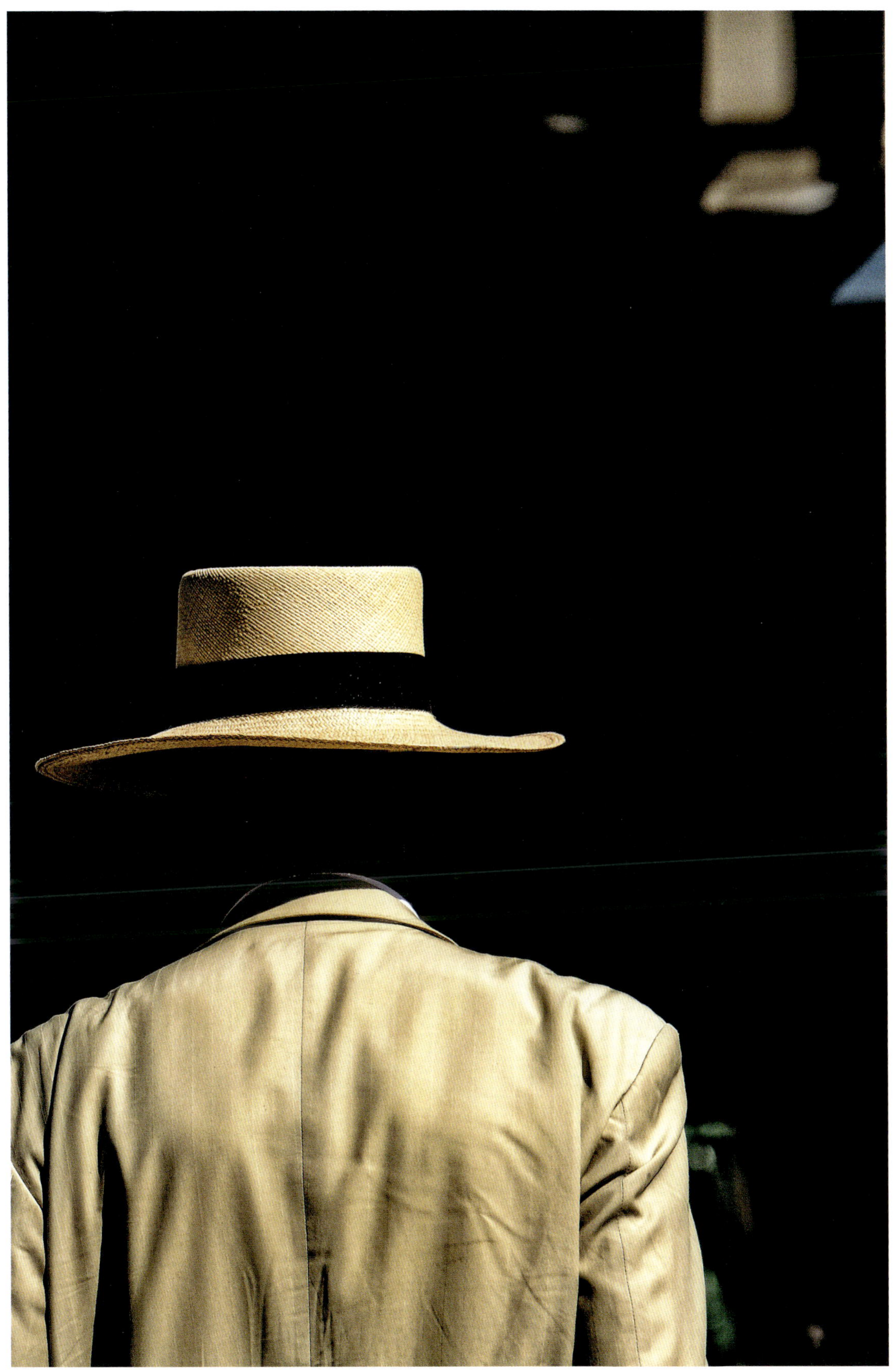

*The Floating Hat*, Paris, France, 2018

# 56

# Sofía Sebastián

I took this picture in New York City during the Veterans Day Parade in 2018. It was one of those beautiful, sunny days in NYC. I watched the men dressed in police uniforms from afar, waiting on a corner. I got excited and quickly made my way to them. I came really close and took several frames. This is the shot that stuck with me, not only because of the perfect arrangement of light and darkness, but for the beautiful layering of hats and shadowy faces.

*Born in Madrid but based in Washington, DC, Sofía's work has been exhibited internationally in both solo and group shows. In 2019, she received the Female in Focus Award from 1854 Media.*

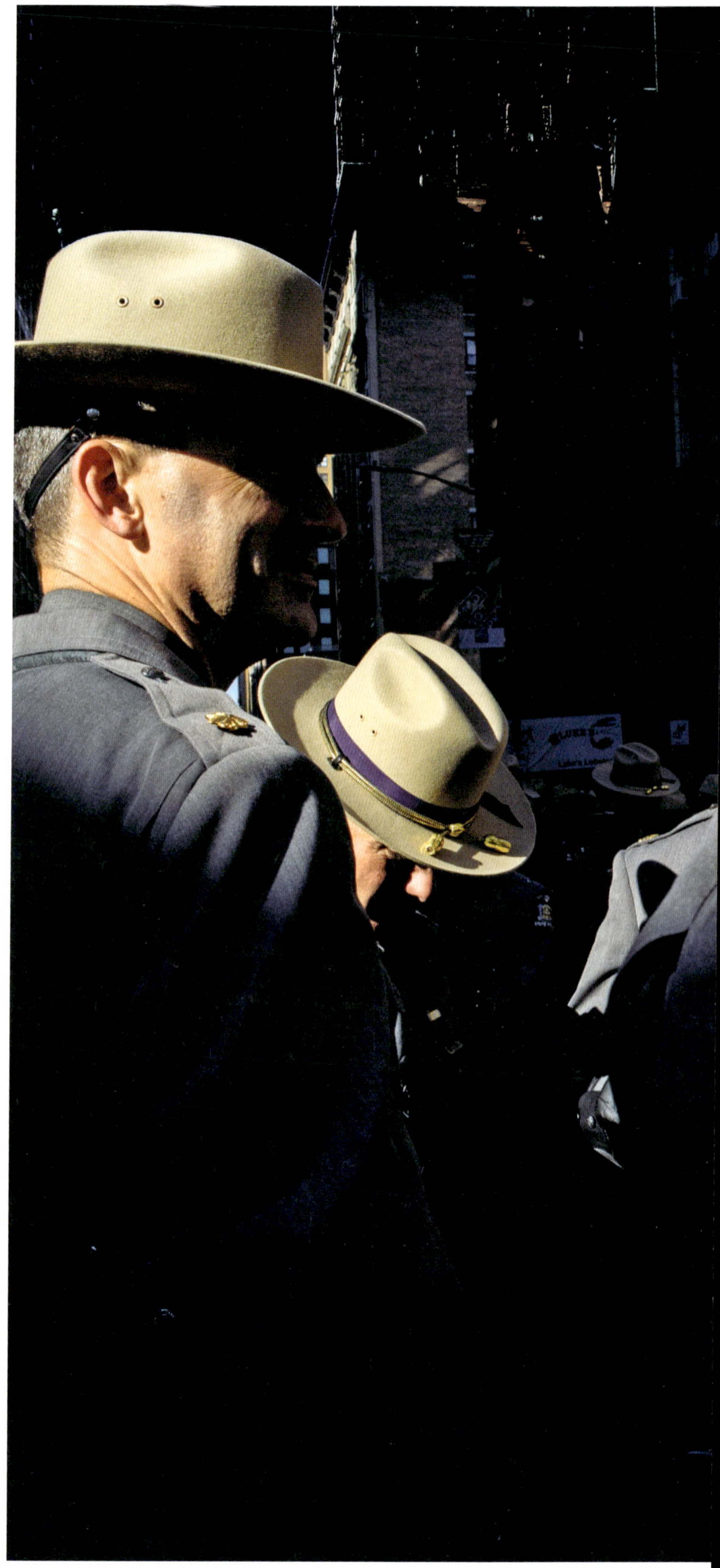

SOFÍA SEBASTIÁN, Spanish

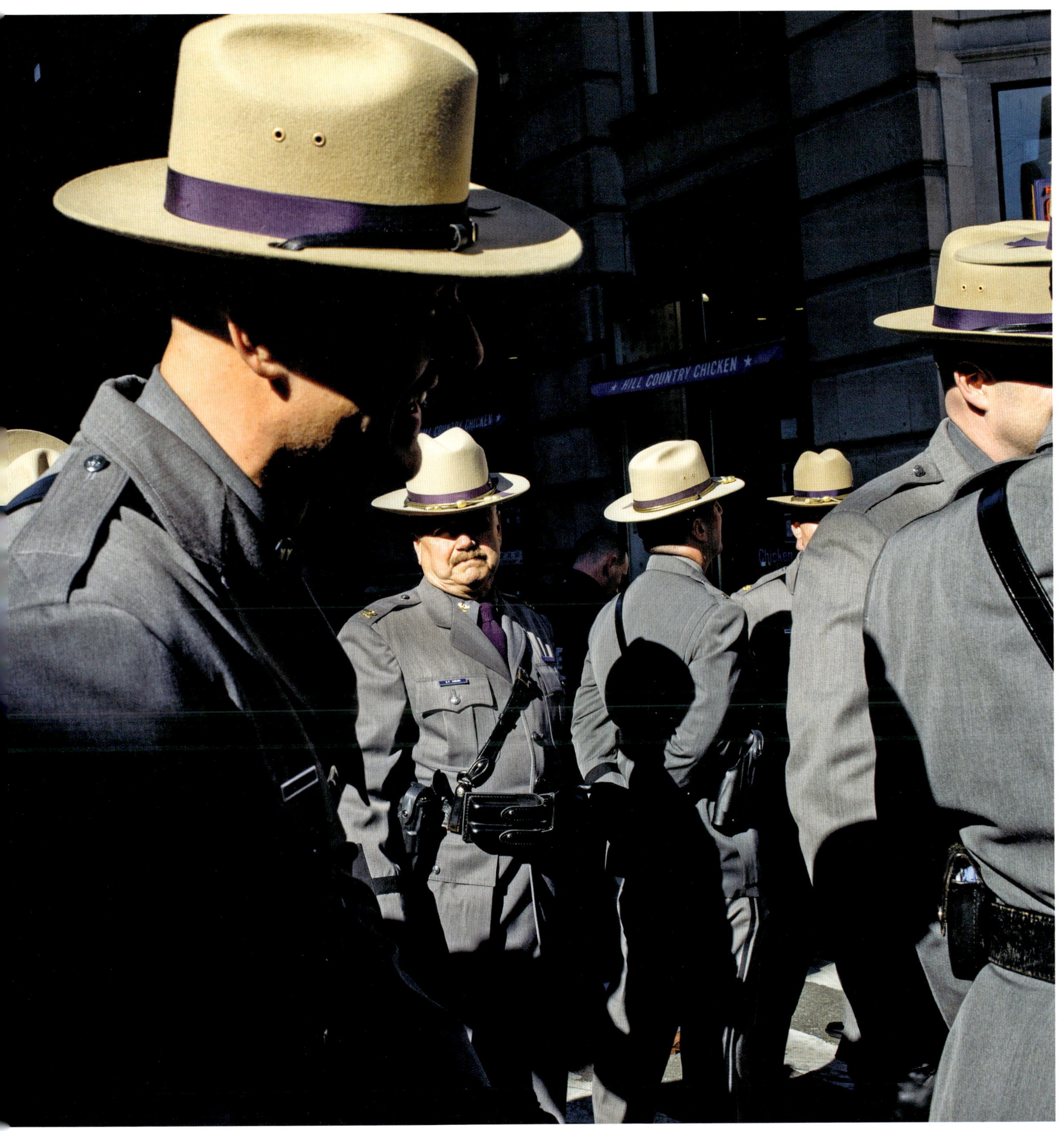

*Law and Order*, New York City, USA, 2018

# 57

# Bambi

Winter was ending and the light in Madrid was golden.
I was walking along Gran Vía and I saw this girl with
golden curls who stood out from the rest of the people, at
least for me. The timing of the gust of wind was pure luck.
This photo always reminds me of spring.

*Bambi is a photographer based in Madrid. She loves to
capture unique characters from everyday life and create
a dreamlike atmosphere with pastel tones.*

BAMBI, Spanish

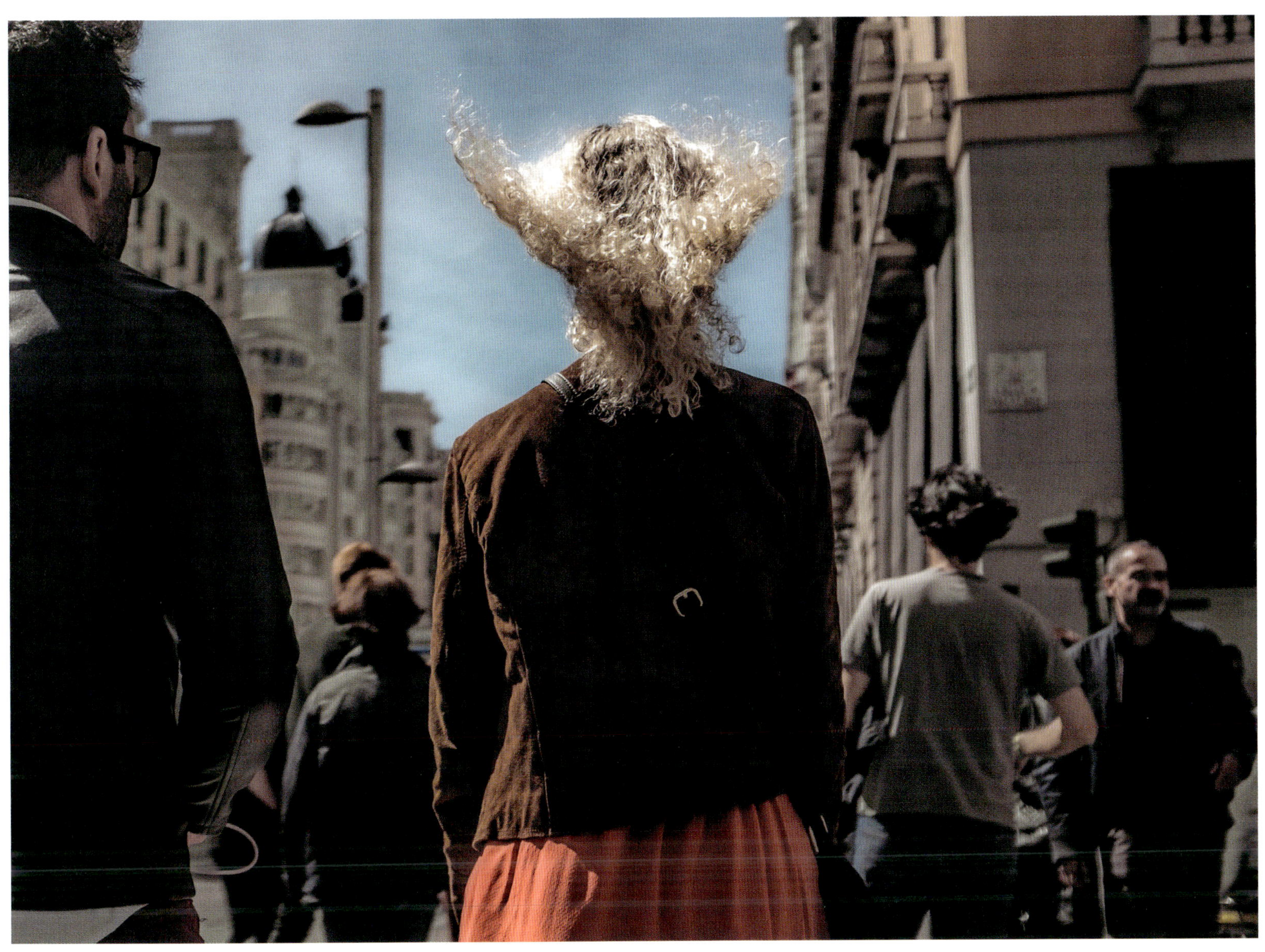

*Spring*, Madrid, Spain, 2017

# 58

# B Jane Levine

In the flash of a few seconds, a woman with red hair walks past me on the street. She stops at the corner before crossing Fifth Avenue and I notice how the shape of her hairdo mimics the pattern on her jacket. Against the backdrop of the colors of the buildings of New York City and the shadows they create, her hair is radiant in the afternoon sun. She has a perfect upswept hairdo, similar to the way my grandmother wore her hair, held in place with hairspray and bobby pins. Her hair and my memory are as fixed as the architecture in the background.

*Jane is a trained biochemist who studied photography at the International Center of Photography and other photography workshops. Her photographs, taken on the streets of New York and other cities, are a composite of the pieces of her life, a self-portrait.*

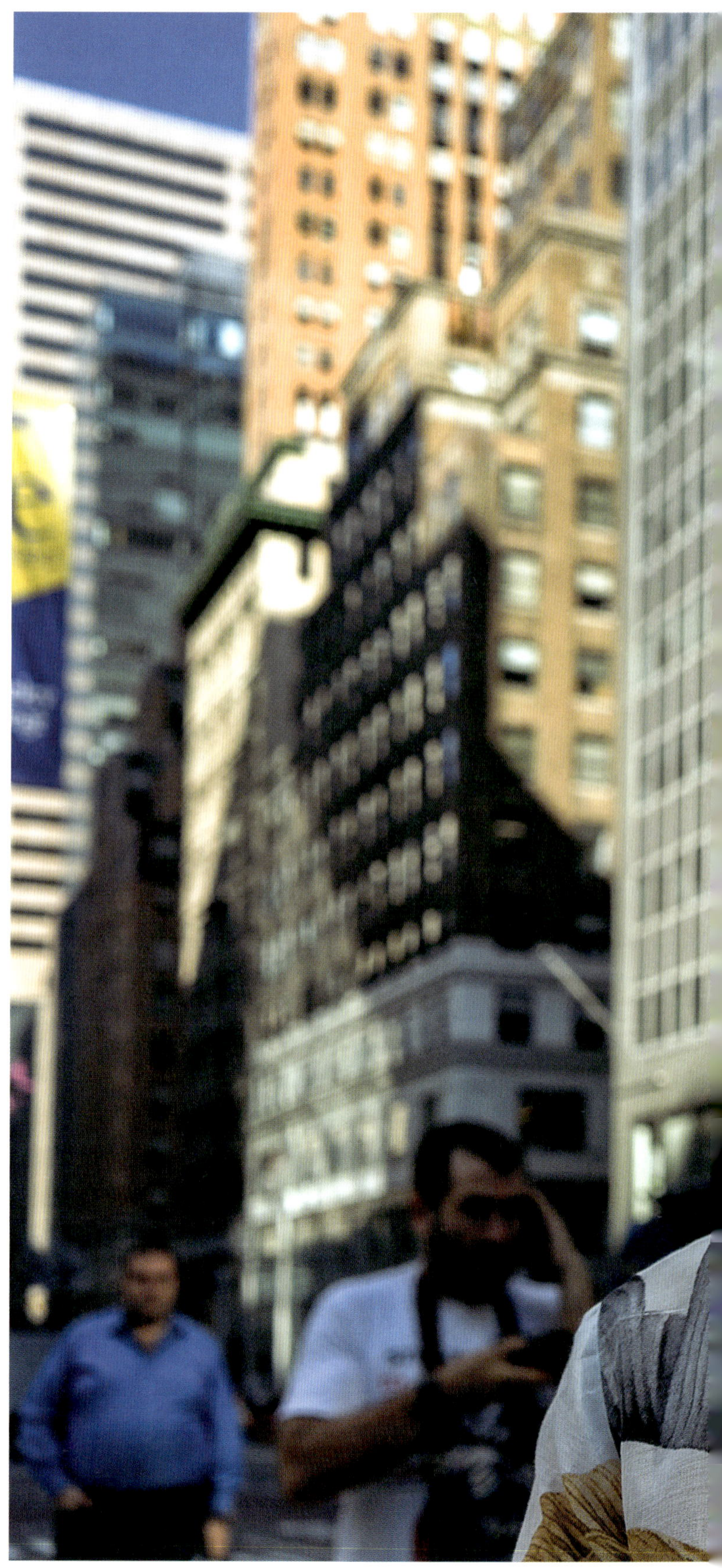

B JANE LEVINE, American

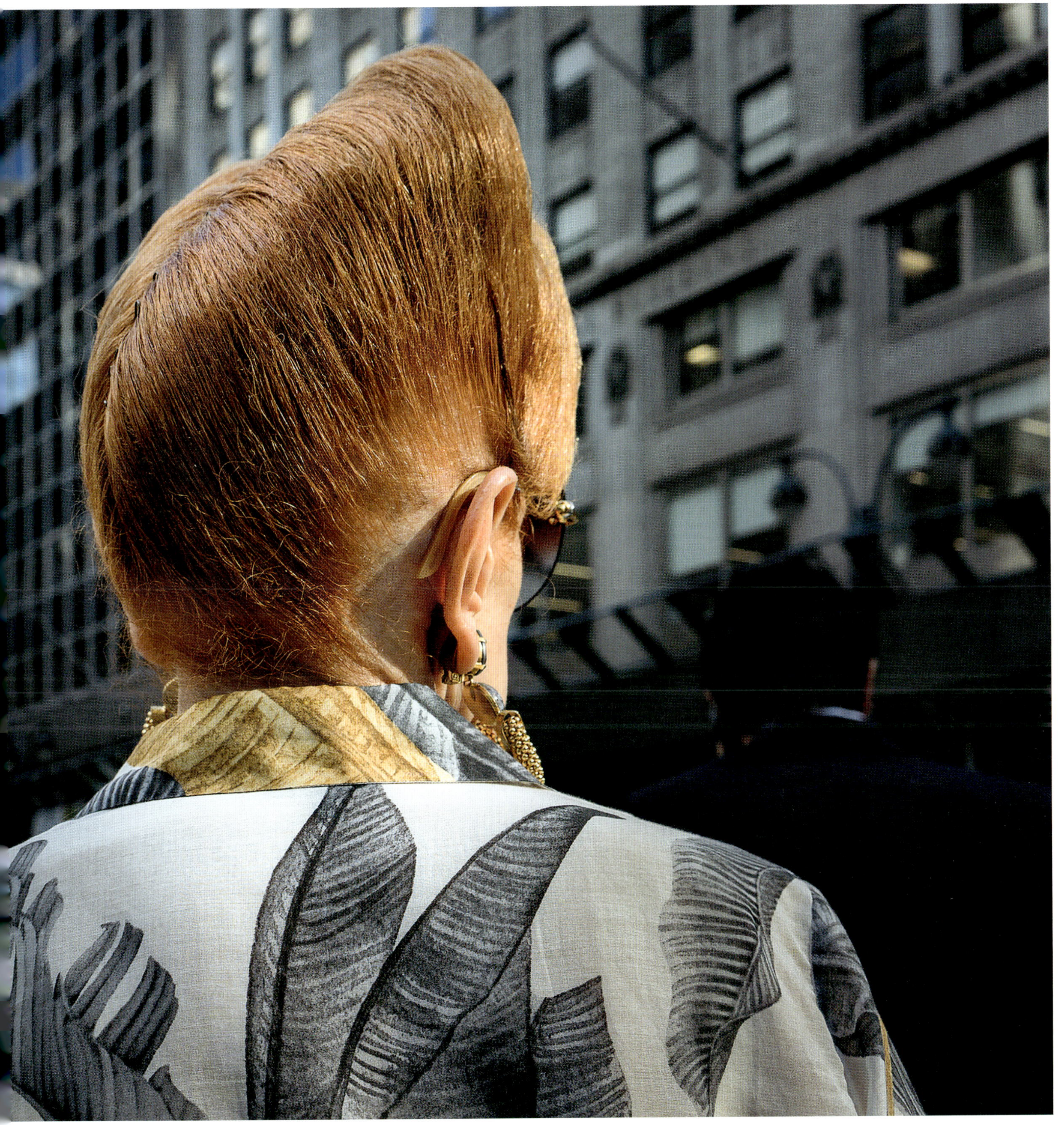

*Red Upsweep*, New York City, USA, 2019

# 59.

# Efi Longinou

It was an ordinary day in the middle of the week. I was strolling on the main street of my neighborhood and thinking about what could make a Wednesday in the middle of winter special. Only a few people were on the streets. I started to feel cold. I walked faster and faster, in the mood to return home.

As I went, I saw a girl drinking coffee in a café. She was alone and looking at the table. I took one step, and then another, and the girl turned and looked at me.

A striking reflection fell on the window and transformed her into a majestic girl, a girl with a crown in her hair. It was my moment to take a photo.

*Efi is an actress for theater, cinema, and television. Her passion is street photography. She has been published in magazines and exhibitions worldwide.*

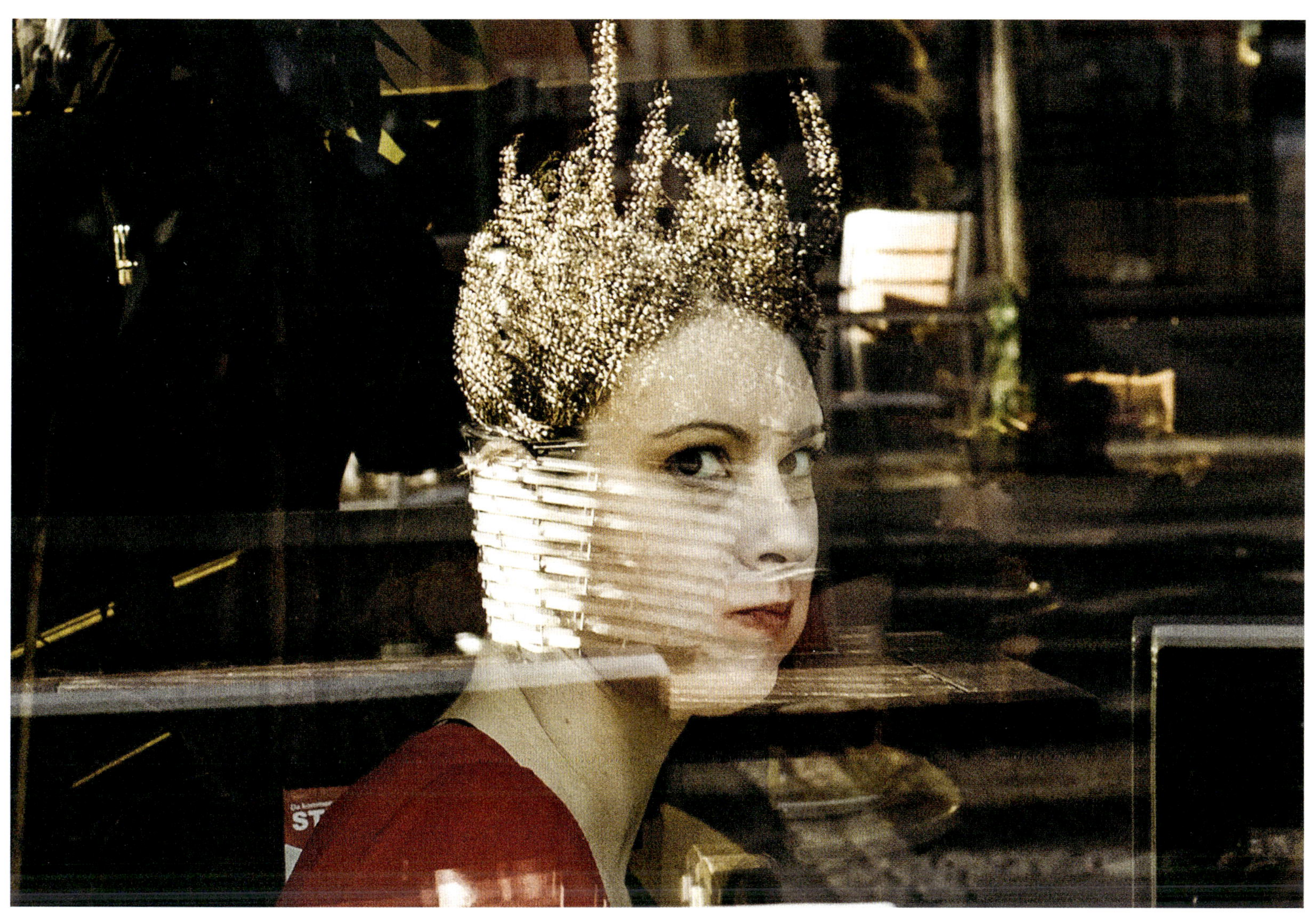

*Untitled*, Berlin, Germany, 2019

# Jane Zhang

I shot this image on one of my daily photo walks. I have gone past this café-restaurant many times, and I always make sure to look at who is sitting at that particular window.

It was one of those rare moments when all the pieces fall into place—the right person in the right place at the right moment. Street photography is exciting because you never know when that confluence of elements will happen.

I clicked the shutter as soon as I saw this lady, and at the same time, she lifted up her glass and made eye contact with me. It was her striking appearance that drew me to her at first instance, and her gaze possessed such warmth and intensity that it stirred my heart. Without saying a word, her presence evoked a strong sense of nostalgia, and with the complementary setting, I felt for a brief moment that I had captured a scene from the old days.

*Jane is a photographer based in Melbourne. Her work often utilizes distinctive light and color, with a focus on capturing emotive moments.*

JANE ZHANG, Australian

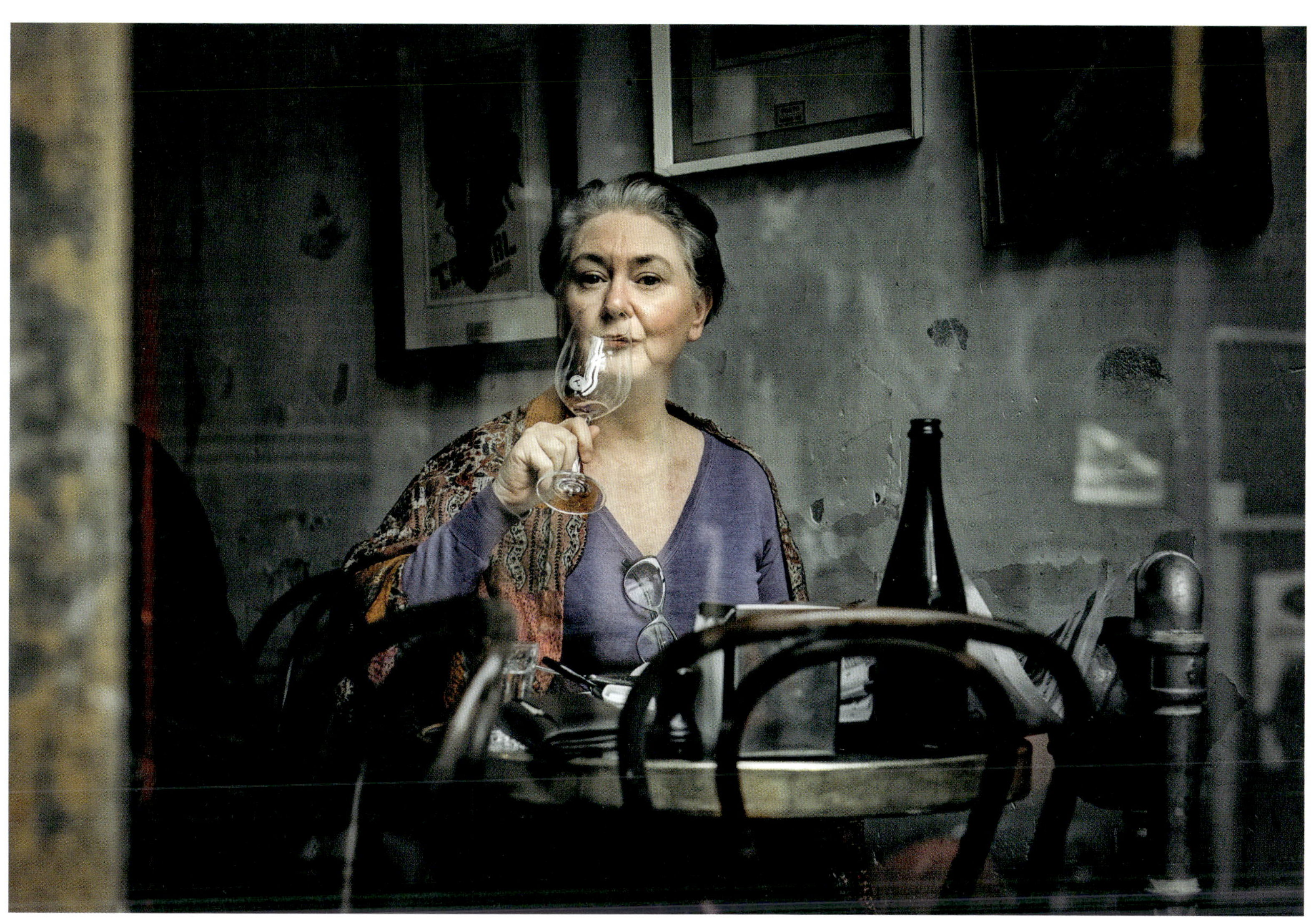

*Lady at the Window*, Melbourne, Australia, 2018

# Marina Koryakin

I took this photo in Tel Aviv, Israel, in a crowded place near the city market at noon. I was attracted by a group of young people who stood out against the background of hurrying people. They were aged seventeen or eighteen, no more, and were holding a wedding ceremony without any official or religious authorities. It was very strange. I was told not to take pictures and to go away, because it was an unauthorized wedding, and besides that they had their own photographer. I had to leave, but I managed to take one shot and I think it works. That is the beauty of street photography. You never know what is waiting for you around the corner.

*Marina was born in Ukraine and has lived in Tel Aviv since 2000. Before she discovered photography in 2015, she had never held a camera. Marina is fascinated by people and mood. Her work has been exhibited in various galleries.*

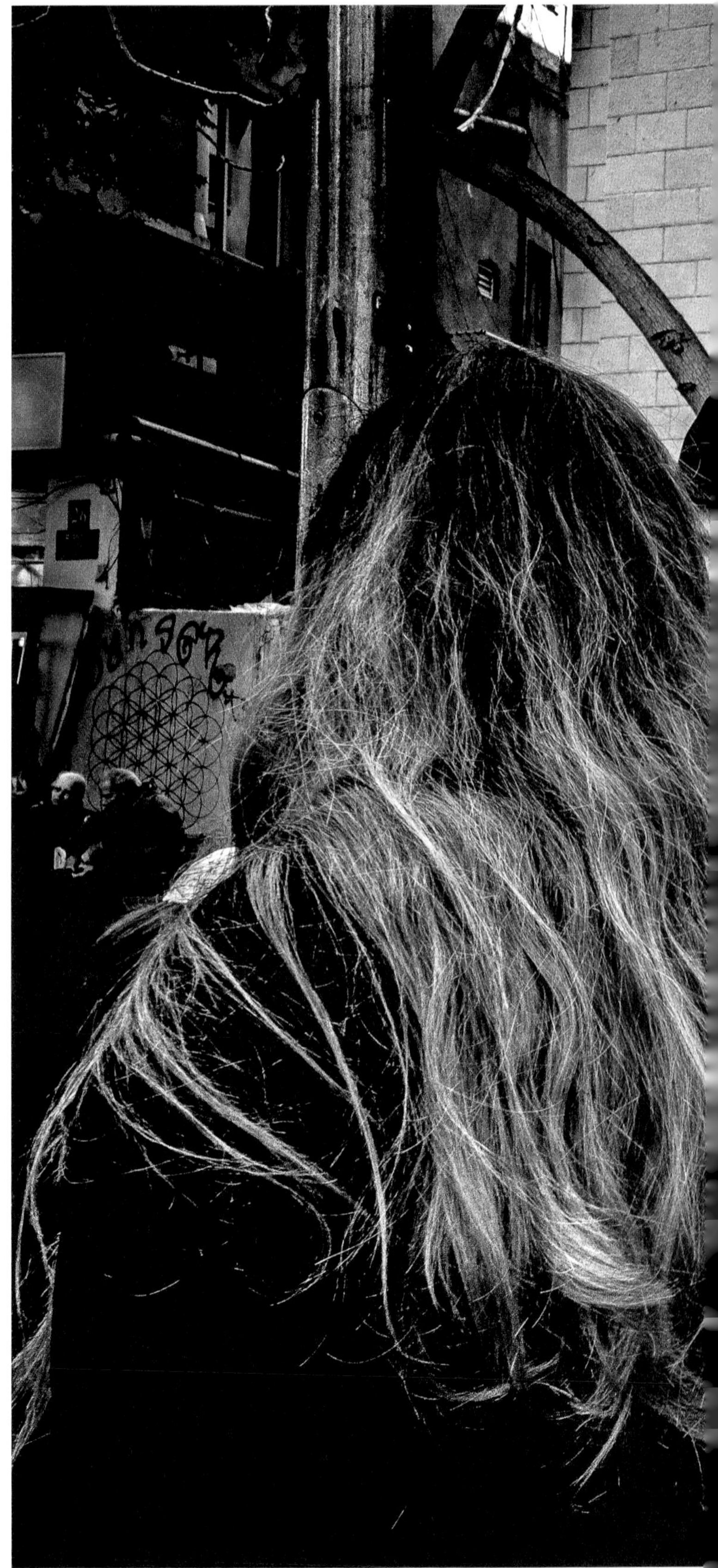

MARINA KORYAKIN, Israeli

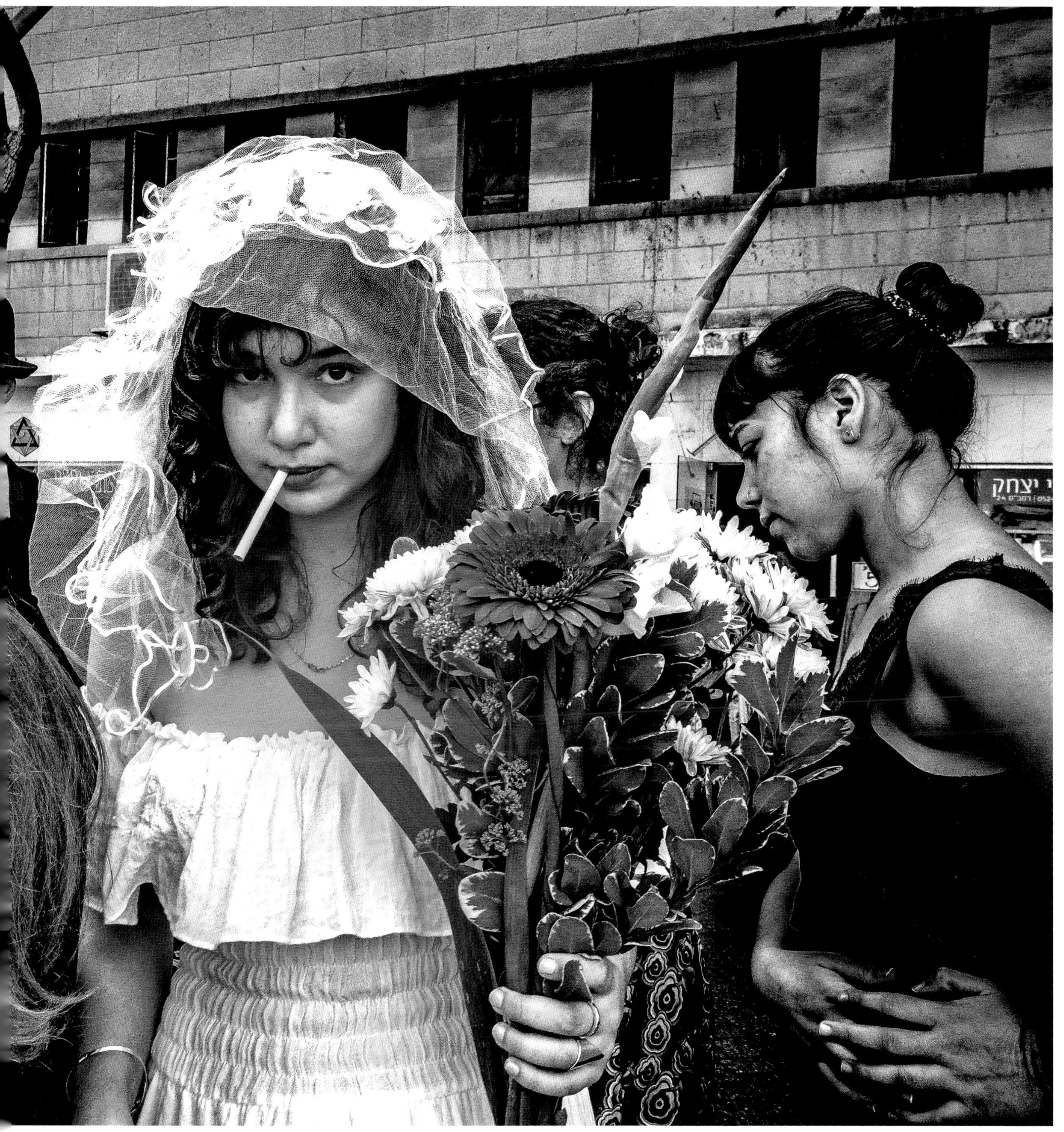

*Untitled*, Tel Aviv, Israel, 2017

# 62

# Hazel Hankin

My three weeks in Tokyo were a street photographer's dream. Exploring the city one day, I was intrigued by the visual possibilities at this designated smoking area near Shinjuku train station. I sat down against a wall and shot the changing tableaus for more than half an hour, waiting and hoping for all the elements to come together in the frame at a peak moment. My patience was rewarded! This is my favorite image from the trip.

*A native New Yorker, Hazel is a widely published and exhibited photographer who is fascinated by the visual spectacle of urban life. She teaches photography at the City College of New York.*

HAZEL HANKIN, American

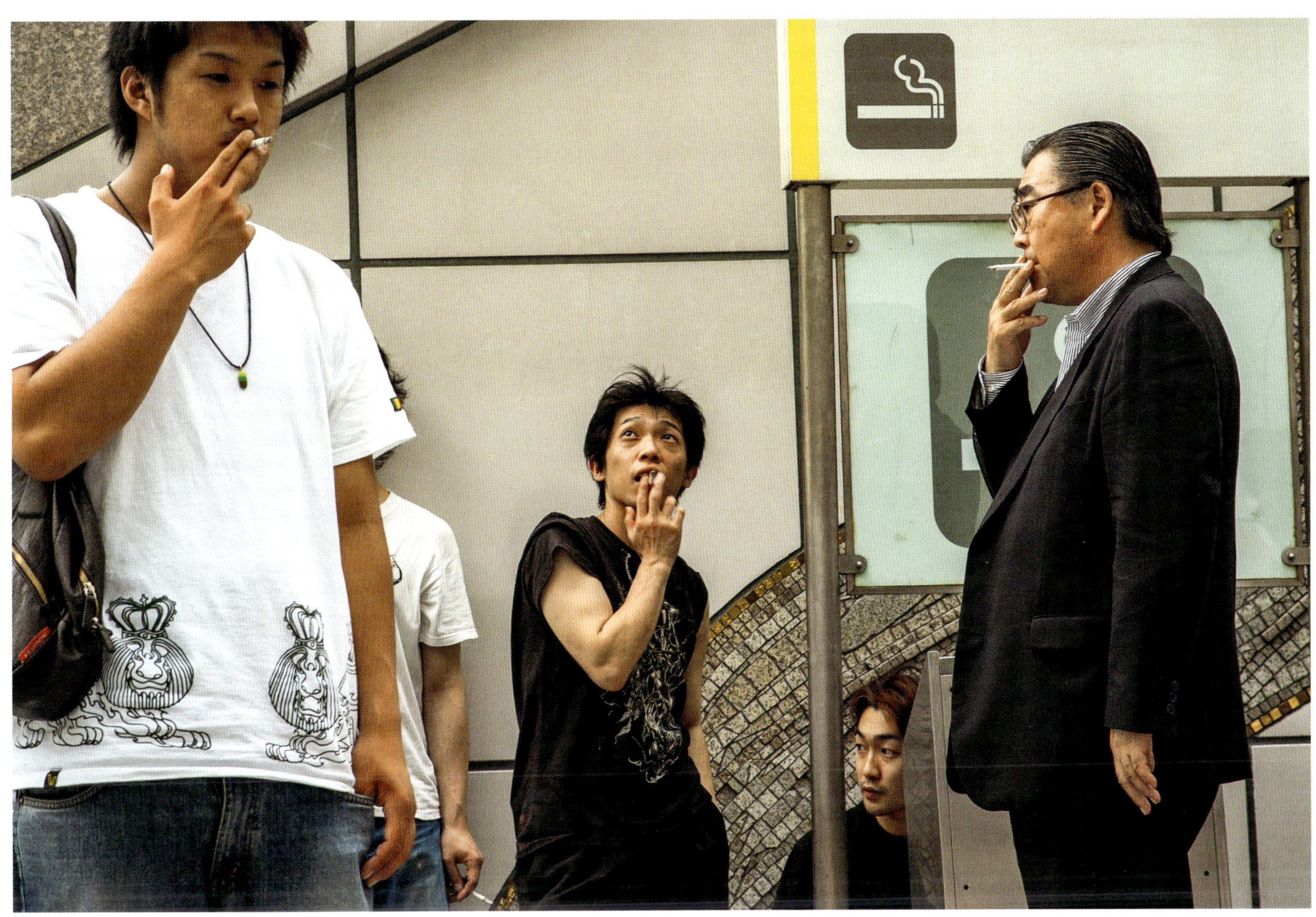

*Tokyo Smokers*, Tokyo, Japan, 2007

# 63

# Dominique Misrahi

On a Saturday afternoon in January I was walking around
Times Square and it was freezing. I decided to wait in a
sunny spot and watch the crowd. I am always looking
for interesting people to photograph, but after waiting for
20 minutes in the cold I decided to move on (I must say
I am not the most patient street photographer … ) It was
exactly at that moment that I saw these two men standing
out from the tourist population like the miracle I was
waiting for. I ran over to them and took this candid shot.
Then I started a conversation, complimented them on
their fantastic style and took more portraits.

*Dominique is a New York-based street photographer from
Marseille, France. She focuses on the varied appearances
of the human condition through her collection of real-life
street portraits.*

DOMINIQUE MISRAHI, French

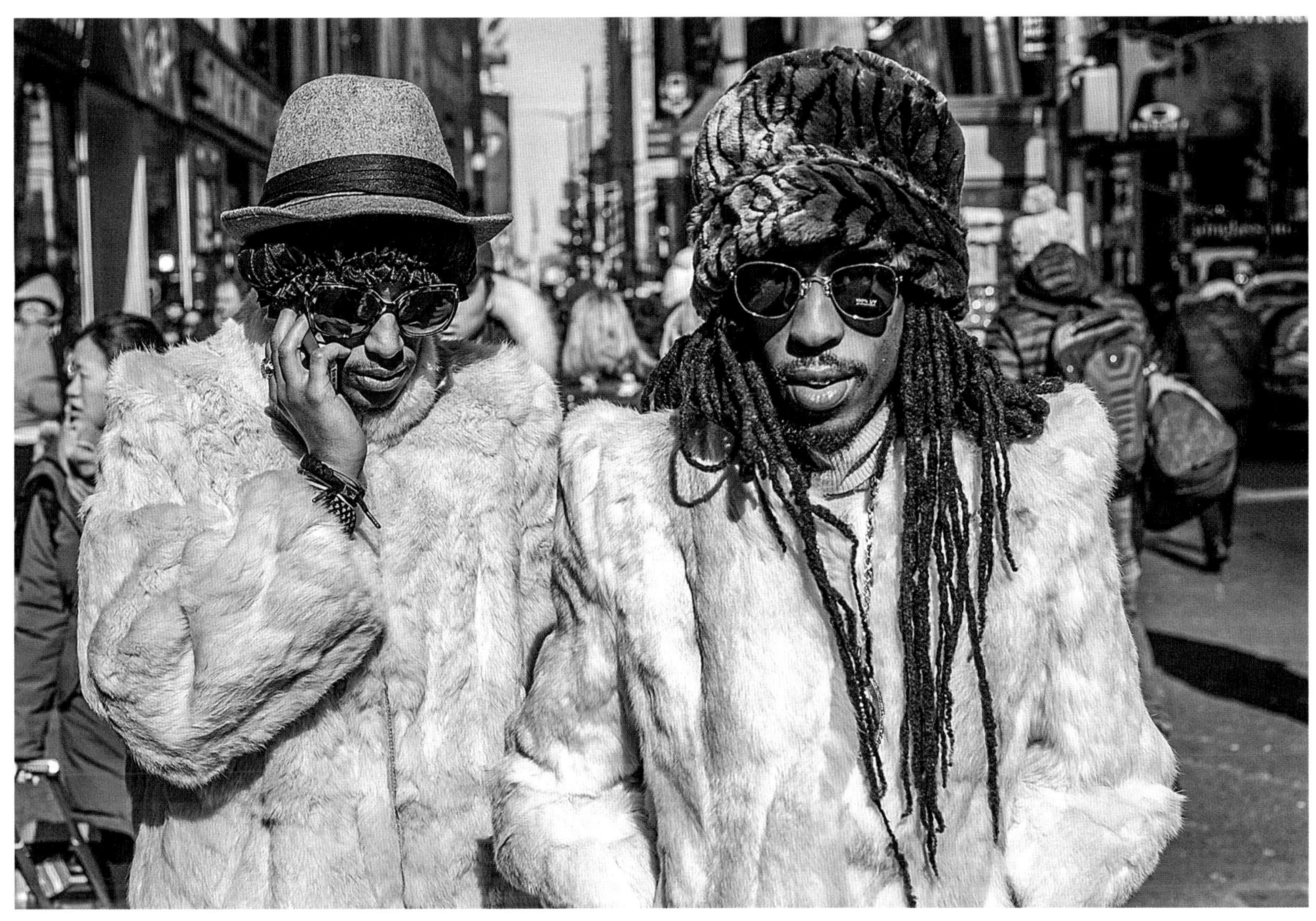

*Young Old School*, New York City, USA, 2019

# 64

# Lou Gilbert

I was observing the flurry of activity from the narrow lane to the crowded street, wanting to capture a moment that reflected the colors and characters of locals going about their everyday lives in Varanasi.

When I saw the upward lines of the banana seller's arms echoing the lines of the buildings and the cohesive positioning of the three subjects, I was pleased I had found my story.

It was only after I looked at the image on camera that I noticed the seated locals in the background, which added another layer to the narrative.

*Lou is a Brisbane-based photographer and photobook maker whose street images have appeared in exhibitions in Australia, Brussels, and New York City.*

LOU GILBERT, Australian

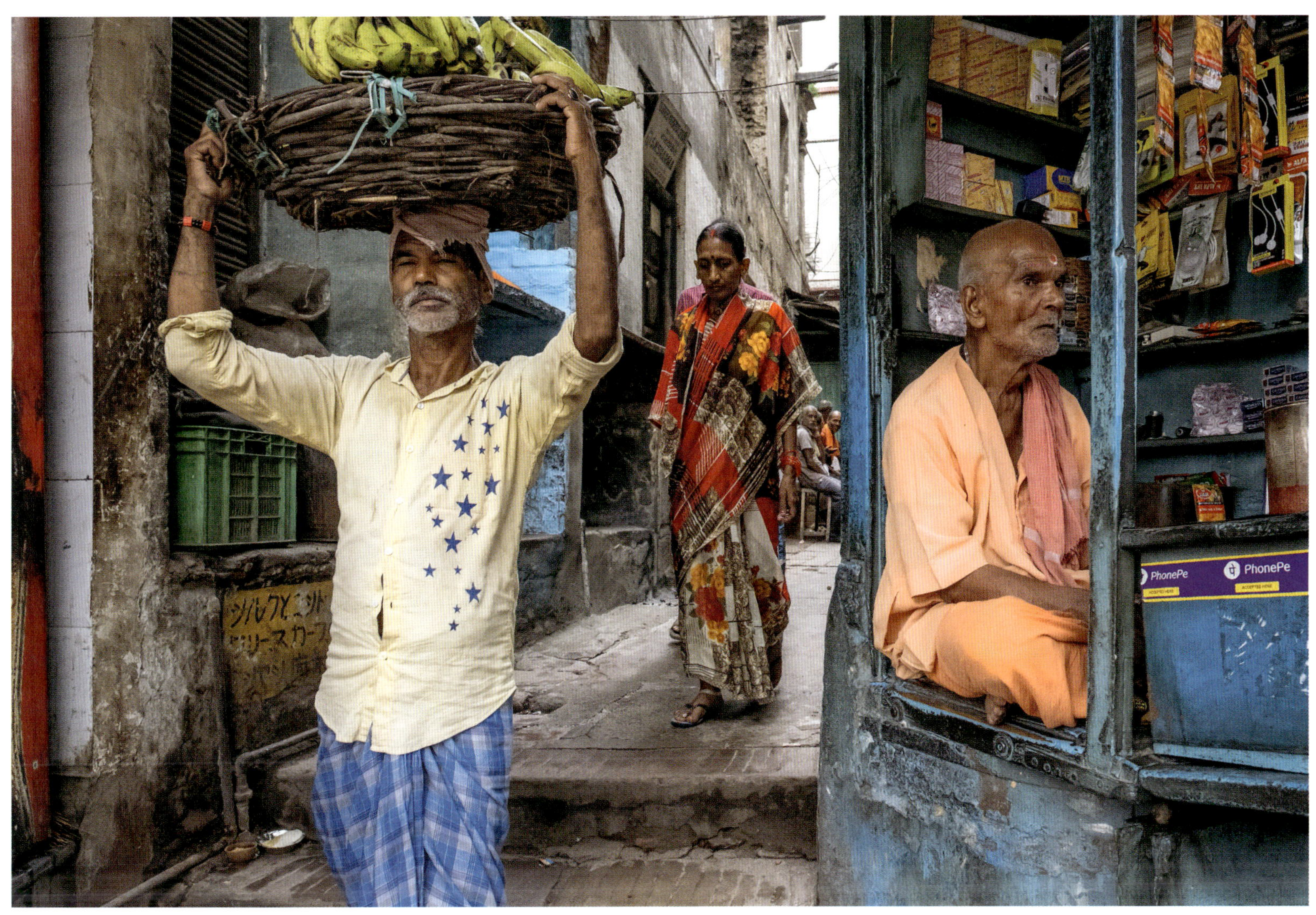

*Untitled*, Varanasi, India, 2019

# 65

# Christelle Enquist

In street photography there are moments: interesting scenes that reveal something about a subject, culture, or place. Then there are exceptional moments when on top of all of the above, light, color, subject, and a deeper meaning come together before your expectant eye.

This was an exceptional moment.

After almost a month traveling through India I was becoming acutely aware of and increasingly unsettled by gender disparity issues. It's not surprising, then, that when I spotted a constant sea of beautifully dressed women walking in the same direction, I was instantly intrigued and curious. I asked one of the women what was going on and she answered, "This is a special day. We are here to inaugurate a temple dedicated to us. It's a celebration of women."

*A photographer and co-founder of The Raw Society, Christelle has a strong focus on street and travel photography. She uses her images to shine a light on the varying cultures across the globe and their similarities.*

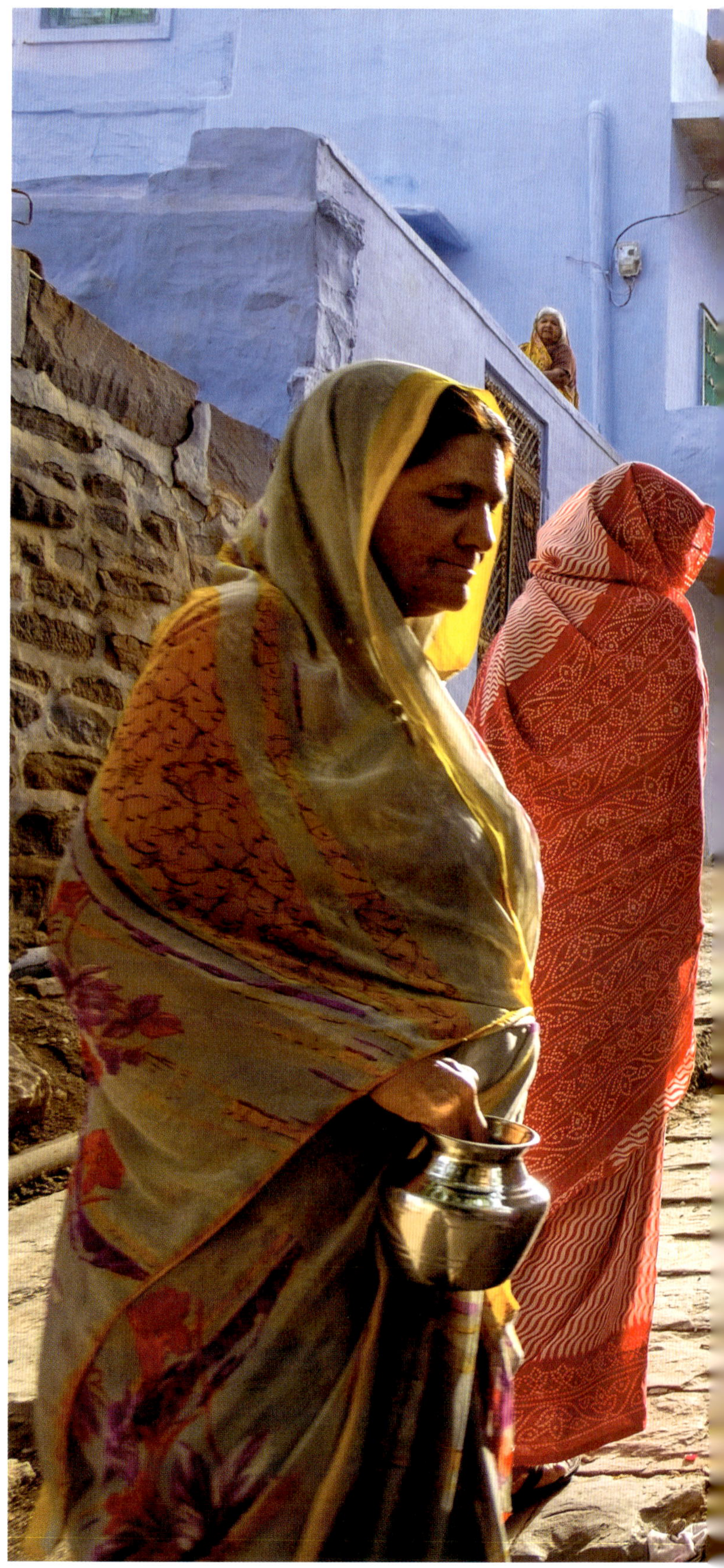

CHRISTELLE ENQUIST, Spanish

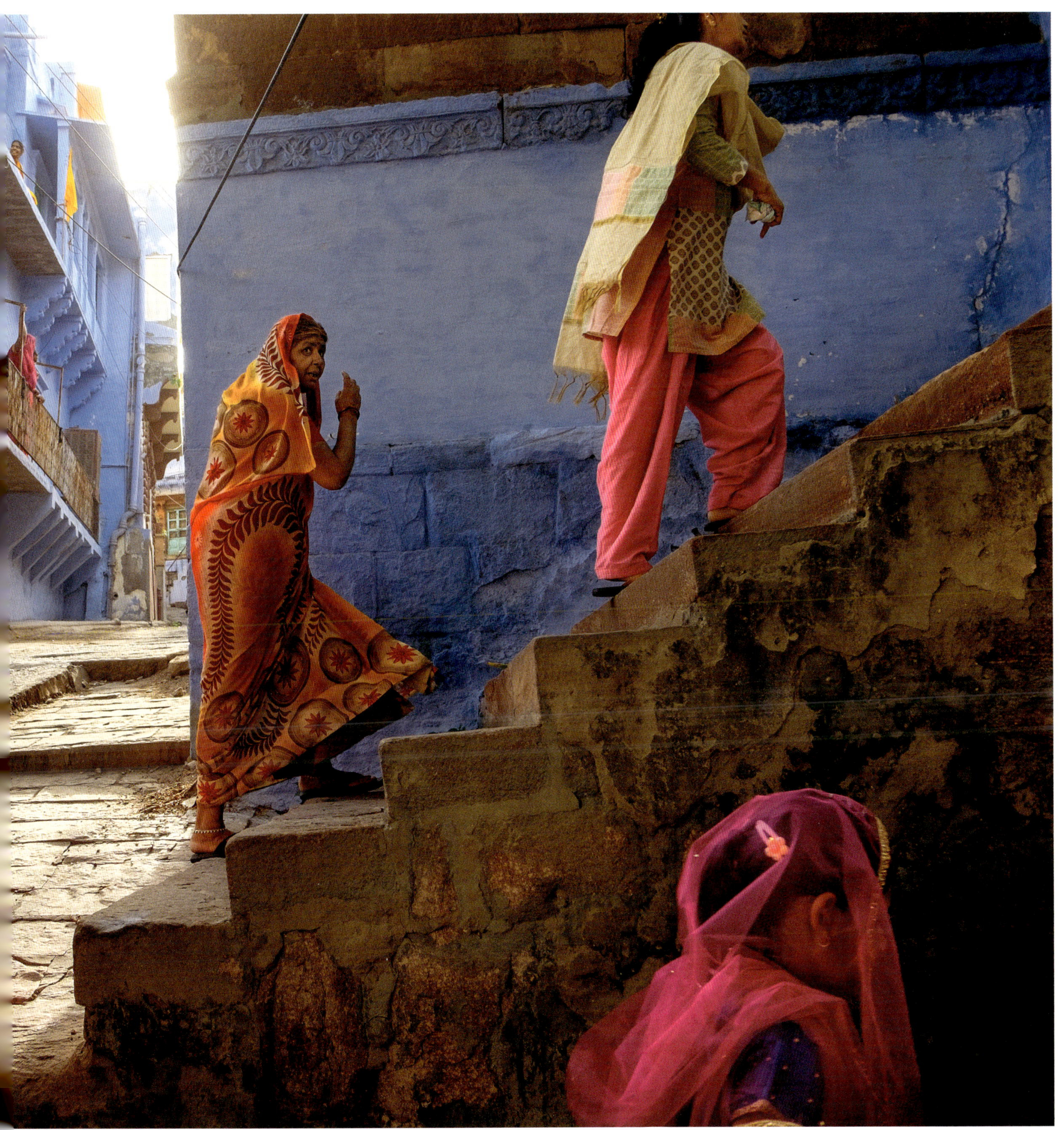

*Ode to Women*, Jodhpur, India, 2018

# 66

# Regula Tschumi

When I saw these two eleven-year-old girls in the late afternoon they were playing a game on a side street in Ghana's capital, Accra. Like many other children in their area, they don't have much time to play because they have to go to school and at home they must help their parents.

I don't know where their skirts came from, but they are not Ghanaian or African dresses. In Accra, these kinds of skirts are sold at the second-hand clothing market, and young girls love to wear them on Sundays in church, or at festivals and family celebrations.

While I was photographing the two girls, they were not distracted by my camera. Maybe my presence made them even more happy and helped to make their game a joyful dance, along with their skirts, in which they looked like two beautiful ballerinas.

*Regula lives in Switzerland but spends several months of each year in Ghana. She has a PhD in social anthropology and works as a freelance photographer, cultural mediator, and educator for art galleries. Her special interests lie in contemporary African art, African religions, and the artistic forms of expression associated with them.*

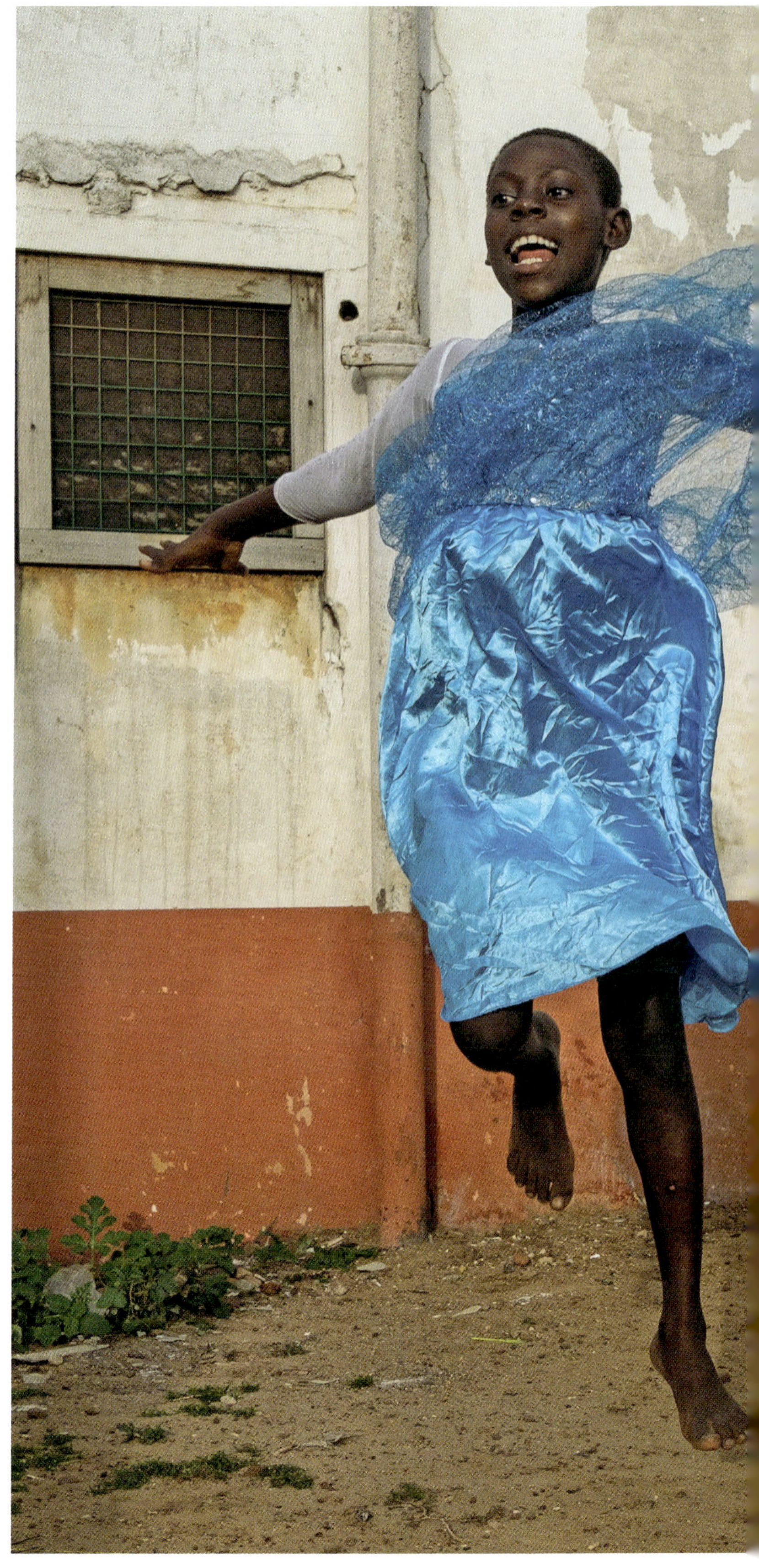

REGULA TSCHUMI, Swiss

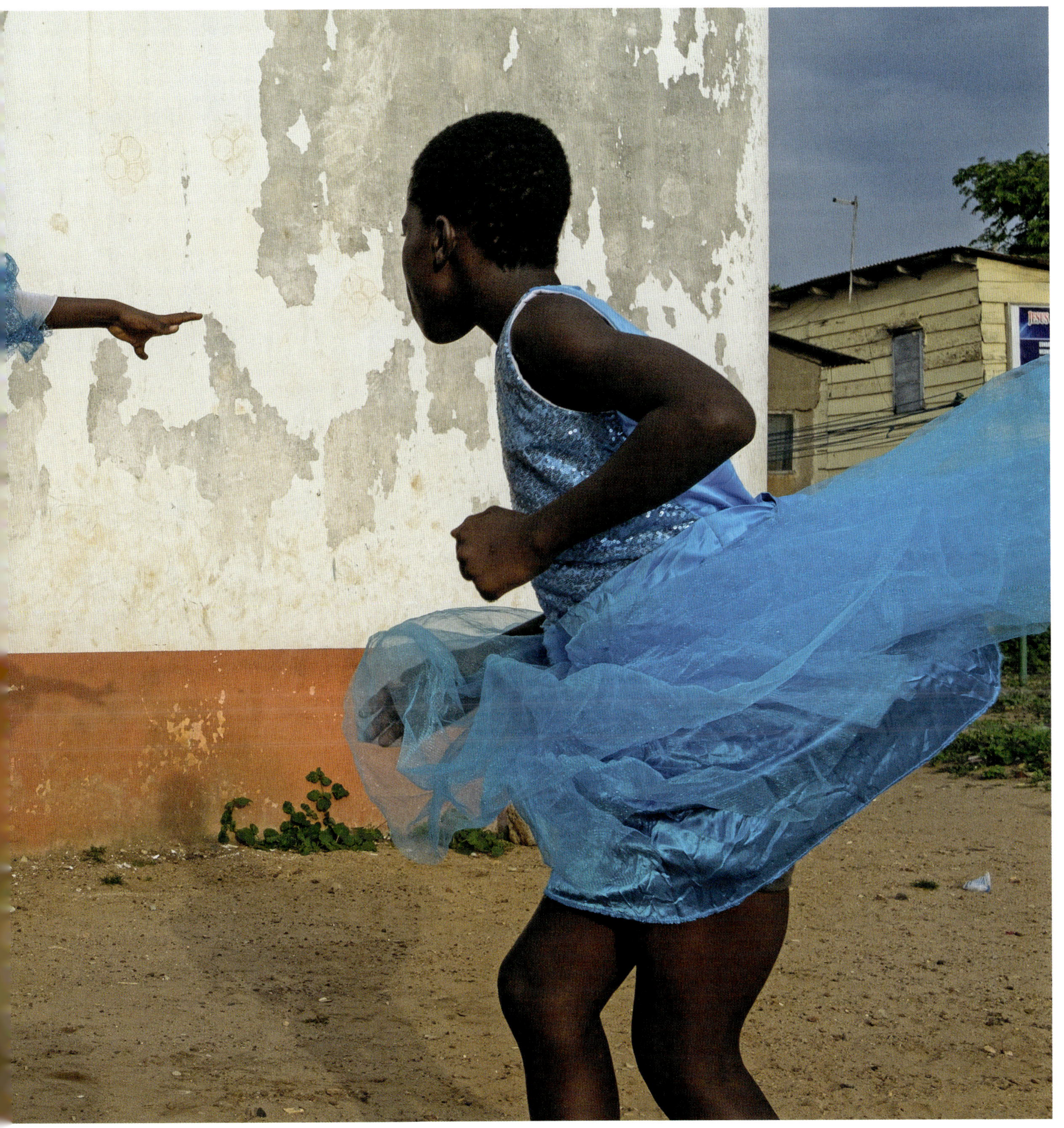

*A Dance of Joy*, Accra, Ghana, 2019

# 67

# Joanna Mrowka

When I was walking in Badami I saw a group of boys playing in tires. This doesn't happen in my country. As the situation was very dynamic, I stayed with them, trying to capture the best moment.

*Joanna is a Polish documentary photographer. She has participated in many group exhibitions, national and international competitions, and has presented several solo exhibitions.*

JOANNA MROWKA, Polish

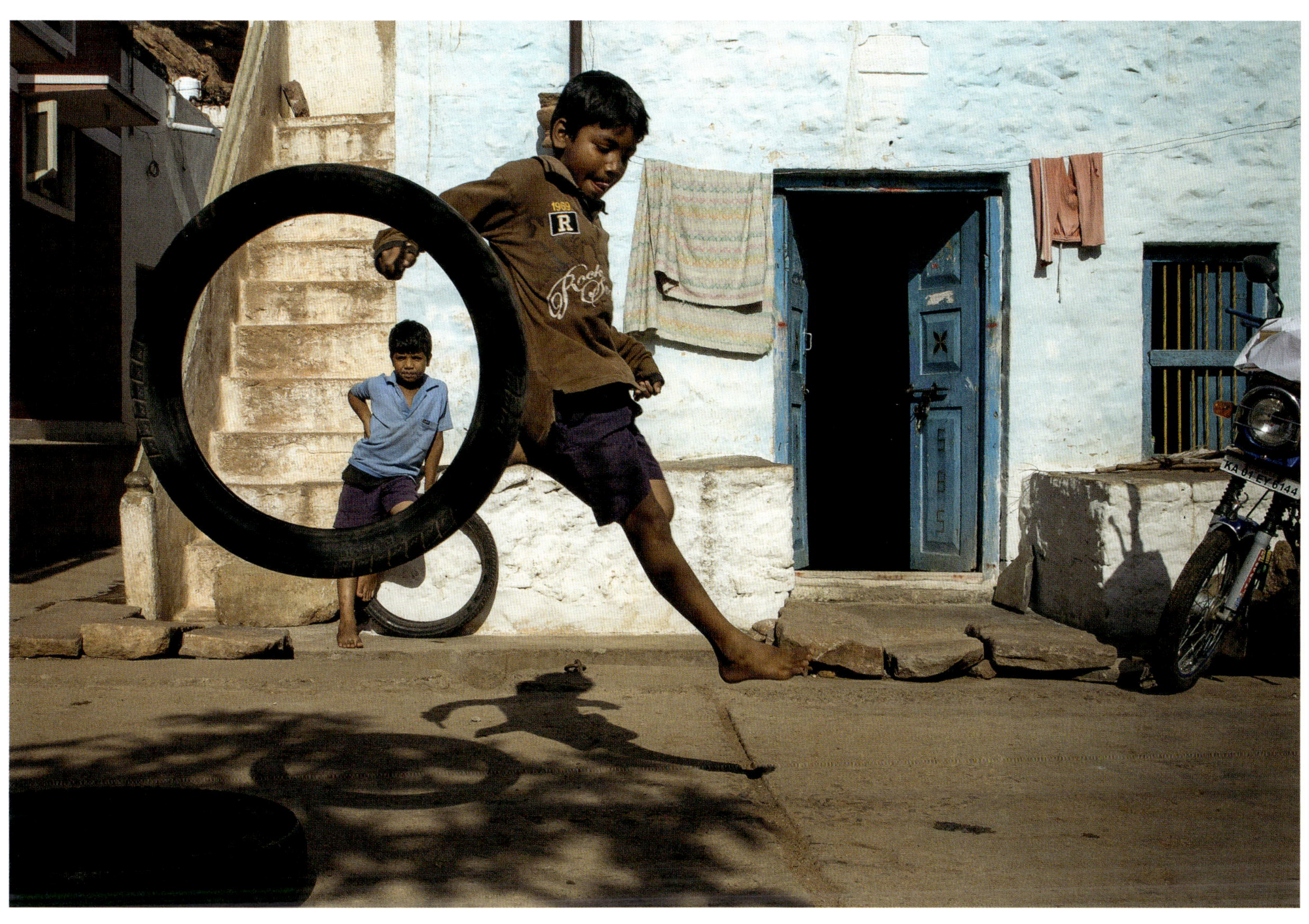

*Play*, Badami, India, 2015

# **68.**

# Lauren Welles

The first time I contemplated shooting at Coney Island, a part of me advised against it; there was nothing I'd be able to add to the visual conversation that hadn't been said before. But the notion that Coney Island is a magical place is not a myth. It's as if the diversity of its denizens—people from all different races, social classes, and ethnicities—join together to create a kaleidoscope of scenes which never allow the visual conversation to end. This photo is the quintessential representation of the Coney Island I see. I love hearing the stories that others see in this photo.

*Lauren is a New York City-based photographer whose work has been featured internationally, including at solo exhibitions in NYC and Sydney, Australia. Her photography often focuses on our commonalities as people.*

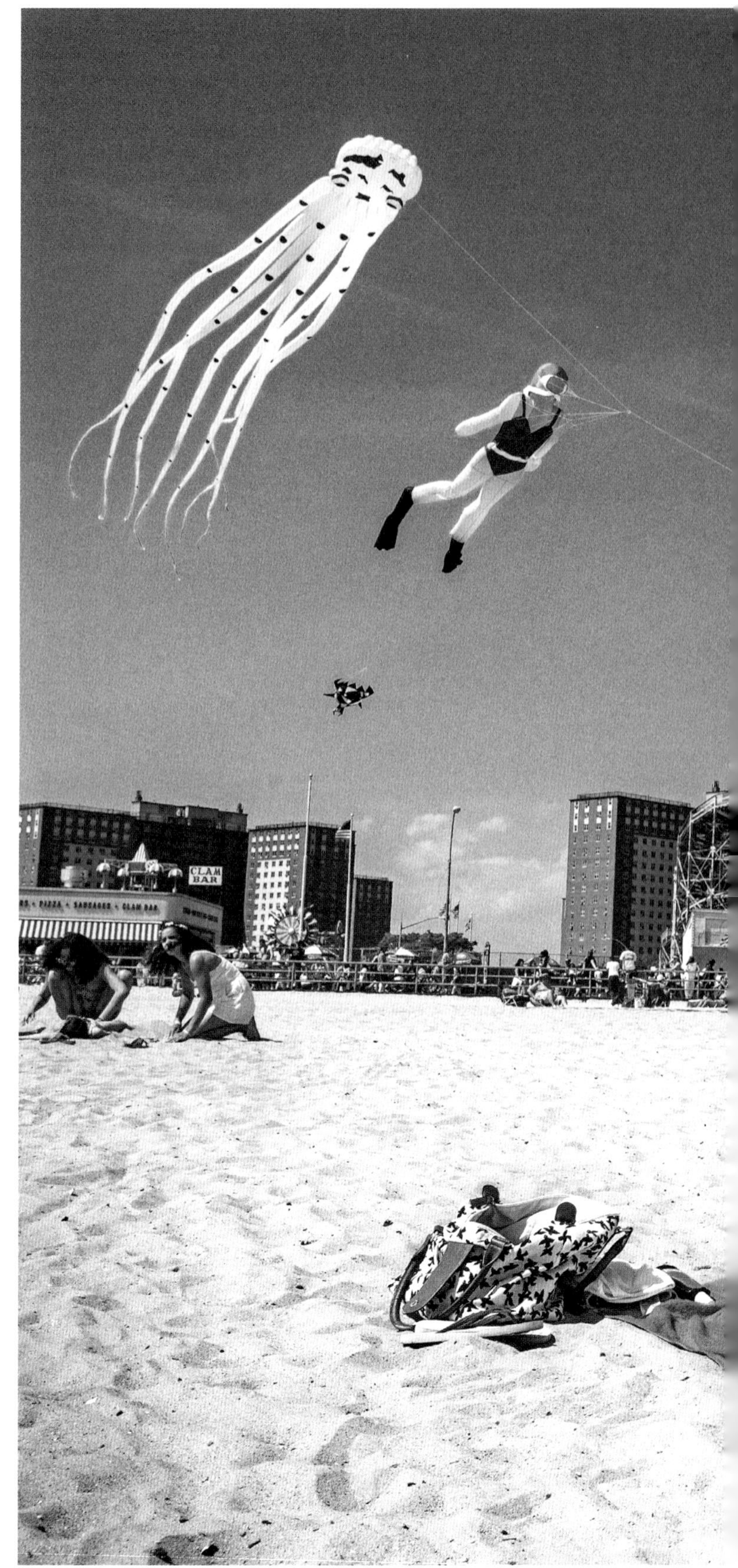

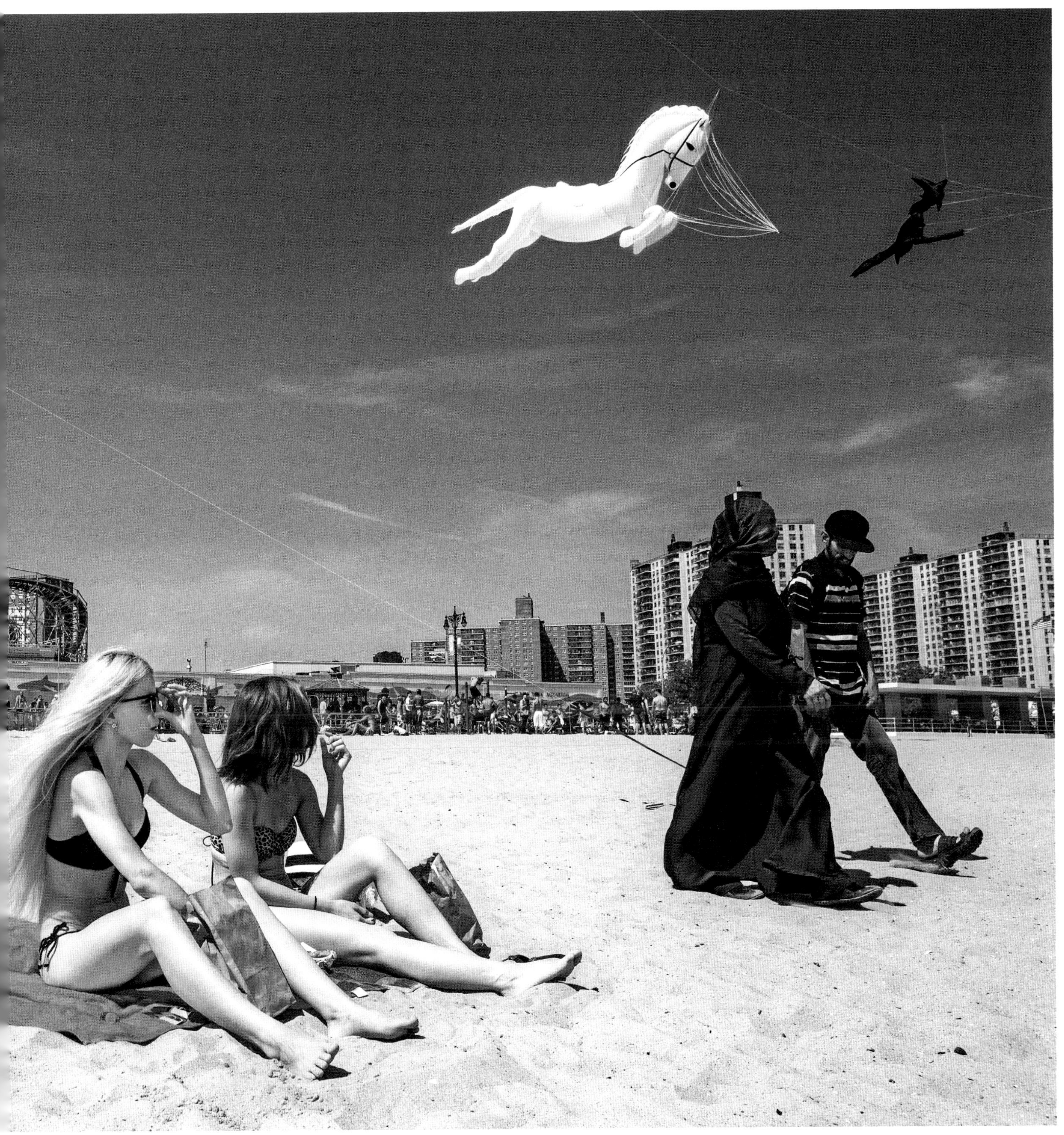

*Beach Culture*, Coney Island, New York City, USA, 2015

# 69

# Mina Noei Noshahr

This photo was taken by me on the streets of Tabriz in 2018. I went to the Mosala to take photos of the faithful praying at the end of Ramadan, and besides the praying, I paid attention to those at the margins of ceremony. I felt that these different types of people—the man in the hat, women wearing the chador, and a young man—could tell a street story.

*Mina is a news, documentary, and street photographer based in Tabriz, Iran. She wanders the streets to find interesting subjects for her long-term self-portrait series "I in the City."*

MINA NOEI NOSHAHR, Iranian

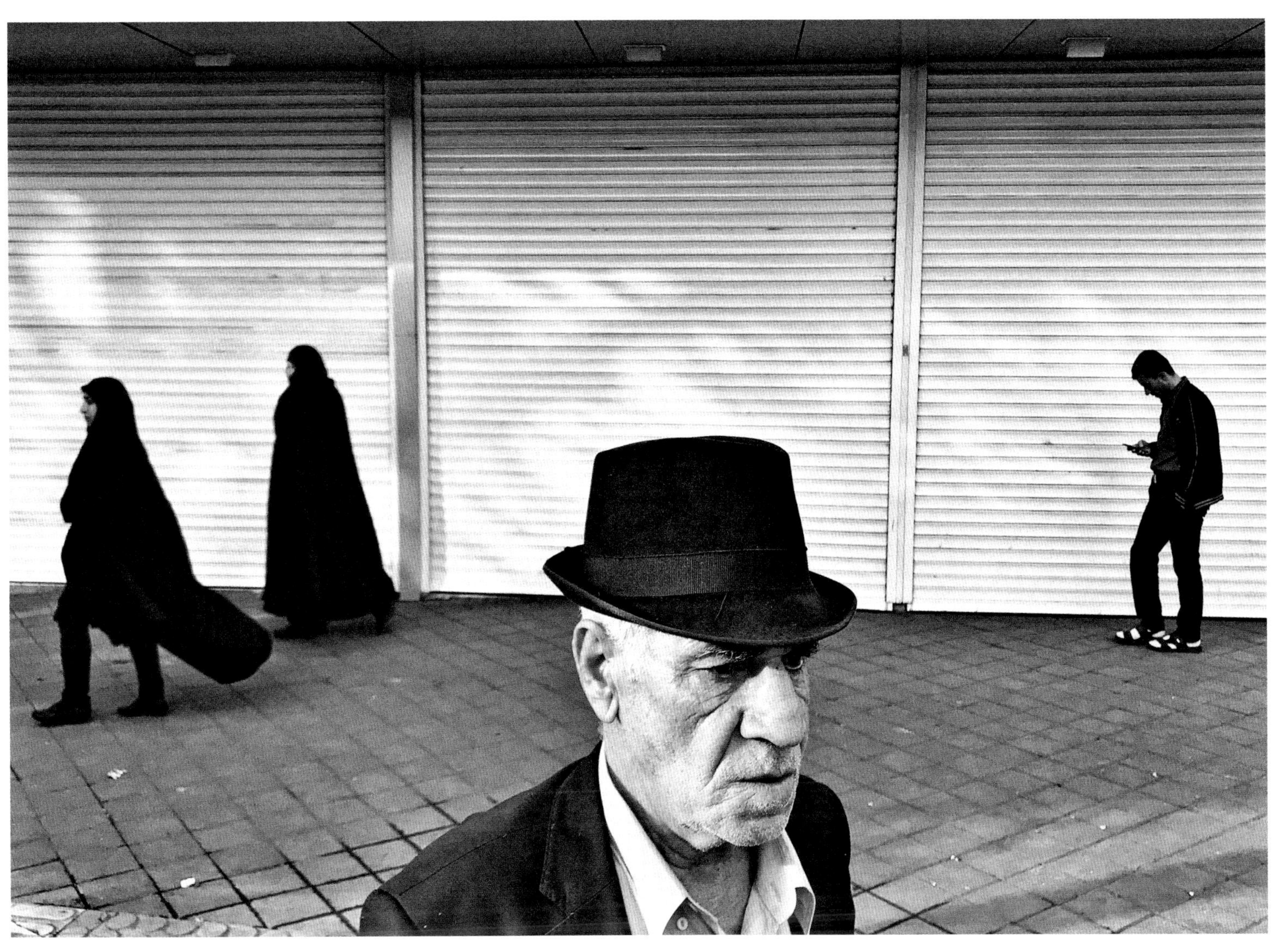

*Tabriz Street Story*, Tabriz, Iran, 2018

# 70

# Debrani Das

One could find this man at the famous riverside of the Ganges of Kolkata beside Howrah Bridge. This very ordinary man comes with a mission. He brings food for pigeons and serves buckets of water to birds every day. Because of pollution and a lower number of trees, Kolkata is losing birds, especially pigeons and sparrows, at an alarming rate. I am happy I captured this moment, when this pigeon saviour looked as if he had disguised himself in a pigeon costume. I waited patiently to get this perfect frame on a chilly winter morning. Every fraction of a second is important in street photography.

*Debrani, winner of the Women Street Photographers Artist Residency 2020 in NYC, is a Kolkata-based street photographer and homemaker. She enlivens her candid shots with soul.*

DEBRANI DAS, Indian

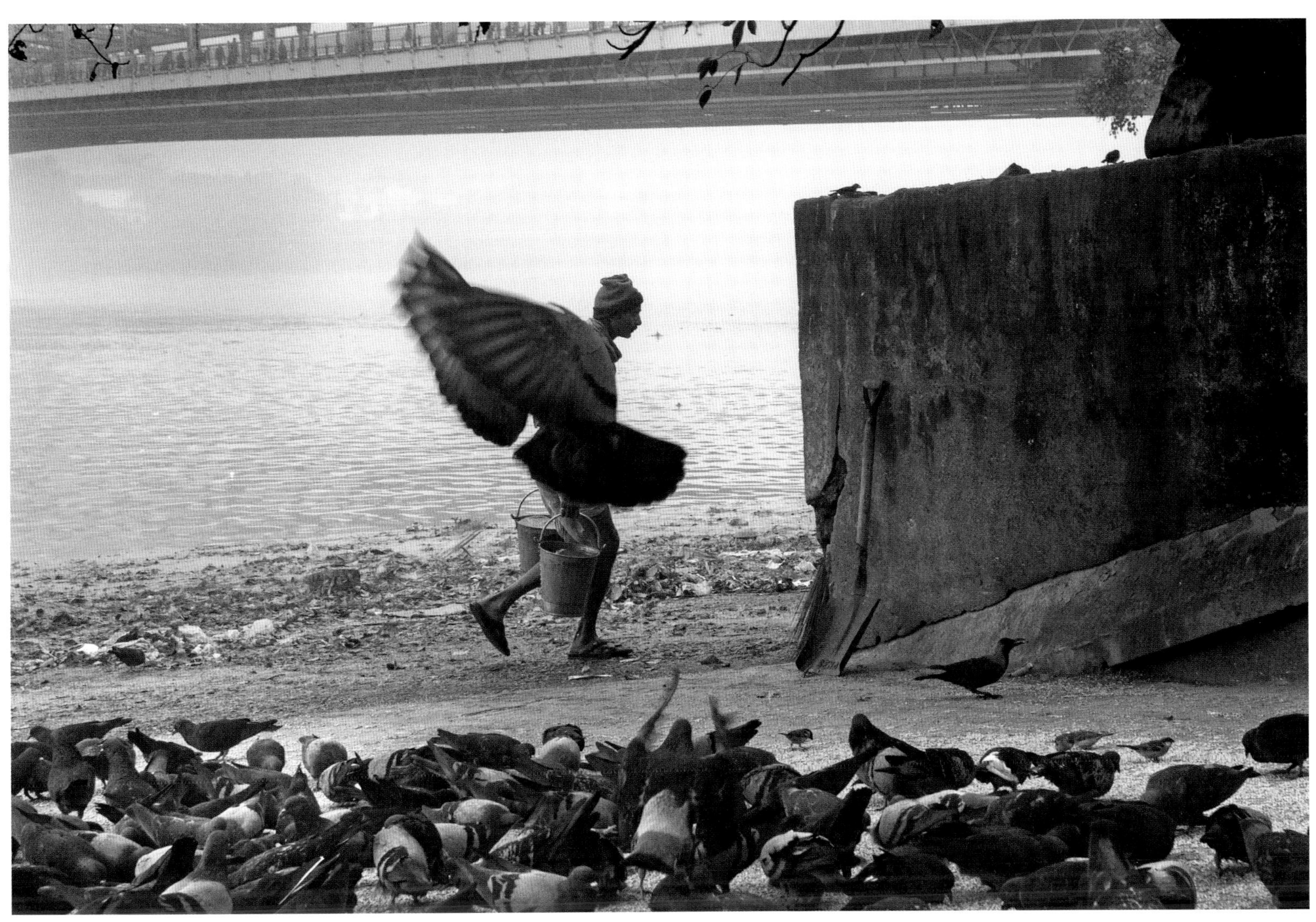

*Bird Man*, Kolkata, India, 2017

# Maude Bardet



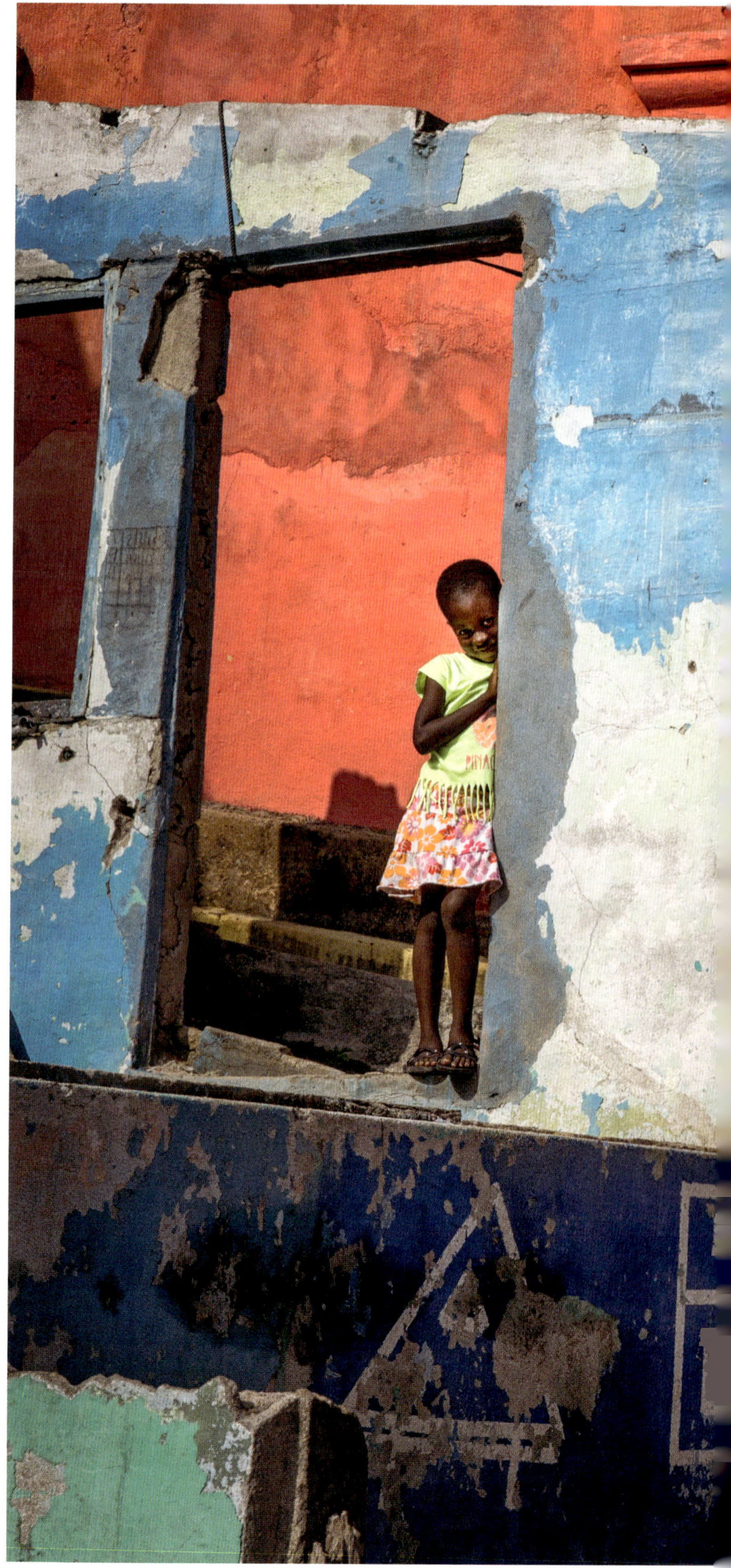

Cape Coast is a city that only reveals itself when you explore its small back alleys. Just a few feet away from the busy thoroughfares lies a maze of narrow paths. The houses there are older and more colorful. Children play while people do their washing, cooking, and hair-braiding in the open.

The mix of colors and energy is what comes to my mind first when I think of the city. I spent two weeks there, which allowed me to see the same neighborhoods again and again, getting to the point where they were not entirely foreign to me anymore. I remember passing by this particular alley very often. I was attracted by the specific combination of colors and architectural elements. I was always hoping someone would stand at the right spot, so the composition would be complete. I got lucky eventually.

*Maude is a self-taught, Netherlands-based photographer. She likes to use strong colors to emphasize the compositional elements in her pictures. Her work has emerged through Instagram and has been exhibited in various cities, including Arles.*

MAUDE BARDET, French

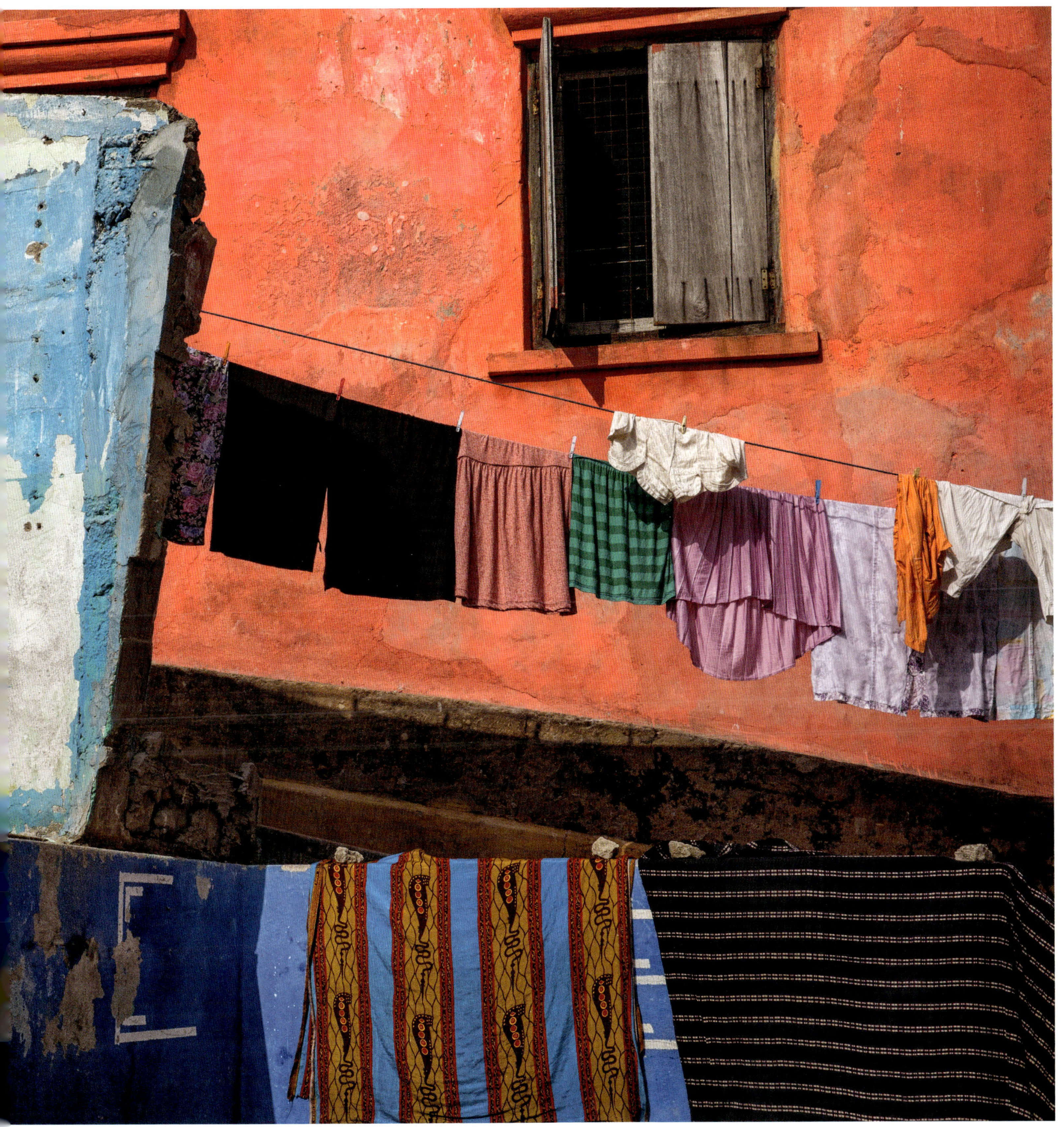

*Downtown Cape Coast*, Cape Coast, Ghana, 2017

# 72.

# Hana Gamal

This photograph was born out of a certain longing for colors. I realized how much I'd missed colors in my life, literally and metaphorically. The image for me is a metaphor of life, representing all its layers, shades, and colors; joys and sorrows, reality and dreams, past and present. I saw in these two women so much grace, strength, determination, and hope; maybe these were the things I longed for at that time, and that's why this was one of the most comforting encounters I've had in my life. As my favorite poet, Leonard Cohen, said, "You lose your grip, and then you slip, into the masterpiece." Over the years, I have learned that photography is not just one of the most beautiful forms of self-expression, but is also an ever-incomplete solitary journey that is both introspective and retrospective. It is the essence of one's vision, dreams, memories, and experiences, a journey that is fluid and constantly changing—just like the artist. An artist is never finished.

*Hana is an Egyptian visual artist. Her work ventures deep into the chaotic, poetic inner world of the human soul and its connection with the outer world.*

HANA GAMAL, Egyptian

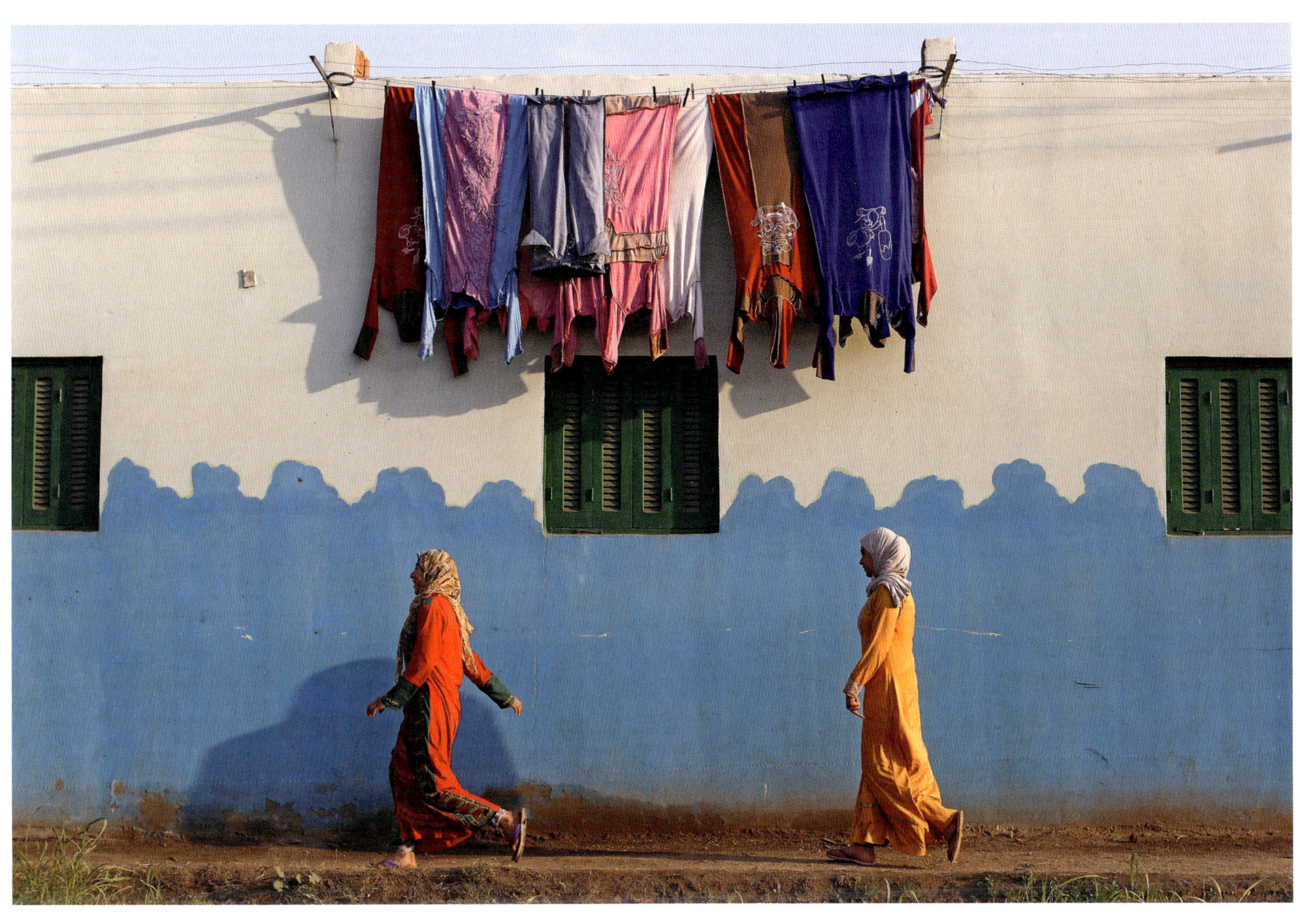

*The Metaphor of Life*, Island of Gold, Cairo, Egypt, 2017

# 73

# Monica Flannery

Studying architecture and seeing how others live
have always been two of my favorite aspects of travel.
I captured this photo on my phone from the top of a
double-decker tourist bus when I travelled to Stockholm
in July 2018.

Initially, I was only trying to capture the lovely green
building with its shuttered windows as the bus sped
by. It wasn't until I got home and examined the photos
that I happily discovered the woman peering out and
the strange item (backbone? seahorse?) in the bottom
right-hand window. Small discoveries of humanity
and mysteries like these are why I love photography so
much—my eyes hadn't even seen these details, but my
camera was able to capture them forever.

*Monica works as an art director and design lecturer.
Her photography of individuals and architecture is often
infused with quirky humor.*

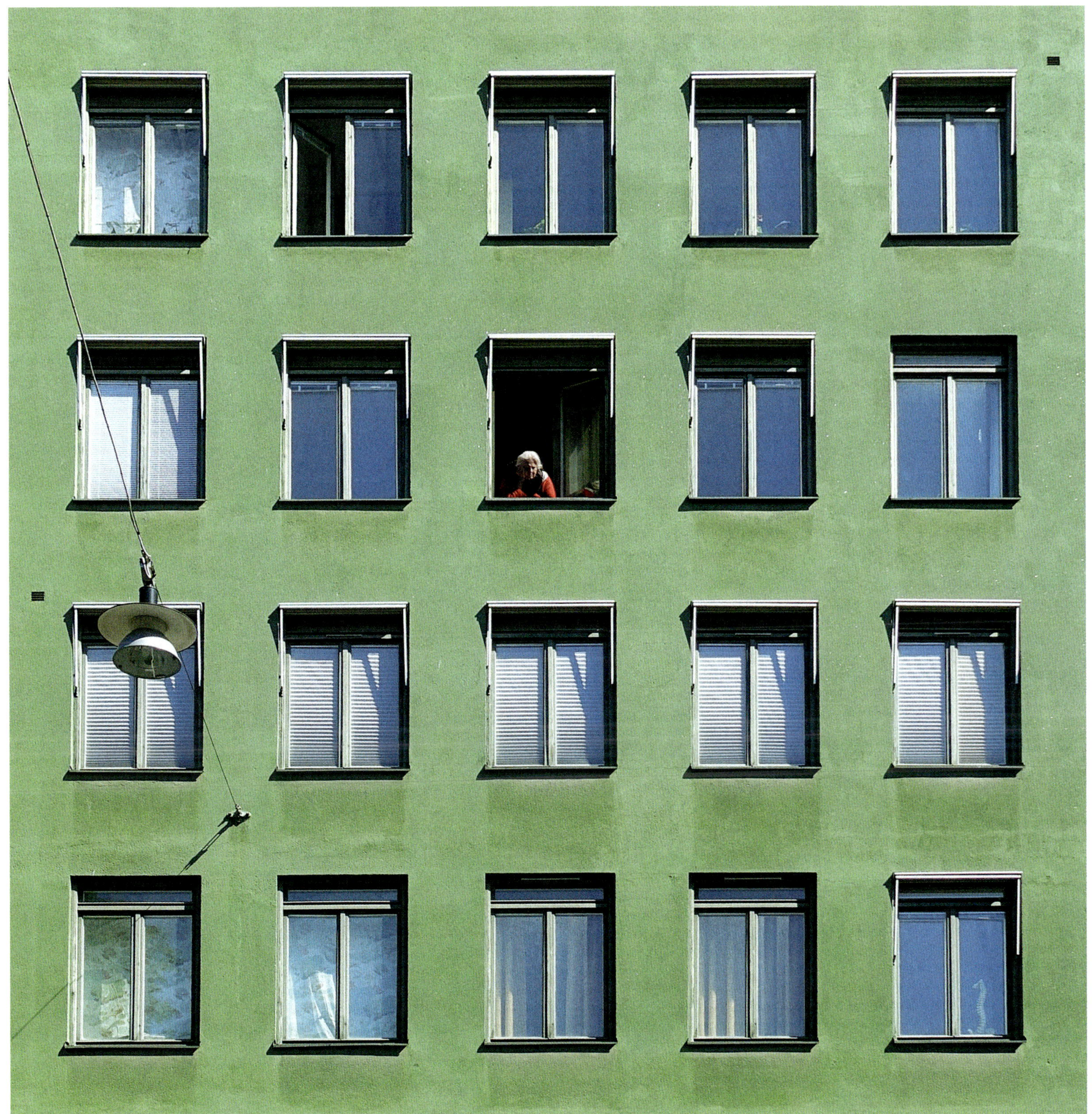

*Window Peep*, Stockholm, Sweden, 2018

# 74

# Laura Reid

As photographer Jay Maisel once said, "I was there. It was there. I shot it." Those words always resonate with me when I am out shooting street photography. It's often about seeing an interesting composition and instinctively shooting it before the moment is lost.

In this scene I was drawn to the strong lines, the color, the textures, and the arrangement of the sunbakers. It was only when I downloaded the image that I saw the angle of the swimmer's arm, which added to the composition. Overall, this photo sums up what summer feels like for me in Australia. I love the strong summer sunlight.

Some people may question whether photos taken at a public swimming pool can be defined as "street photography." My belief is that any photo taken in the public realm can fall within the street-photography category. These are the streets I feel most comfortable shooting.

*Laura is a Sydney street and lifestyle photographer. Her work often features architectural elements and coastal locations.*

LAURA REID, Australian

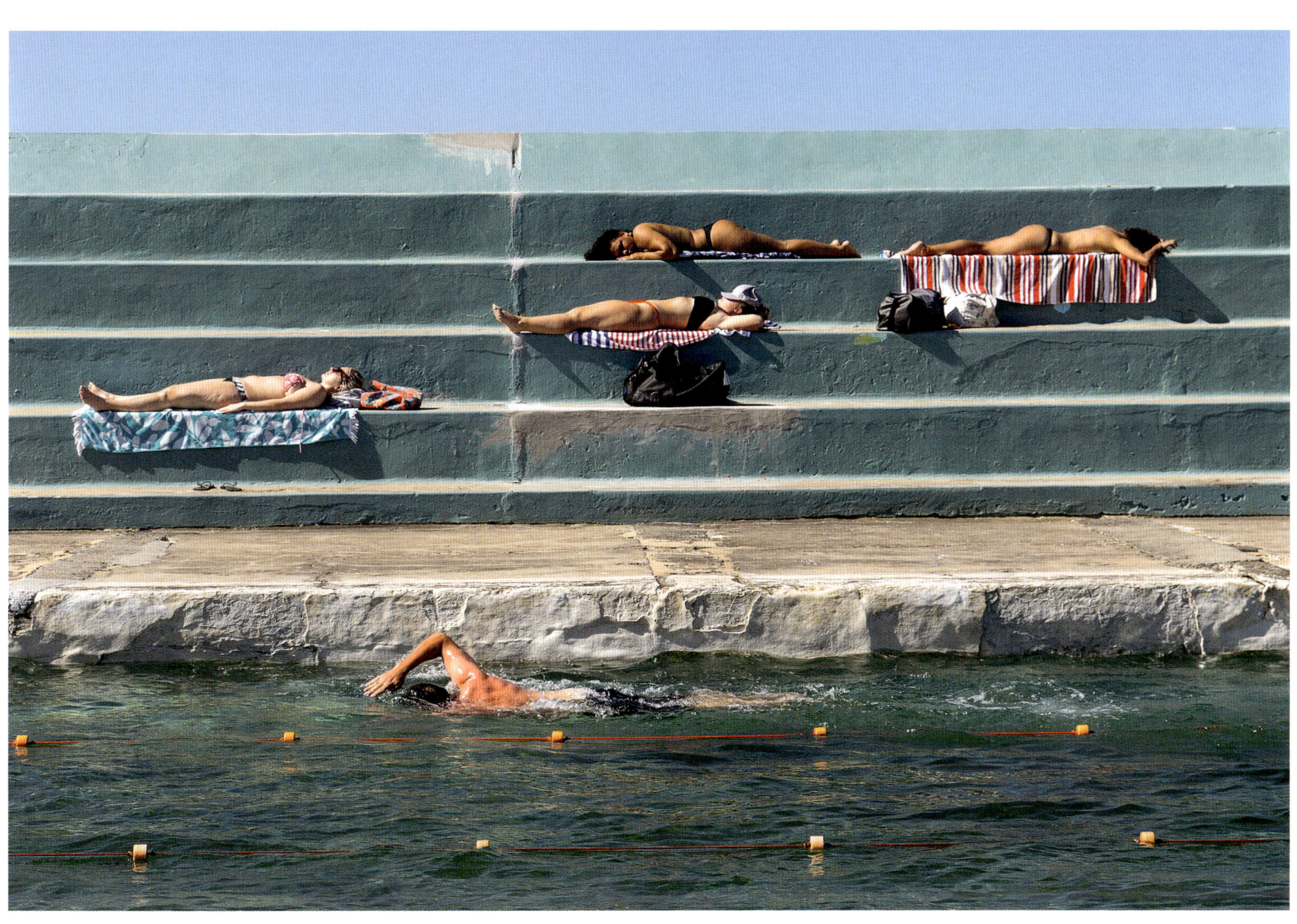

*Sun Worship*, Newcastle, Australia, 2017

# 75.

# Deb Achak

*The Queue* was captured in Maui, Hawaii, in 2016. I swam out to Black Rock with the intention of photographing jumpers as they descended into the water. During a lull, I found myself in a unique position to capture the perfect line of bodies moving from one corner of the frame to the other. Young underwater swimmers on the left make their orderly way below the surface, emerging on the right to scramble up the popular rocky outcropping.

My goal while shooting is to react to what is in front of me, even if it's not what I set out to capture. Photographing from the water presents a myriad of technical and physical challenges, but the hard work is worth it during moments such as this.

*Deb is a street and conceptual photographer. Her street photography, captured while swimming off beaches worldwide, is rooted in her lifelong fascination with water imagery and beach culture. Her work is represented by Winston Wächter Fine Art.*

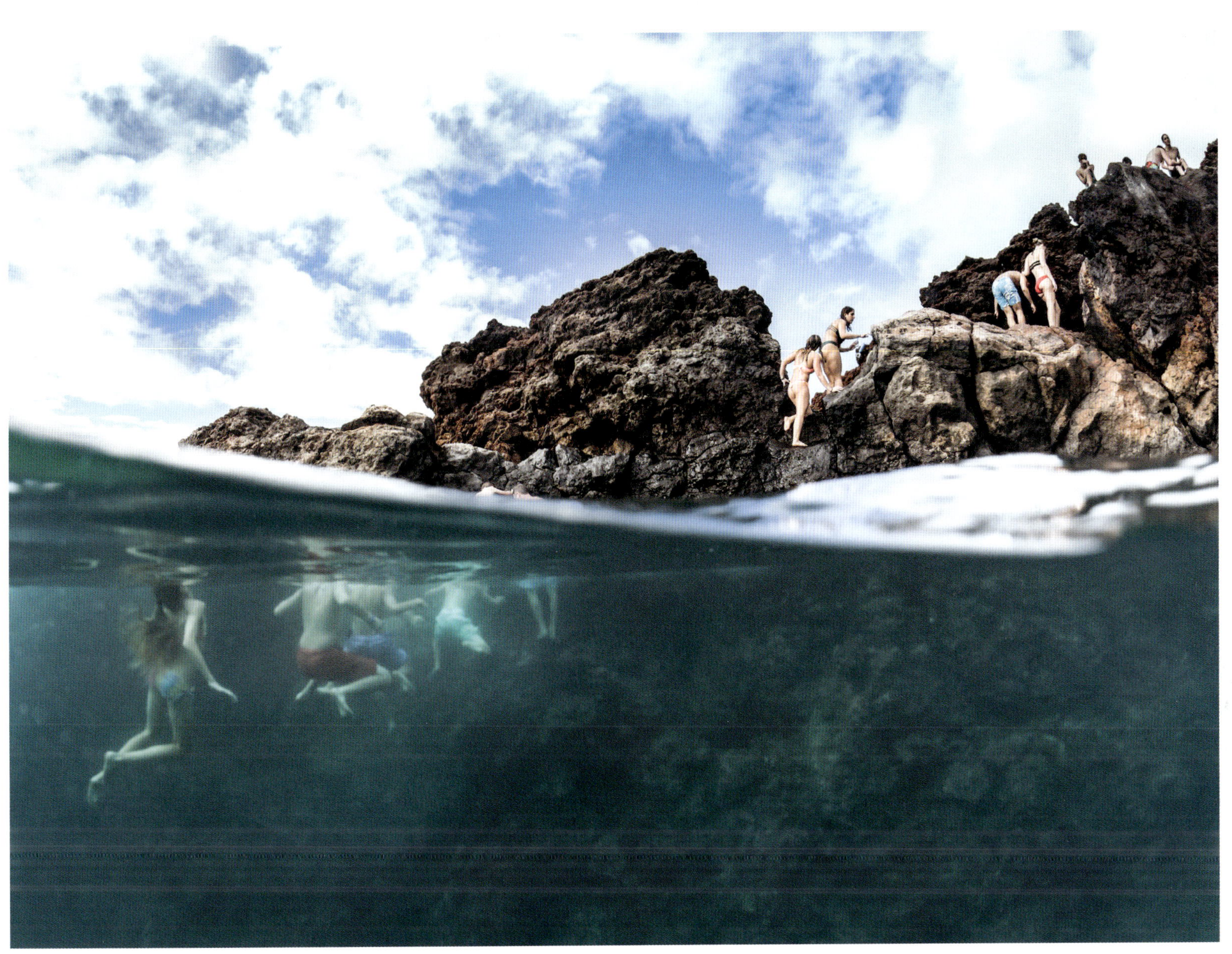

*The Queue*, Maui, Hawaii, USA, 2016

# Kirsty Greenland

I was at the beach and was watching this man in front of me get into his wetsuit and apply sunscreen. It fascinated me the way he was twisting his body and I like the abstract result in this photo. At first glance it is clearly a human figure but the viewer is encouraged to question the form and create their own meaning from it.

*Kirsty is a teacher based in Perth, Australia. Previously she lived in Asia and the Middle East for nearly fifteen years, and her desire to document her travels and the communities she lived in led her to street photography.*

KIRSTY GREENLAND, Australian

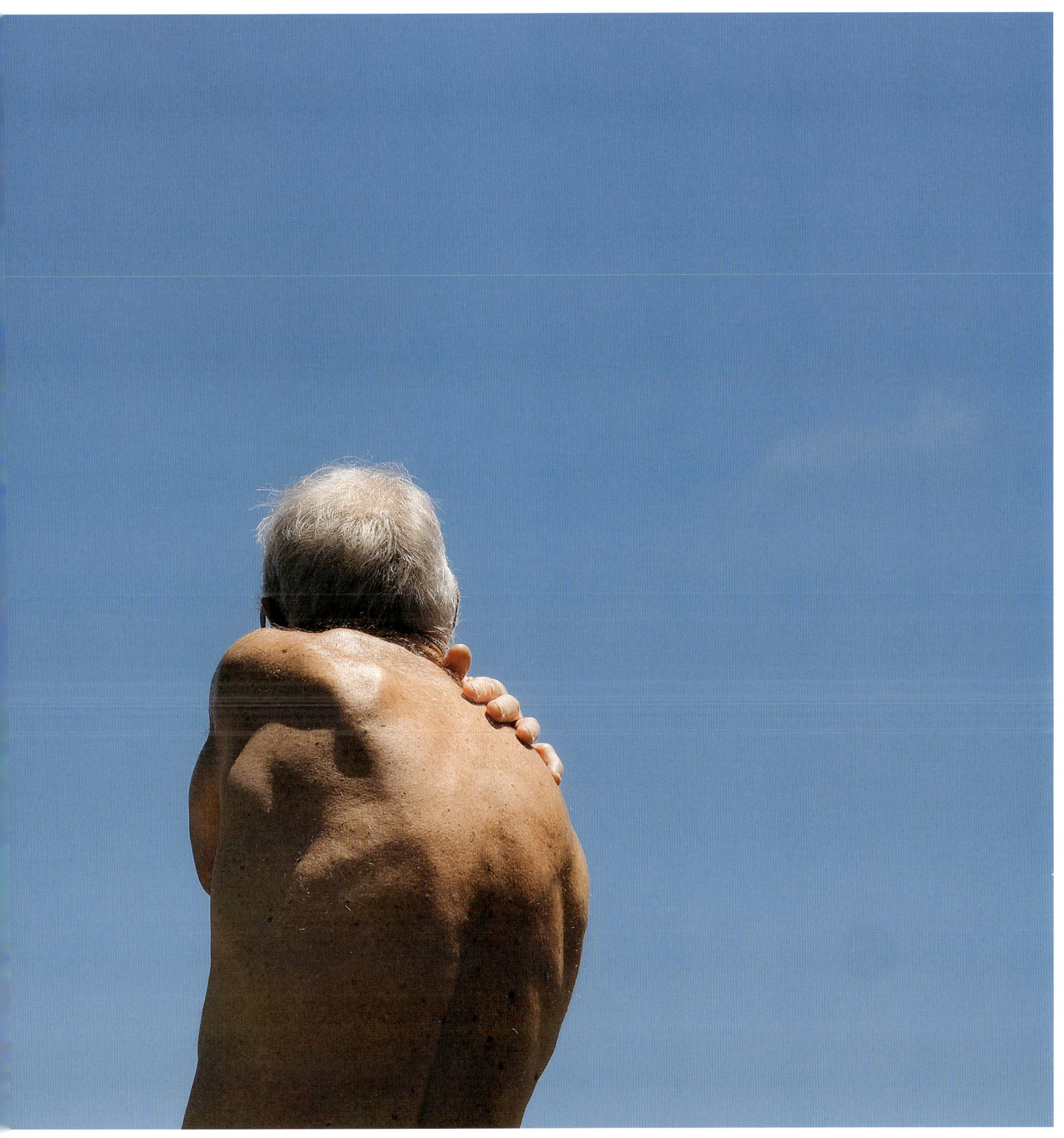

*Untitled*, Victoria, Australia, 2019

# Catherine Matthys

I love to find intriguing and unexpected moments in the everyday, wherever in the world I may be. This was certainly one of those. I grew up with the iconic vibrant red Coca-Cola branding, and the familiarity and attraction of it was still with me when I happened across this photoshoot in Fez, Morocco. The centuries-old character of Morocco provided the backdrop for this juxtaposition of East and West. The fabulous subject, perfectly styled, provided the "quirk" to make this scene particularly surreal. I love to wonder what history may lie behind the red-painted roller door.

*Catherine is an Australia-based photographer who travels and documents people and places through her images. She trained at Edith Cowan University and is often featured on online photographic platforms.*

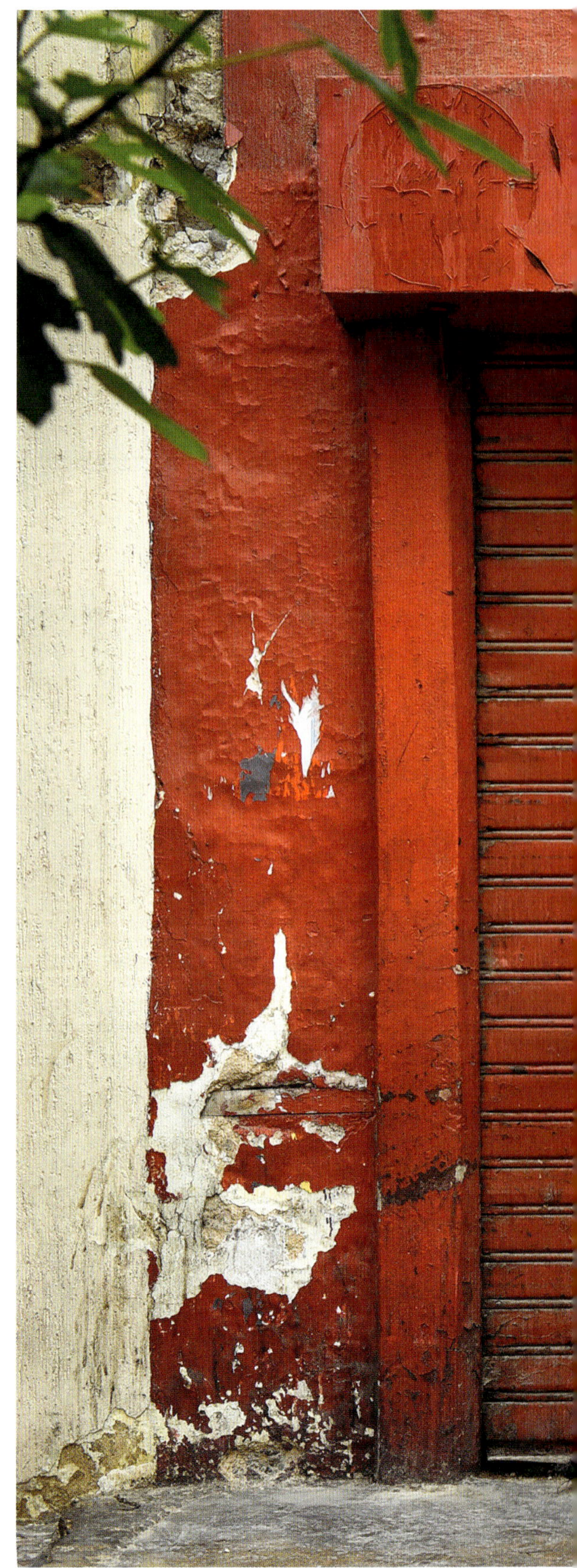

CATHERINE MATTHYS, Australian

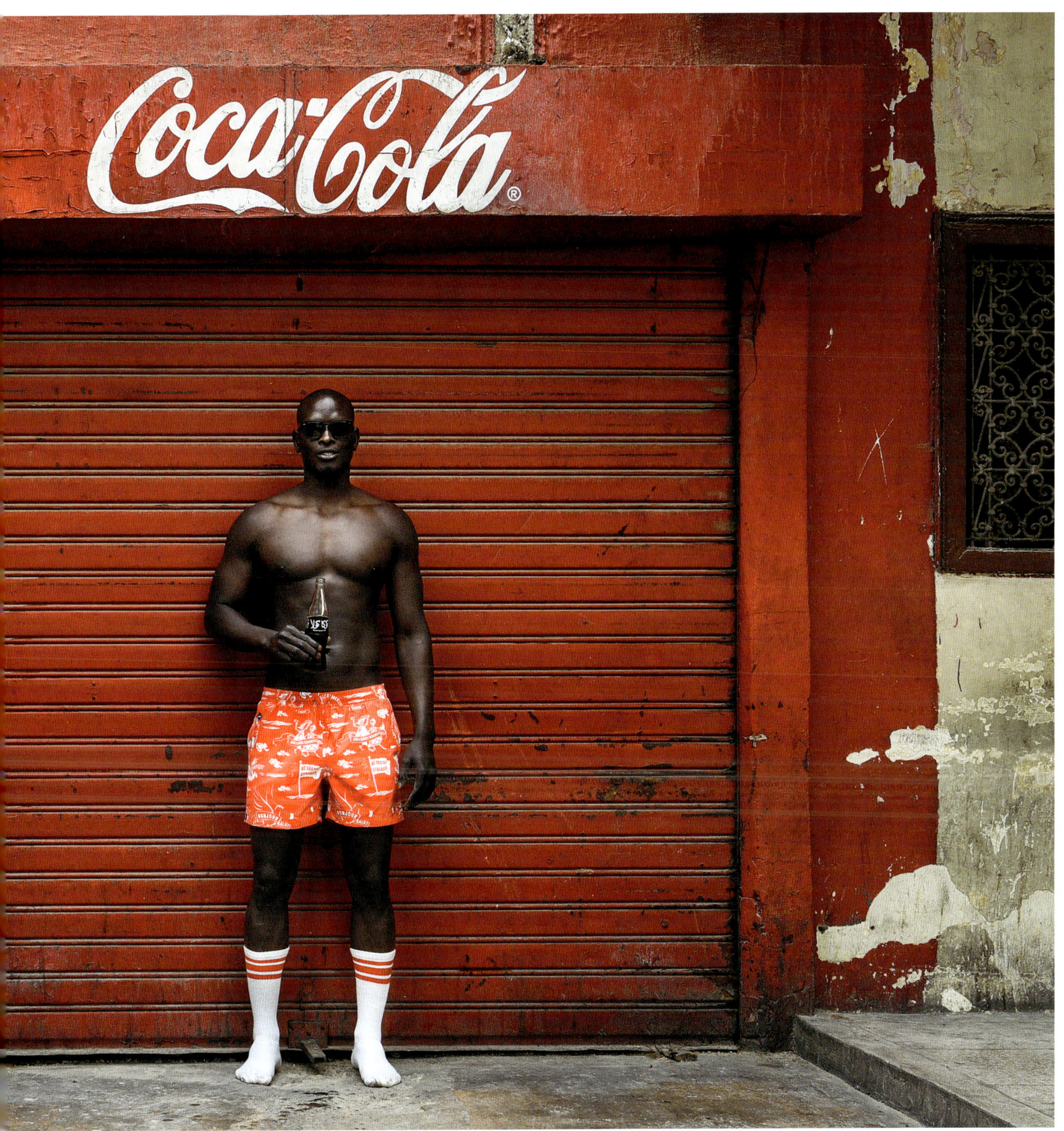


*The Real Thing*, Fez, Morocco, 2018

# Julia Coddington

While shooting in Sydney's late winter light, I spied these red shoes skipping over the curb and crossing into the shadow. Chasing after them, I managed to catch up just in time as the shadow floated off into the darkness. The wispy form of the shadow has an almost magical, ghost-like quality. I imagined I was that shadow, floating along invisibly, capturing moments as closely as possible, and being right there with the subject, within the scene, and then completely within that final image.

This photo is from my *Into the Light* series. Much of my work is brighter and more colorful, but I'm also strongly drawn to the interplay between light and shadow.

*Julia is a photographer whose street work is an intimate exploration of humanity, as she captures emotion, gestures, and movement using light and colour.*

JULIA CODDINGTON, Australian

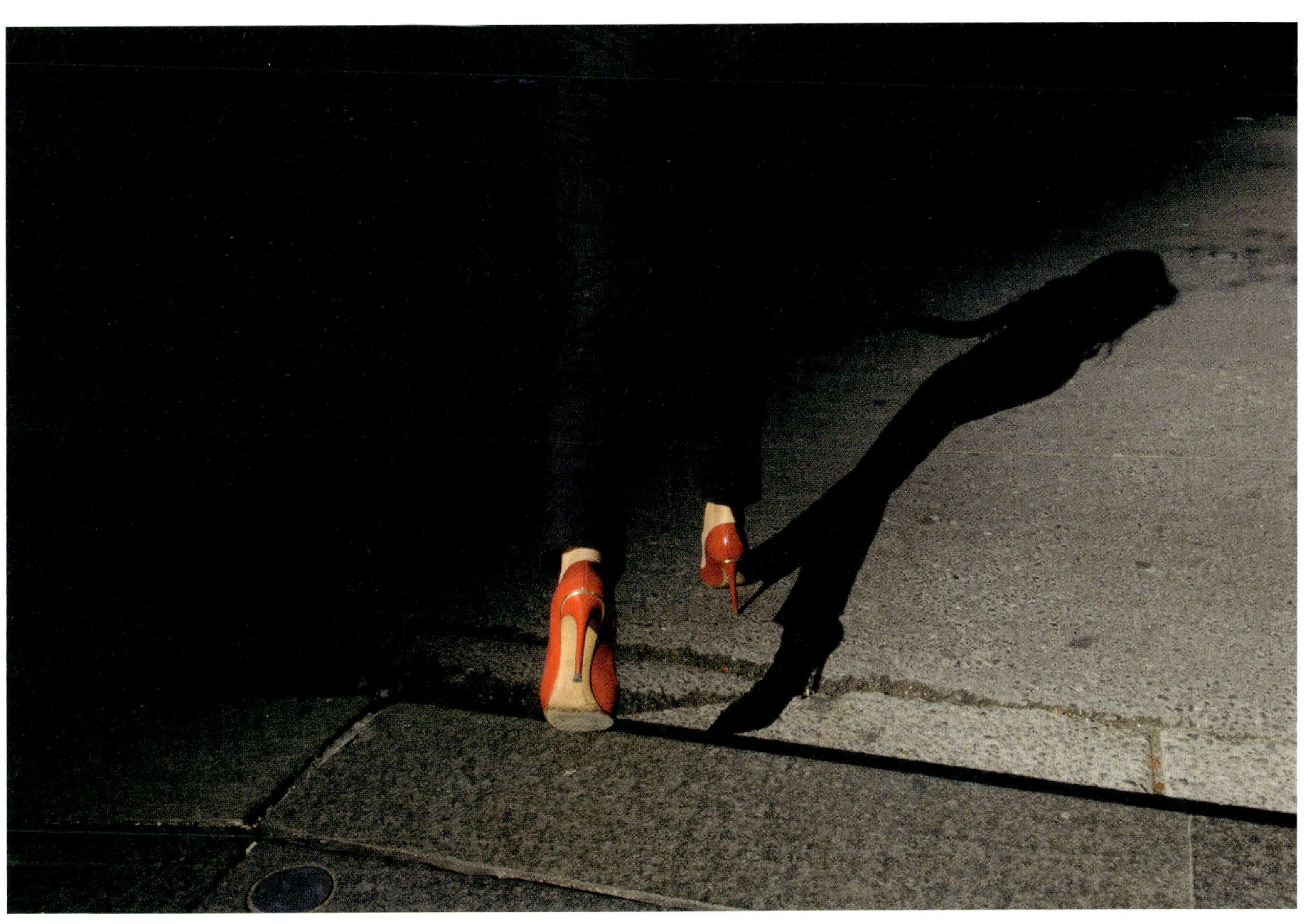

*Red Shoes*, Sydney, Australia, 2018

# 79.

# Orietta
# Gelardin Spinola

The color red is one which I feel extremely attracted to.
I saw a lady with a long red dress and her shadow, so I
took a few shots. I thought the beautiful Roman light and
the darkness of the pavement, making the dress stand
out, would have been enough for the shot. When a man
approached the scene waiting to cross the road, I realized
that his silhouette was just sitting at the bottom of her
dress. It was exactly what I needed, and I left the spot
with some hope of having caught an interesting moment!

*Orietta is a graphic designer and passionate street
photographer. She is a member of La Calle Es Nuestra,
a street photography collective based in Madrid, Spain.*

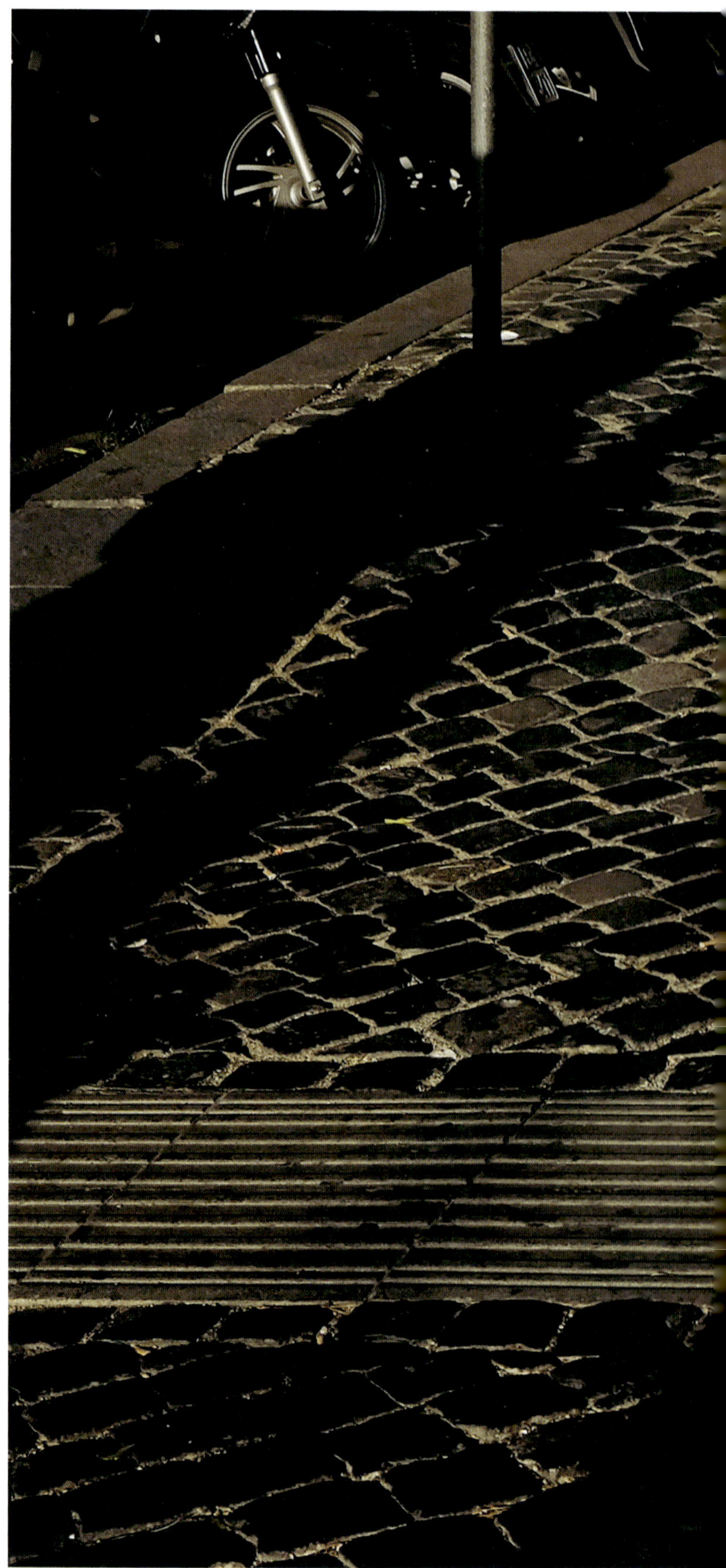

ORIETTA GELARDIN SPINOLA, Italian/American

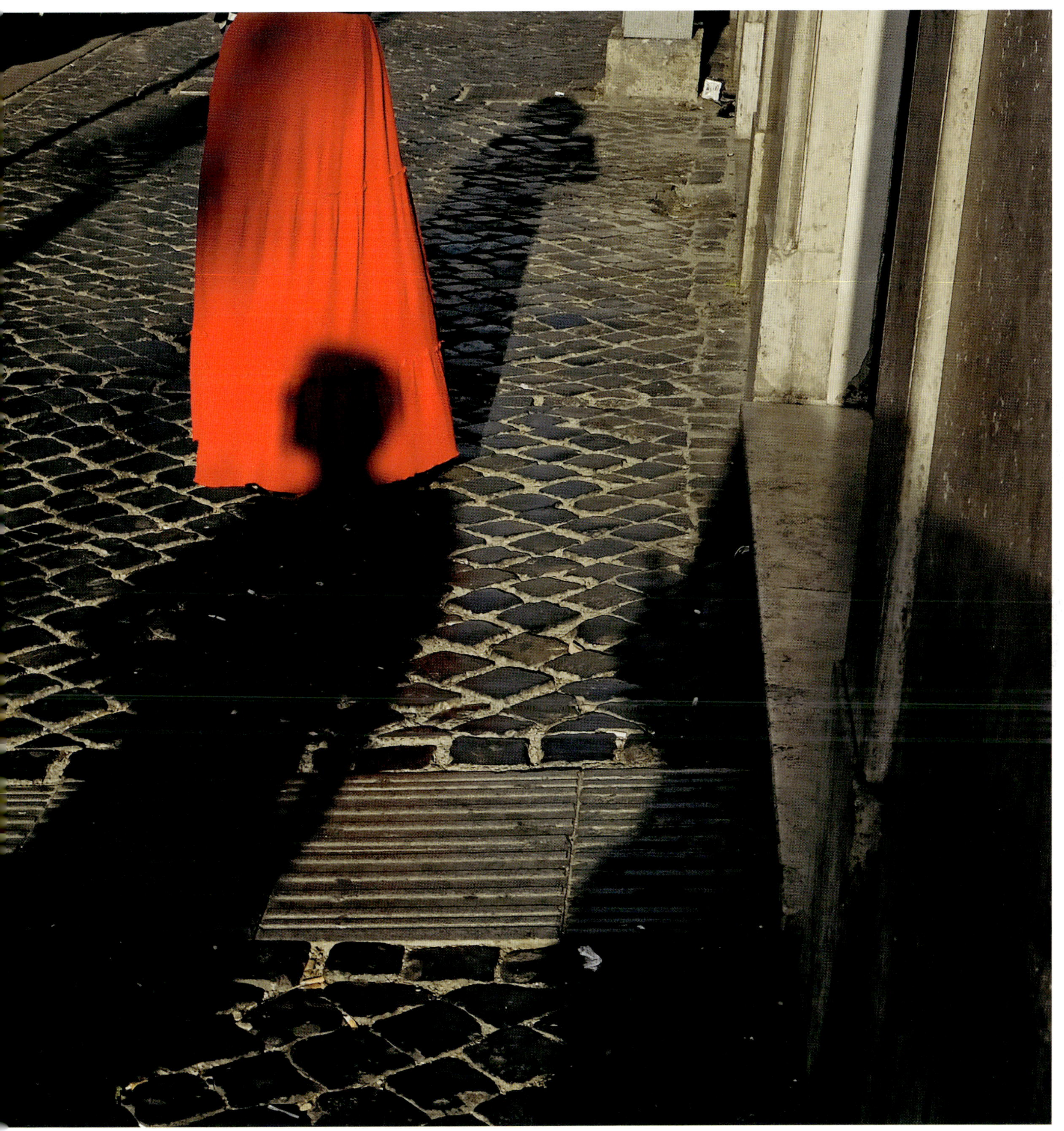

*Largo di Torre Argentina. Roma*, Rome, Italy, 2017

# 80.

# Jana Kupčáková

The street is one big stage for me and I really enjoy capturing this crowded and dynamic show. I like to be aware of interesting plays of light and shadow, humorous or artistic elements, facial expressions, gestures, color contrasts, and situations that often last only for a moment. I try to tell a short story with each photo. I really love to take pictures in Italy as well as loving the country itself, its history, culture, and natural resources. Italians are nice, smiling, open-hearted people; they have a sense of beauty and an amazing ability to enjoy life to the full. The light in this part of the world is almost always favorable, the colors are rich, and the architecture is photogenic. What more could you want for a good shoot?

This photo was taken at Easter in my favorite Italian city, Venice. I love it for its simplicity, art galleries, and color contrasts. It reflects the colors of the Italian flag and at the same time refers to the cultural traditions of the city.

*Jana is a graduate of and, since 2014, a lecturer at the School of Creative Photography in Prague. In 2012, she received the title "Photographer of the Year" from* FotoVideo *magazine.*

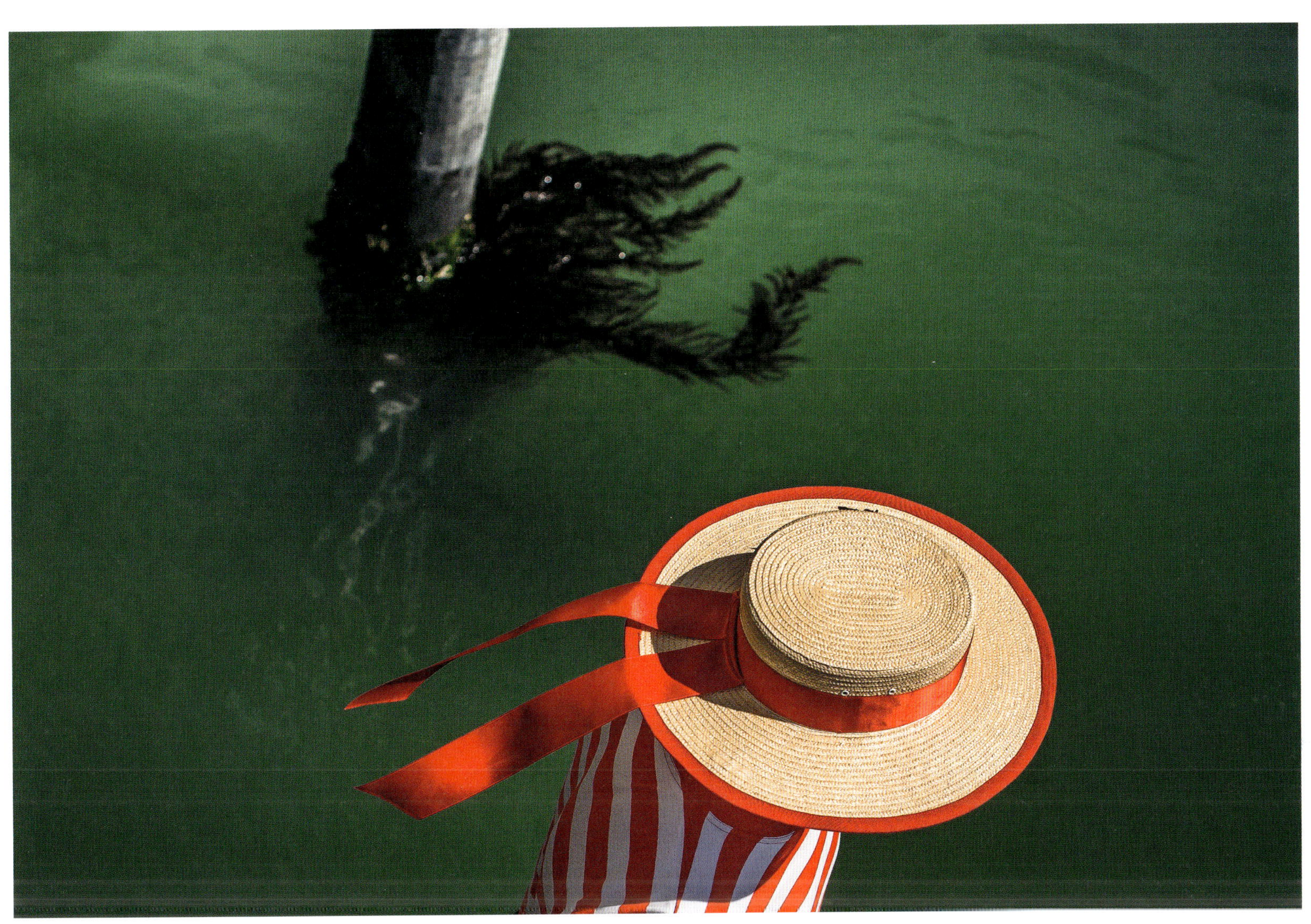

*Gondolier*, Venice, Italy, 2019

# 81

# Olga Karlovac

This photograph was taken in Zagreb, the capital of Croatia, through a tram window on a rainy day while the tram was leaving the station. In the moment, everything felt a bit disturbing and in motion. It is an intuitive shot.

*Olga is a Croatian-born, self-taught photographer who is known for her self-published photo books. She exhibits worldwide.*

OLGA KARLOVAC, Croatian

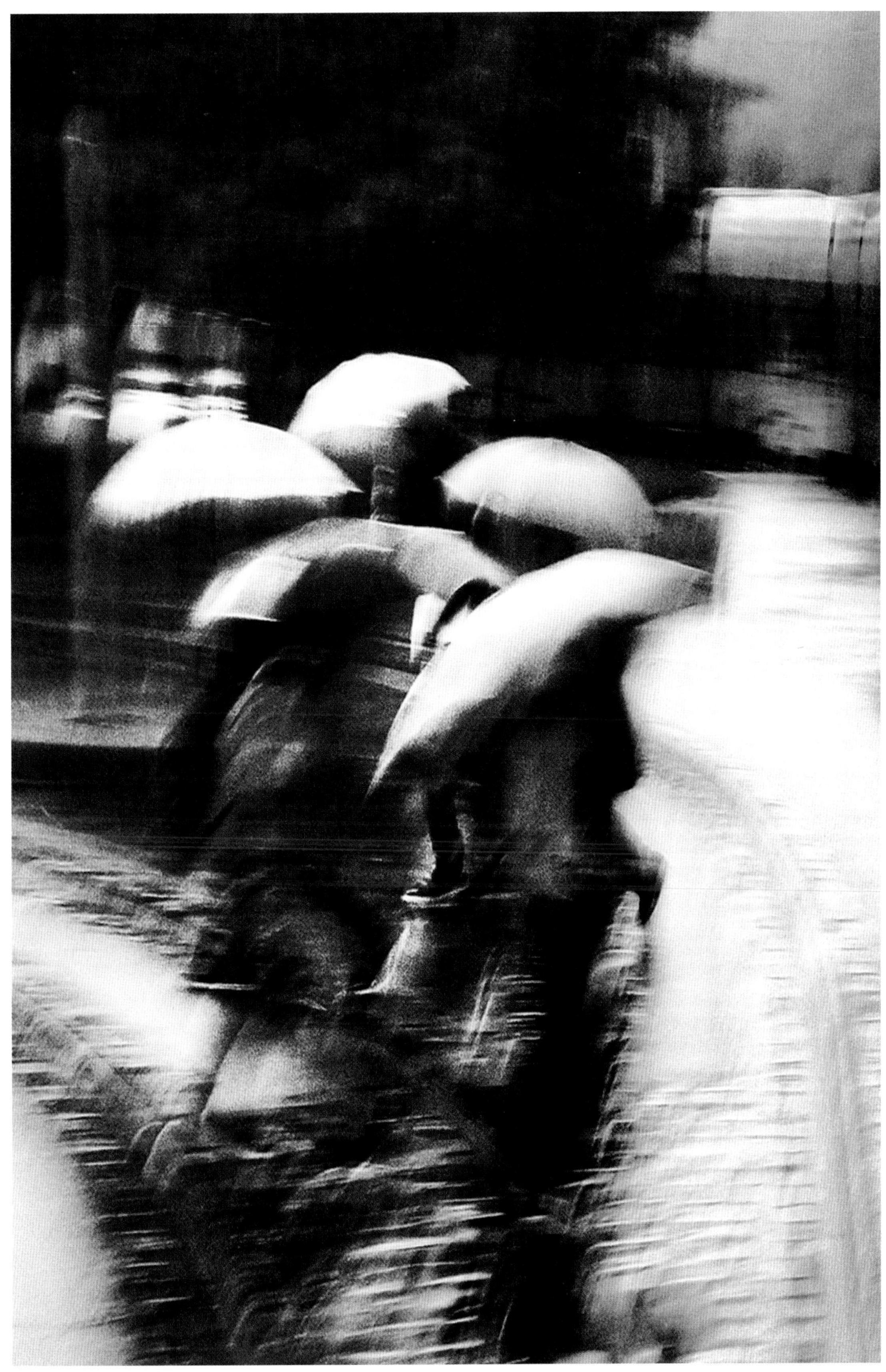

*Escape*, Zagreb, Croatia, 2018

# 82

# Christina Noerdam Andersen

This photo is from my first trip to New York City, which I had anticipated since I took up street photography.

I stood on this street corner for hours, so excited to have found the iconic NYC steam. I loved the way the steam transformed the scene into something otherworldly. As a photographer I am not so much interested in reality as I am in portraying a parallel world that exists right alongside ours. I consider the anonymous silhouettes to be all of us.

*Christina is a self-taught photographer based in Copenhagen, Denmark. Her images often focus on solitude and melancholy in an urban environment.*

CHRISTINA NOERDAM ANDERSEN, Danish

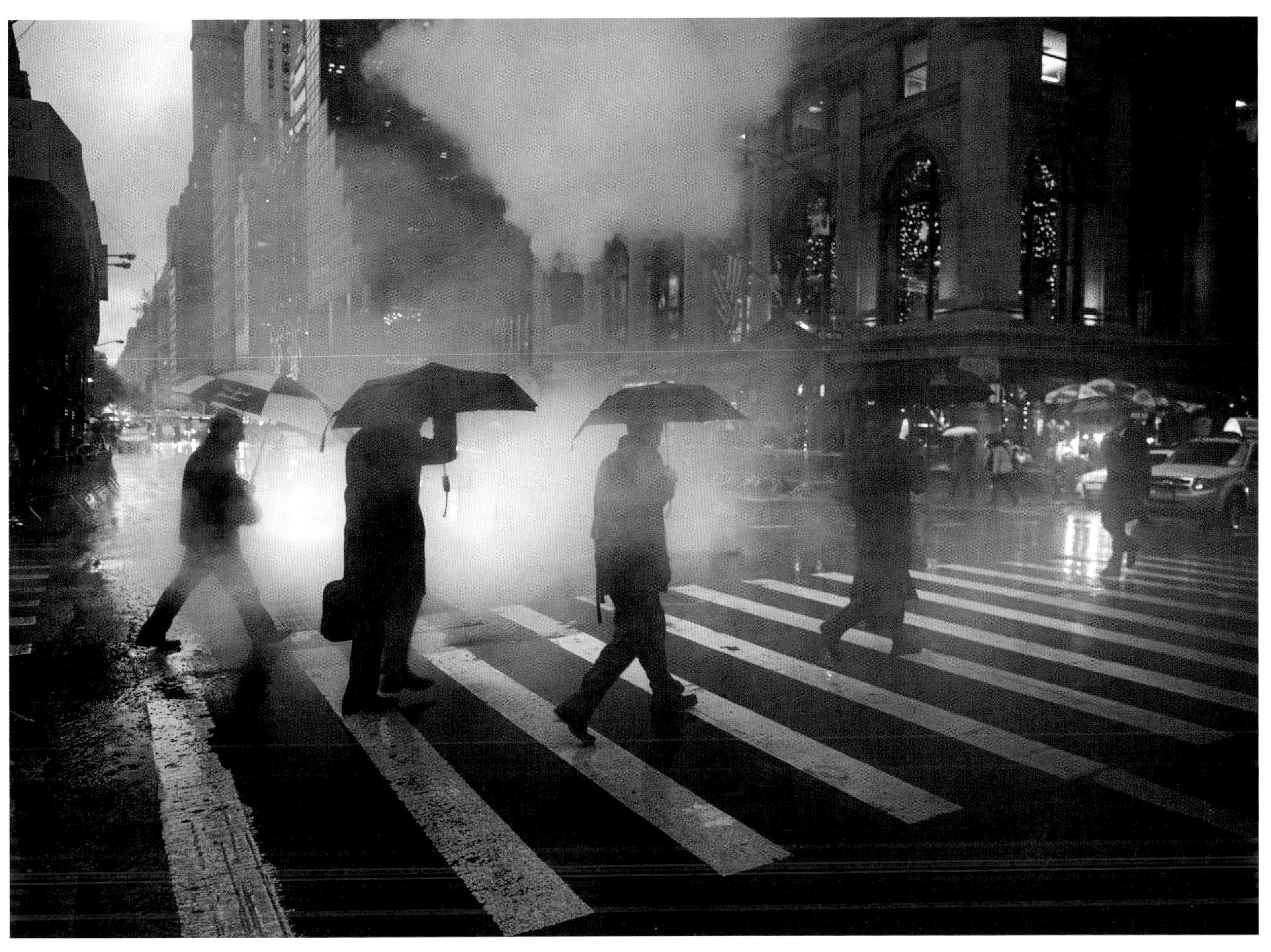

*After Dark*, New York City, USA, 2016

# 83

# Mavis CW

New York is a city I feel very connected to. You can feel the rich history of street photography as you walk around the city and the vibrancy of life offers something unexpected every day. Alongside the yellow cabs and skyscrapers, steam is a part of everyday life that's quintessentially New York—the result of an energy system that started in the 1880s and now reaches more than 100 miles underneath the city, serving nearly 2,000 buildings.

In 2019, I was heading off to watch the Columbus Day Parade on Fifth Avenue. A huge plume of steam caught my eye. The air became still. There was a brief break in the clouds, and all of a sudden the bright midday sunshine illuminated the steam as it rose toward the sky. After I captured the moment with one frame, the sun vanished behind the clouds.

I like the temporary nature of the elements in the scene and how they relate to the pace of change and buzzing energy of the city.

*Mavis is a London-based photographer working with traditional methods. Her photography examines everyday life in cities, using the streets as her visual landscape.*

MAVIS CW, British

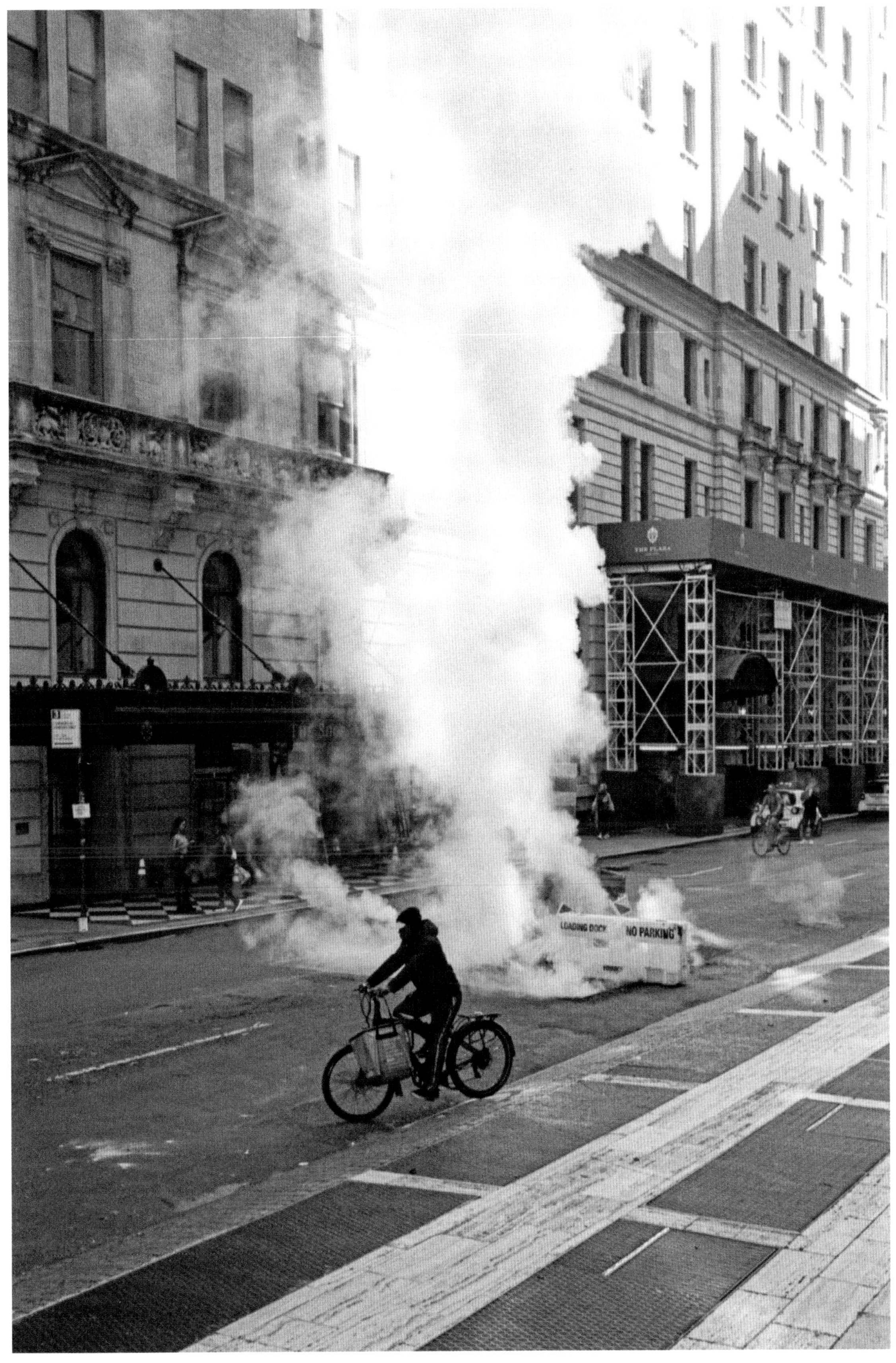

*58th Street, New York*, New York City, USA, 2019

# 84

# Priscilla Falcon Moeller

I took this photo in Thailand when the nation was in a one-year period of mourning. King Bhumibol Adulyadej had just died and everyone was wearing black. We found ourselves living through moments of beauty and hardship. I met the boys' mother in a small community outside the city of Bangkok and she soon introduced me to her family. I immediately felt connected to them. Grief, love, and family seemed to band us all together. The photograph is a result of one of the daily moments of joy within a time of national hardship, a true reminder that there is always beauty in the ordinary.

I remember feeling that fate had brought us together, and that when I found them I couldn't let them go.

*Priscilla is an emerging Mexican photographer whose work has been awarded by the* British Journal of Photography, Portrait of Humanity, Magnum Photos, *and the* Worldwide Photography Gala Awards.

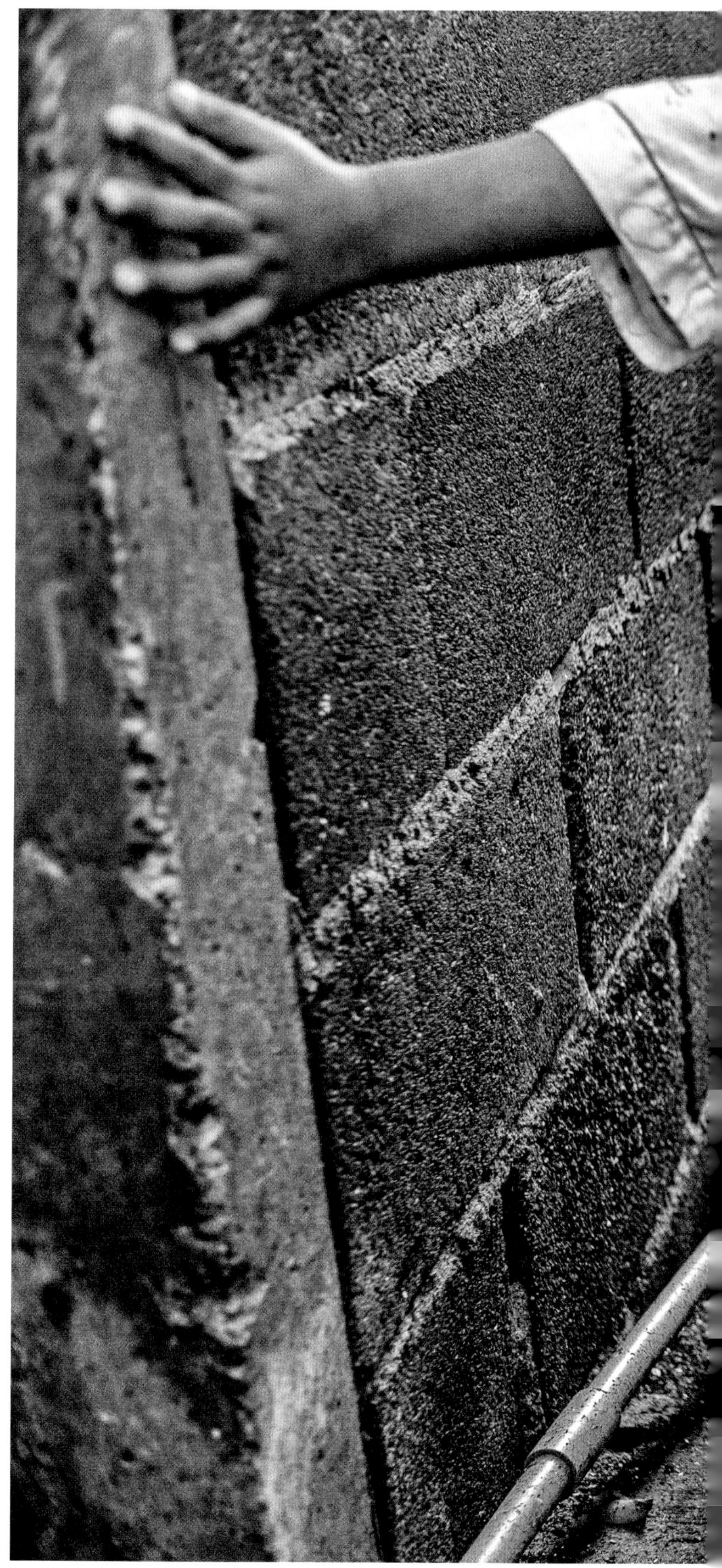

PRISCILLA FALCON MOELLER, Mexican

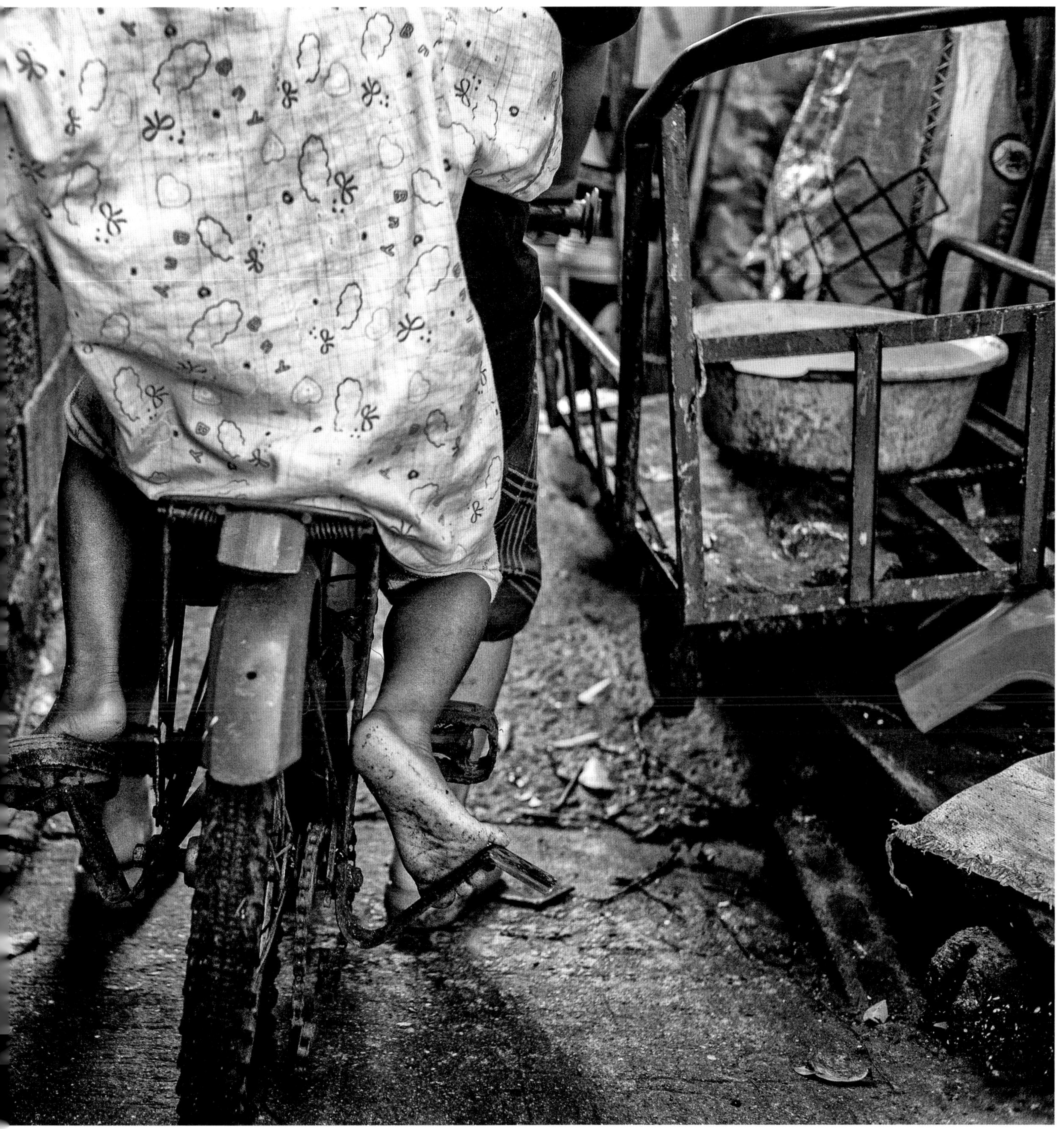

*Untitled*, Bangkok, Thailand, 2016

# 85.

# Linda Hacker

The main focus of my photography is exploring the
mysteries and ambiguities of the world around me, using
filters and reflections to abstract, skew, and make the
transparent opaque. For me, much of the joy and excitement
of exploring the city comes from the serendipity of
encountering photos. I always carry a camera with me.
I spotted this scene when I was attending open art
studios in an old manufacturing building in the Dumbo
neighborhood of Brooklyn, New York. I often find that
looking at art readies my mind to see new photographic
possibilities. On this day, I was walking down a hallway
and saw the light reflected beautifully on the highly
polished floor. Then I had only to wait for the right person
to walk by and cast their shadow into the waiting light to
complete the photo.

*Linda is a Brooklyn-based fine art and street photographer.*
*She is a member of the artists' roster at Soho Photo Gallery*
*in downtown Manhattan.*

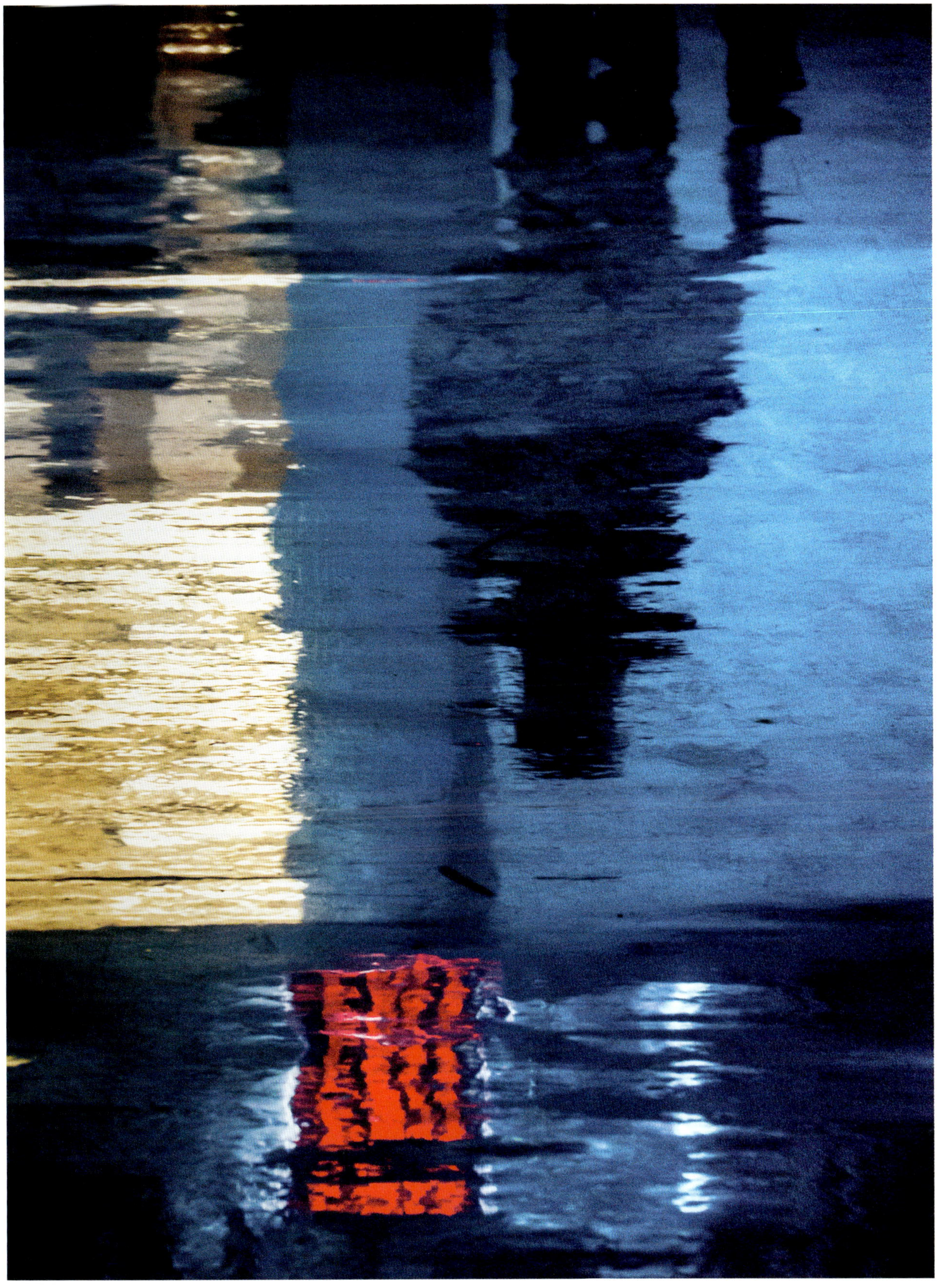

*This Way Out*, Brooklyn, New York, USA, 2019

# 86

# Linda Wisdom

This "American diner" restaurant in central London
had been in this location since 1987 until it was sadly
replaced by another restaurant in early 2019. The glowing
neon lights had always impressed me at night time, as
it literally lights up this street corner like a beacon. One
night, during a photo walk, there was a sudden downpour
of rain. This was the first time I had noticed just how
amazingly reflective the nearby paving was, turning the
whole corner into a mirror of rainbow colours. I knew I
had to make an image of the scene, despite getting totally
drenched. It was worth it.

*Linda is a self-taught, professional photographer based
in London. Her street photography focuses mainly on
storytelling and the nuances of human nature.*

LINDA WISDOM, British

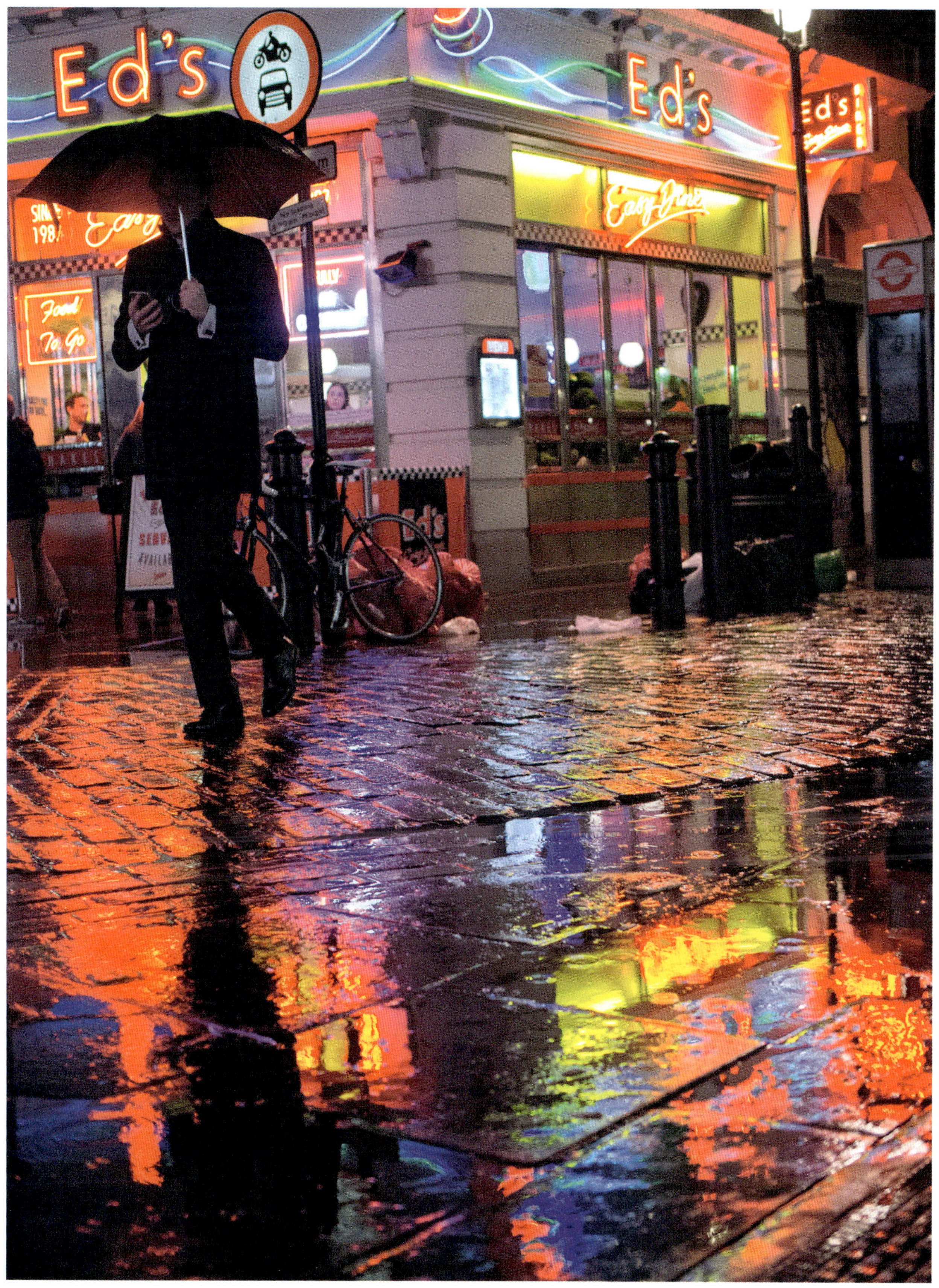


*Ed's Diner at Night*, Soho, London, England, 2016

# 87

# So.aSa

A hot summer day. The sun burned the facades of the buildings. The colors were bursting. The areas of light and shadow were perfectly aligned. I remember crouching to find the best angle, to draw the frame with the screen of my iPhone. This young woman appeared. She seemed happy. Her light step contrasted with the weight of the heat. I'm sure she was on a date.

*Asa is a mobile photographer based in Corsica. Her work is focused on anonymity on the streets. She has been published by Apple,* Fotografiska, Aesthetica *magazine and others.*

SO.ASA, Corsican

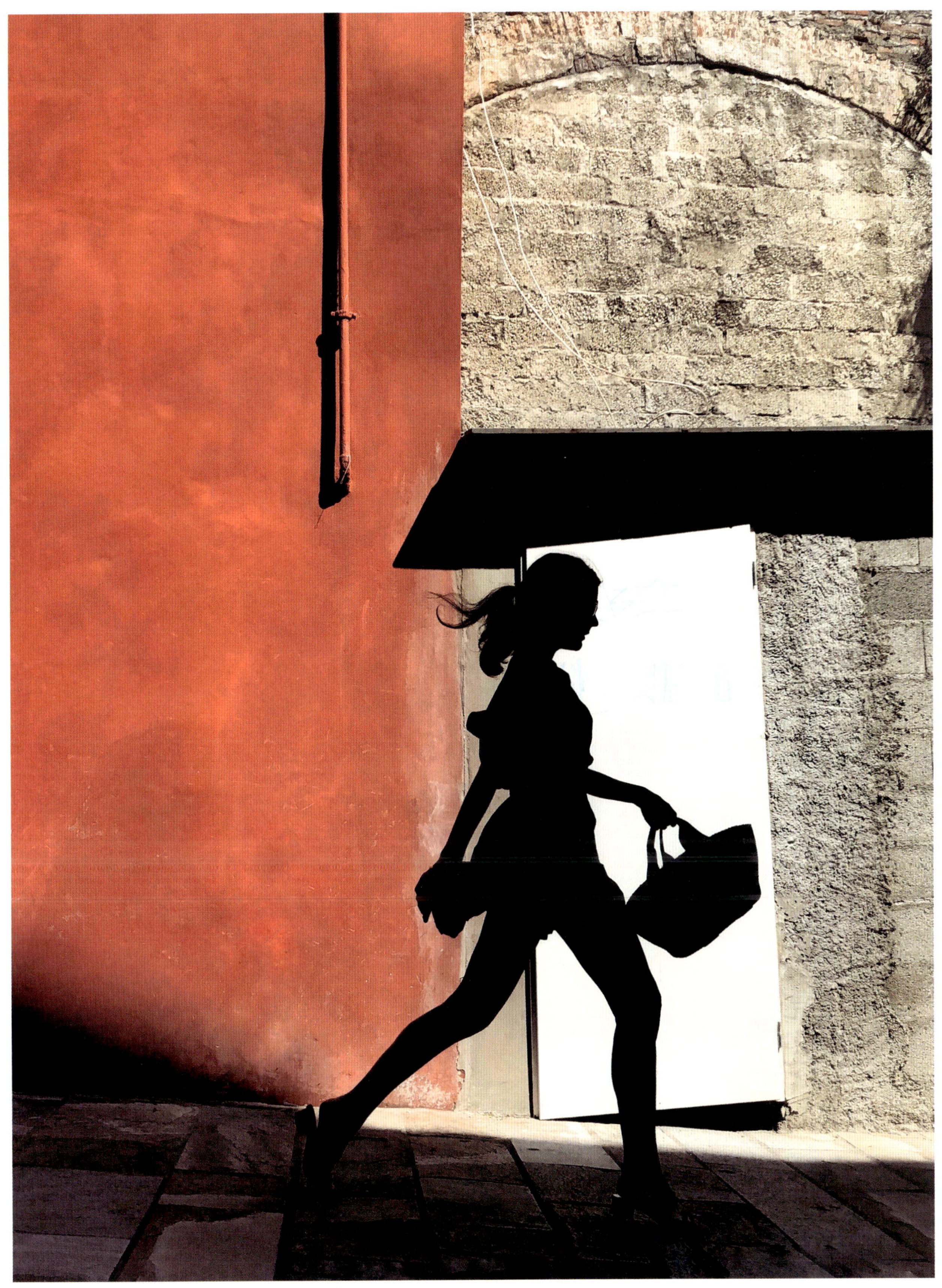

*Rendez-vous*, Bastia, France, 2018

# 88

# Nanda Bayler

I have always been fascinated by faith. When I lived in Delhi, I was in contact with Islam for the first time, and this beautiful religion deeply intrigued me. I took this picture on one of my many visits to mosques in Old Delhi. The compositions of shadows and faces are fertile ground for inspiration and imagination. The gaze of the faithful immersed in their prayers, often unaware of their surroundings, is one of my favorite subjects. I always wonder what is going on in their minds.

*Originally from Brazil, Nanda's work is inspired by the continuous chase for spontaneity, searching for shots that possess the magic of authenticity.*

NANDA BAYLER, Brazilian

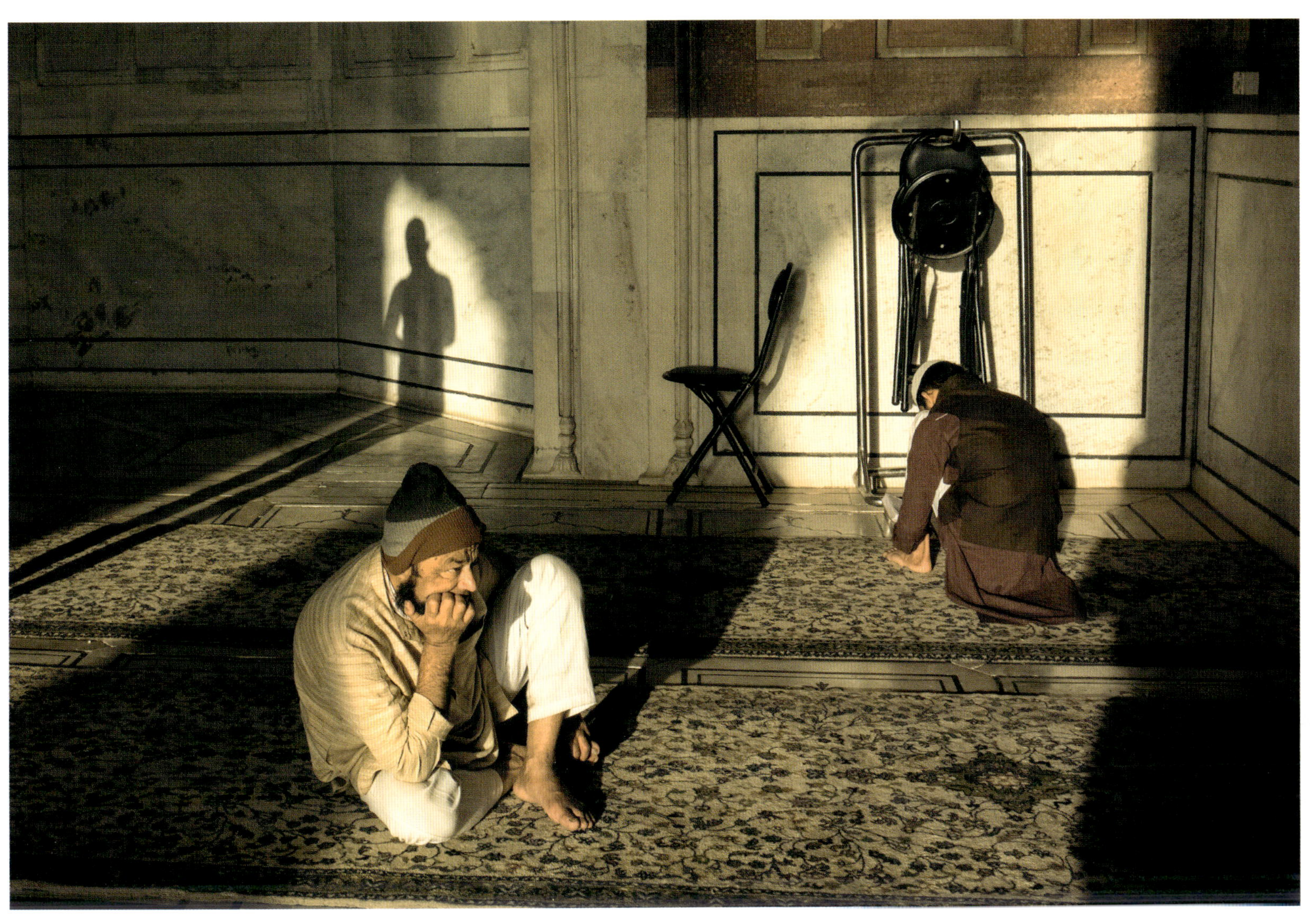

*His Gaze*, Old Delhi, India, 2019

# 89

# Olesia Kim

The photo was taken in Khiva, the old city in Uzbekistan (ex-USSR). In general, it's not permitted to take photos at the local markets there because the government of Uzbekistan regards them as ugly and shameful.

*Olesia is based in Tyumen, Siberia. She has a wide visual vocabulary and women are often central to her pictures.*

OLESIA KIM, Russian

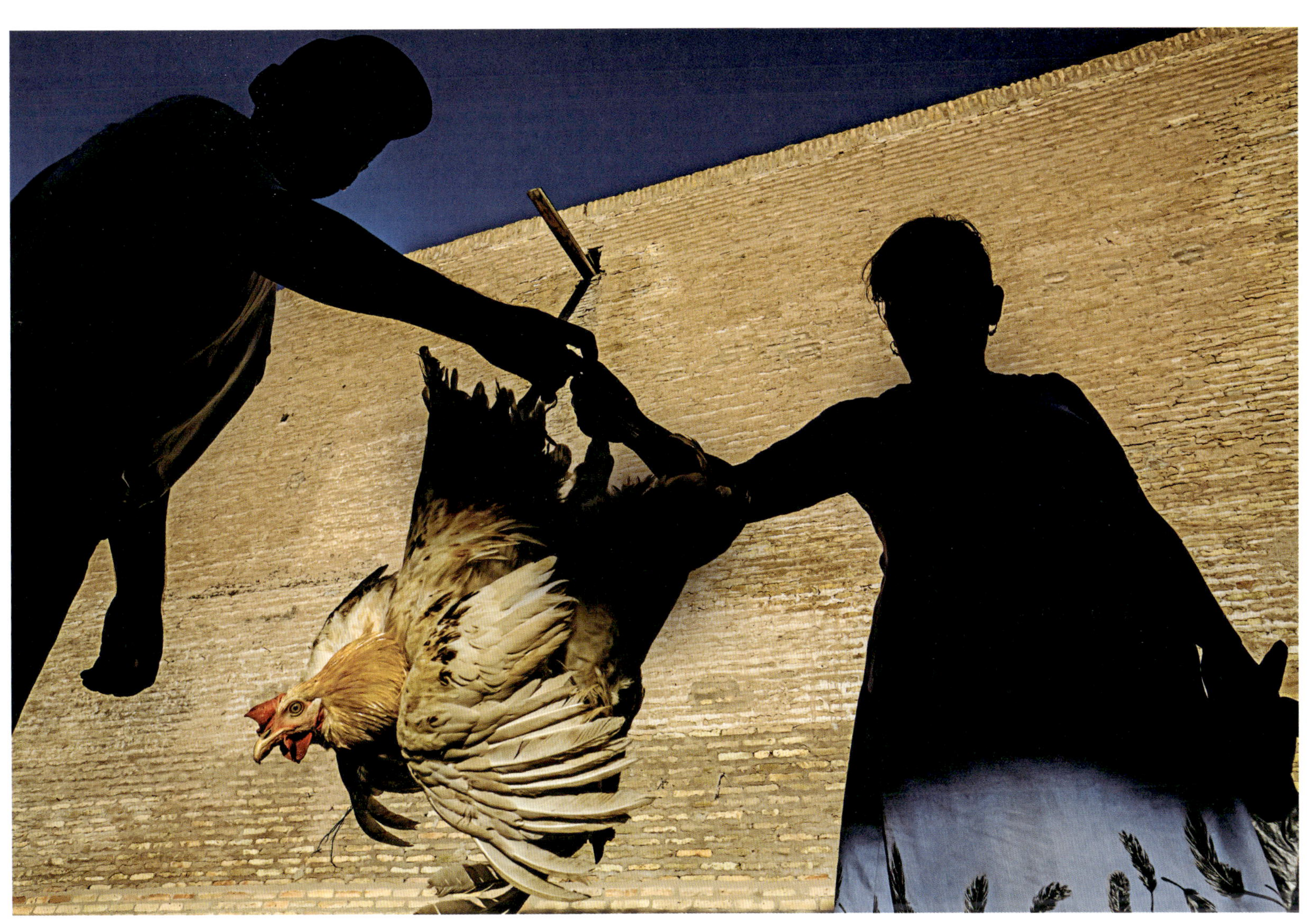

*Untitled*, Khiva, Uzbekistan, 2015

# 90

# Jutharat Pinyodoonyachet

This photo is important to me. I was confused about my career path so I went to Coney Island in the morning to clear my head. It was a bright day but there weren't many people around as it was winter. I was walking on the boardwalk when I saw this man. It took me a while to get close enough to take the photograph. I was lucky that he didn't stop stretching when I reached the perfect distance for shooting. I was so delighted when I got the photo. It made my day.

*Jutharat is a Bangkok-born photographer. She works as a photojournalist and is based in New York City. She loves to capture people's moments in ordinary life.*

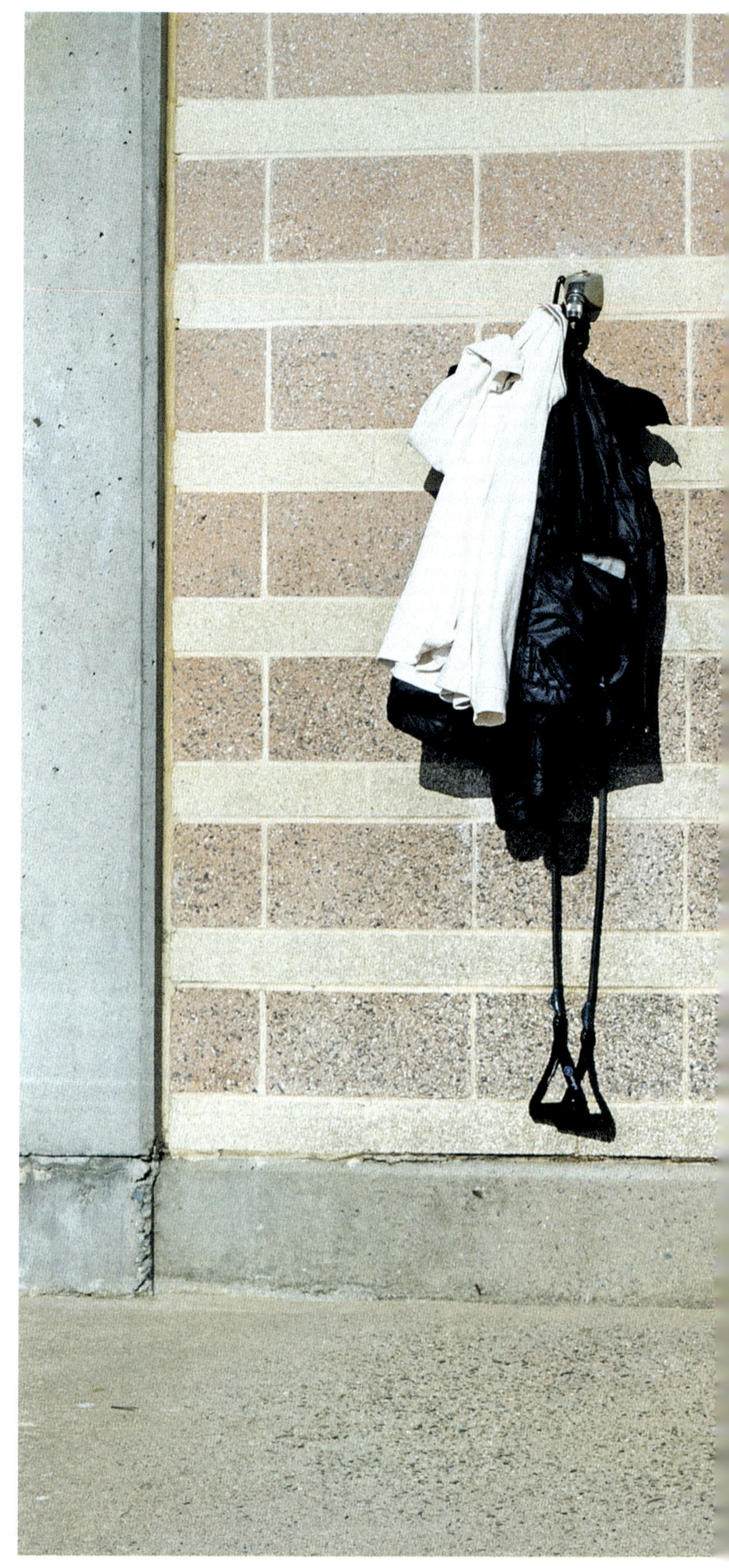

JUTHARAT PINYODOONYACHET, Thai

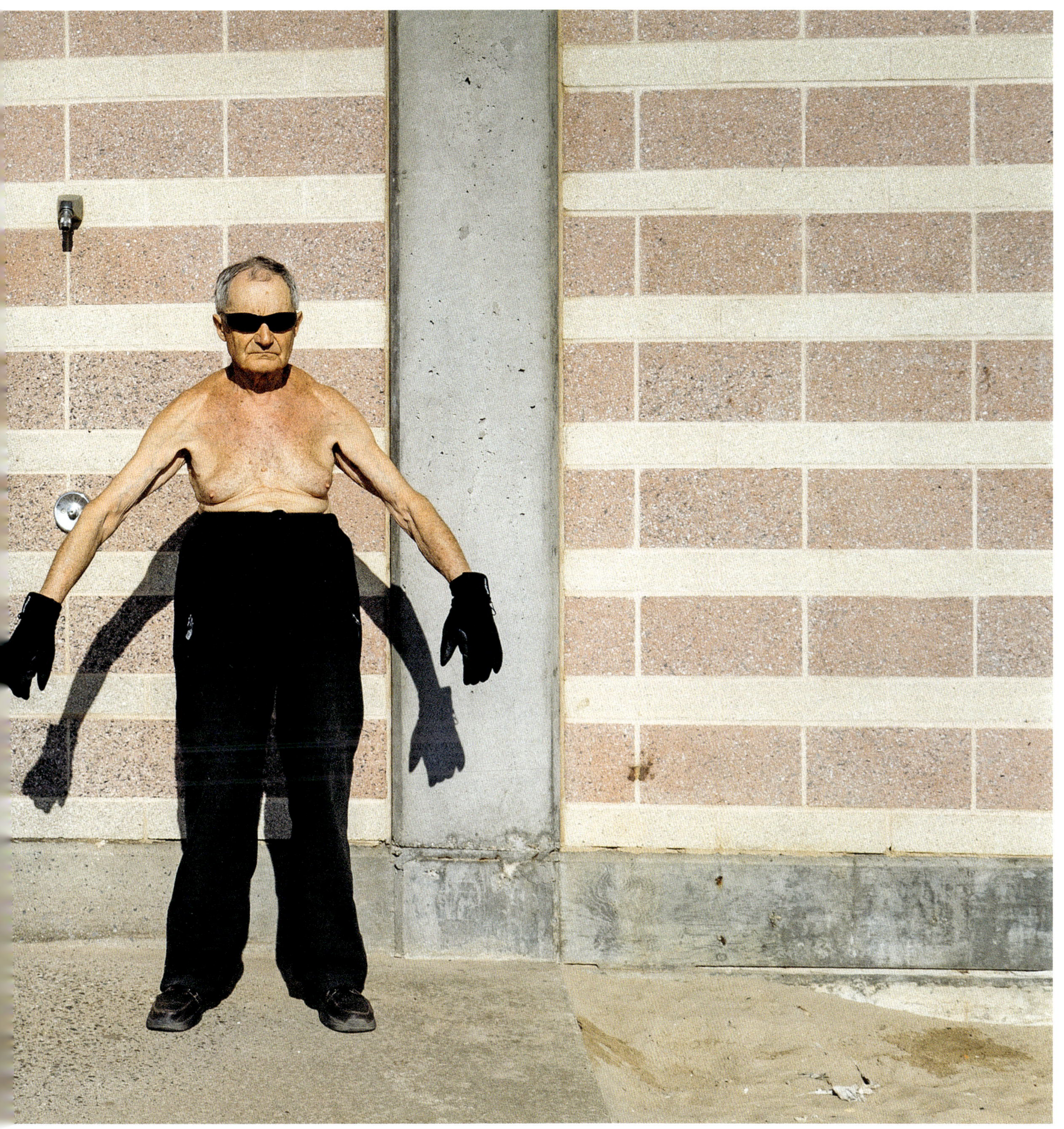

*Mind Flayer*, Coney Island, New York City, USA, 2017

# 91

# Michelle Rick

I wrote an essay for an undergraduate writing workshop imagining my father as a boy in Coney Island. Even though Coney Island is one of my favorite places to shoot, I'm not sentimental about it. I try to avoid nostalgia in my photography, with the possible exception of this picture. My father was a boy in the 1930s and '40s. When I saw these boys, with their crewcuts and milk-fed swagger, I realized that he could have been one of them, just as any one of them might be him eighty years from now.

*Michelle came to photography in 2009 after working in publishing and film. Her images often focus on the dynamic streets of her native New York.*

MICHELLE RICK, American

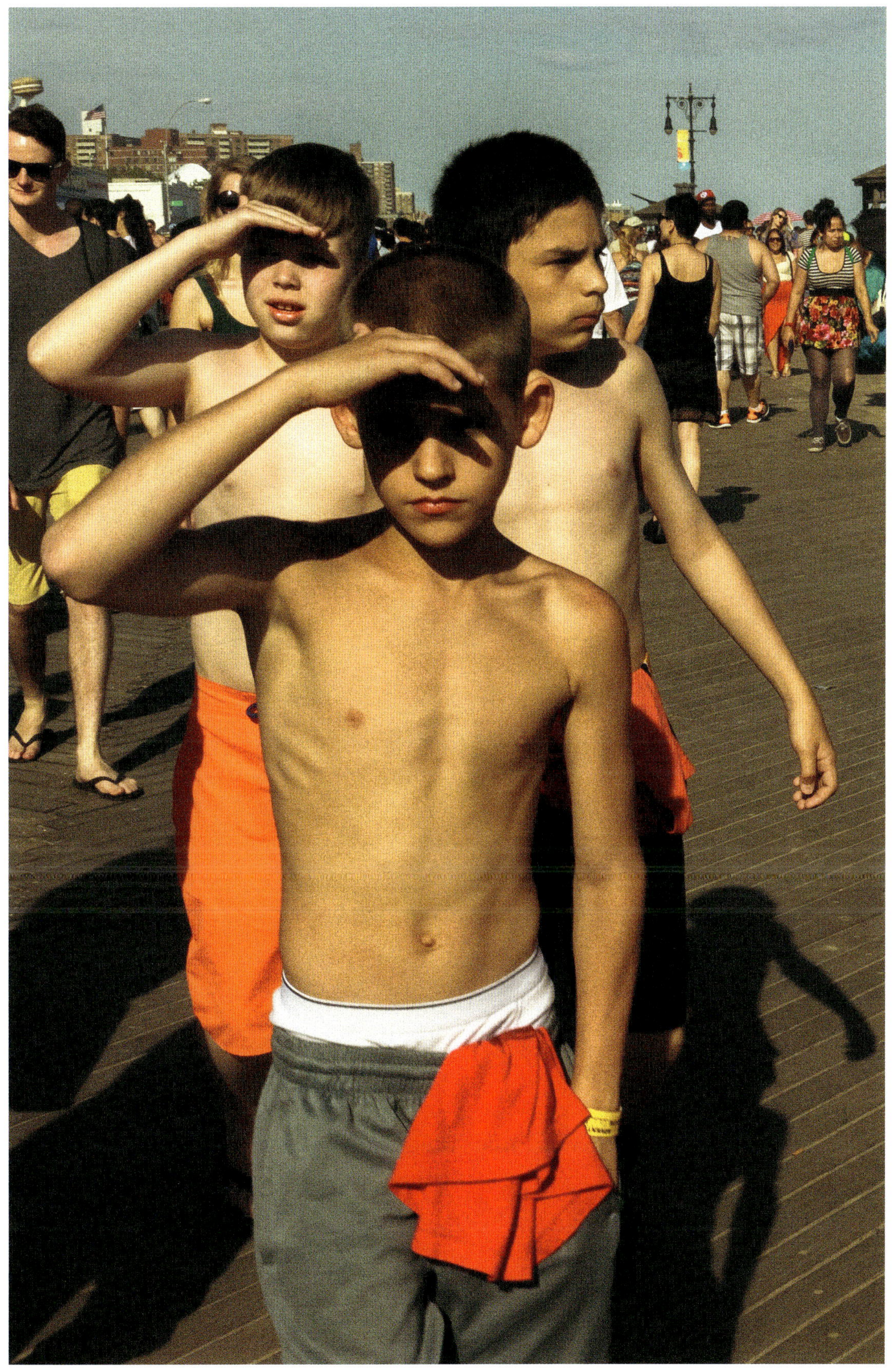

*Untitled*, Coney Island, New York City, USA, 2014

# 92

# Heike Frielingsdorf

I took this picture during a visit to a carnival. Taking photos there always thrills me; I'm drawn to the artificial worlds, the happy children, and the perceptible human longing. My memories of childhood drive me there.

The situation shown in the picture appealed to me emotionally and I reacted instinctively. The whole scene lasted for only a few seconds and so I felt very happy and grateful to have had the chance to capture this "decisive moment."

For me it is an image that tells a story and makes other people's feelings tangible—with a dose of humor. It is so nice to see how the father seems to be trying to protect his little daughter. When I look at his expression, I'm sure he briefly believed that there was a risk, even though he knew that the stream is part of a funny water game. Perhaps this is why viewers of the picture are a bit confused and don't immediately recognize whether it's a funny or a serious moment.

*Heike is a Cologne-based photographer who loves to stroll through the streets, moving around as if on a huge stage and trying to capture the complex game of life.*

HEIKE FRIELINGSDORF, German

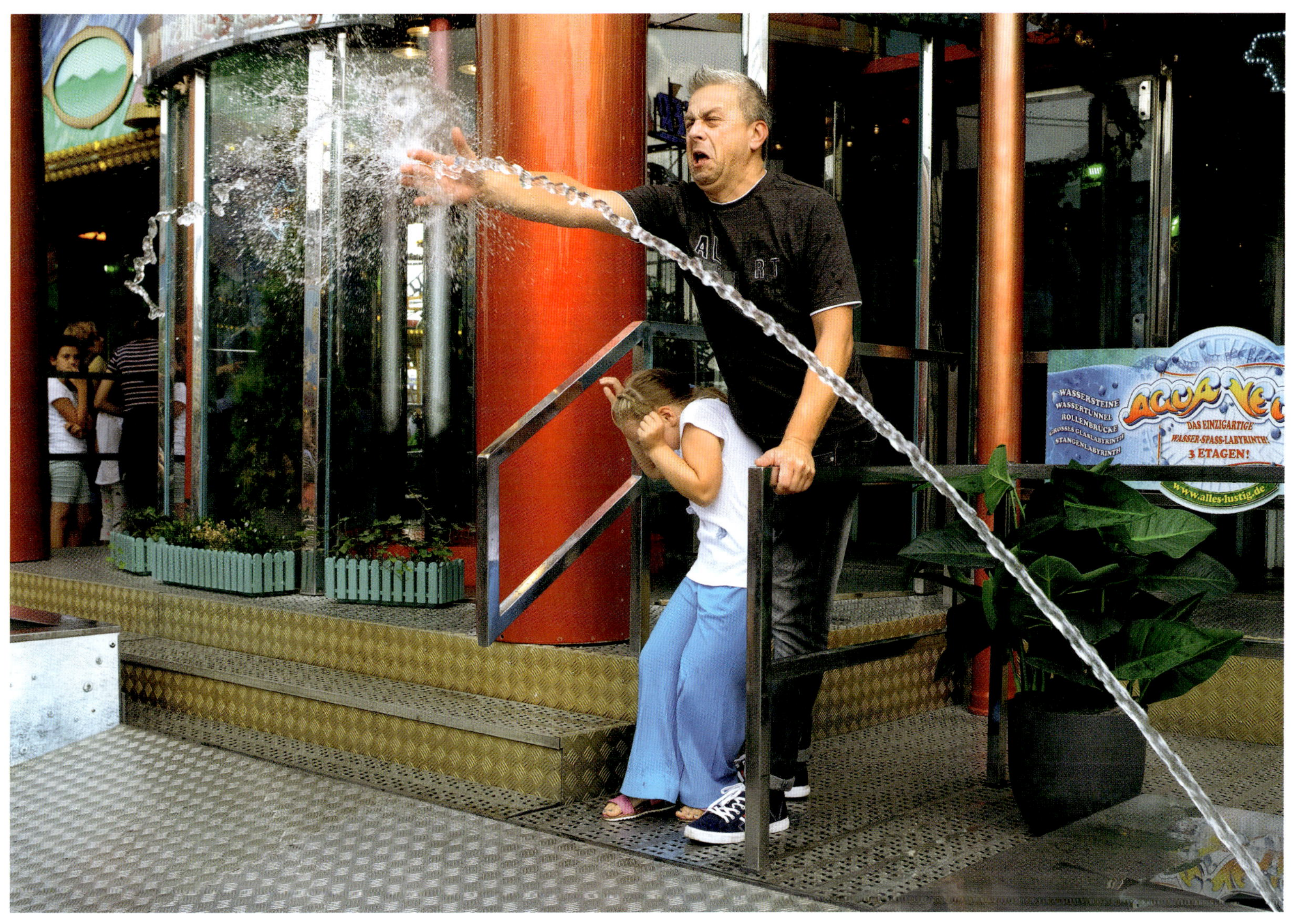



*Untitled*, Dusseldorf, Germany, 2019

# 93

# Orna Naor

For the last thirteen years, Israeli women from the
Machsom Watch organization have helped bring women
and children from Palestinian villages to the beach; for
most of them it's for the first time in their lives.
Their fear and anxiety soon change to joy and laughter.

*Orna is a street and documentary photographer based
in Tel Aviv, Israel; her work focuses on emotional issues
and moments.*

ORNA NAOR, Israeli

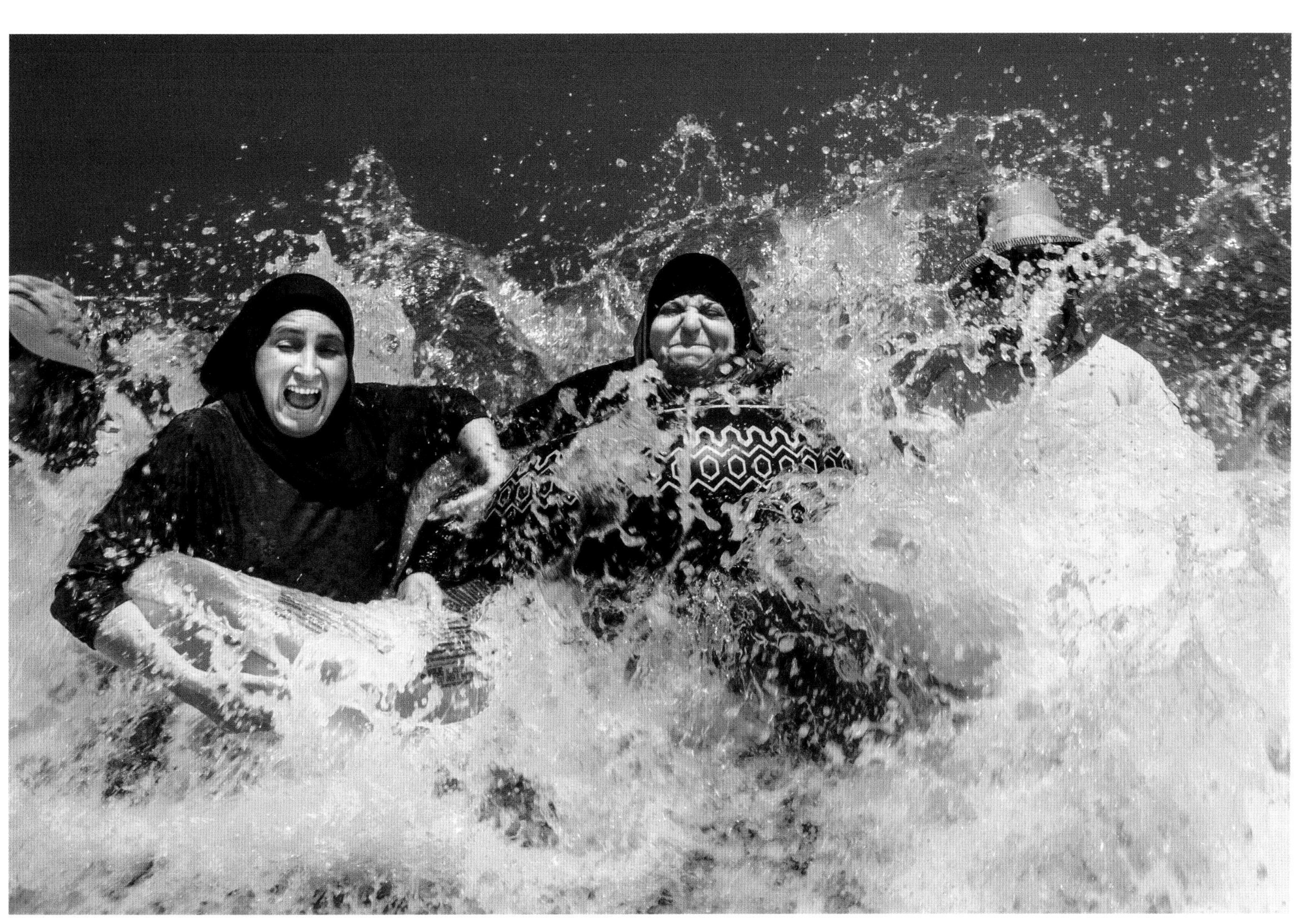

*Women of the Sea*, Tel Aviv, Israel, 2019

# Sonia Goydenko



# 94

It may not look like it, but this photograph was taken in late December. The weather was 25 degrees Fahrenheit with wind gusts at 30 mph, but that didn't stop this Coney Island Polar Bear. If anything, the colder the better. These incredibly brave souls come together every winter Sunday in Coney Island to take a dip in the freezing water. I've photographed them in sandstorms and freezing rain, on Christmas and Valentine's Day. It continues to amaze me how these people go into the ocean every week, no matter the weather. What an incredible community.

*Sonia is an award-winning, internationally exhibited NYC-based street photographer. The magic and spontaneity of the streets keep her photographing and educating others.*

SONIA GOYDENKO, American

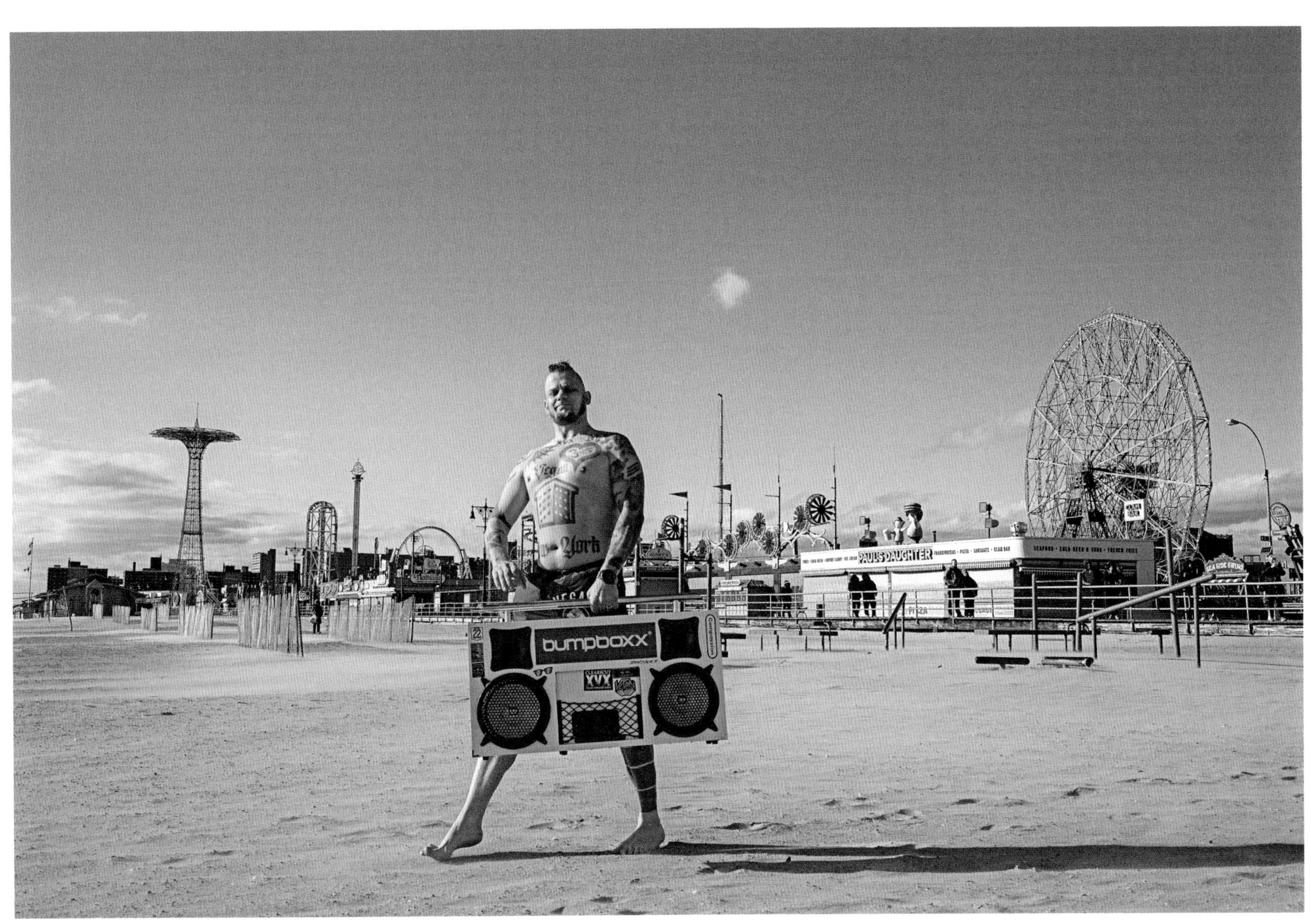

*Coney Island Polar Bear*, Coney Island, New York City, USA, 2019

# Sandra
# Cattaneo Adorno

I took this photo in Ipanema on a strange day: The sea was very rough and the undertow was so strong that the bathers were hesitating to get in. A thick, ominous mist hung over the beach and was colored by the sunset.

*Sandra has been passionate about photography since she discovered it at the age of sixty. Her work has been exhibited internationally, won numerous awards, and been published extensively. She has published two photo books.*

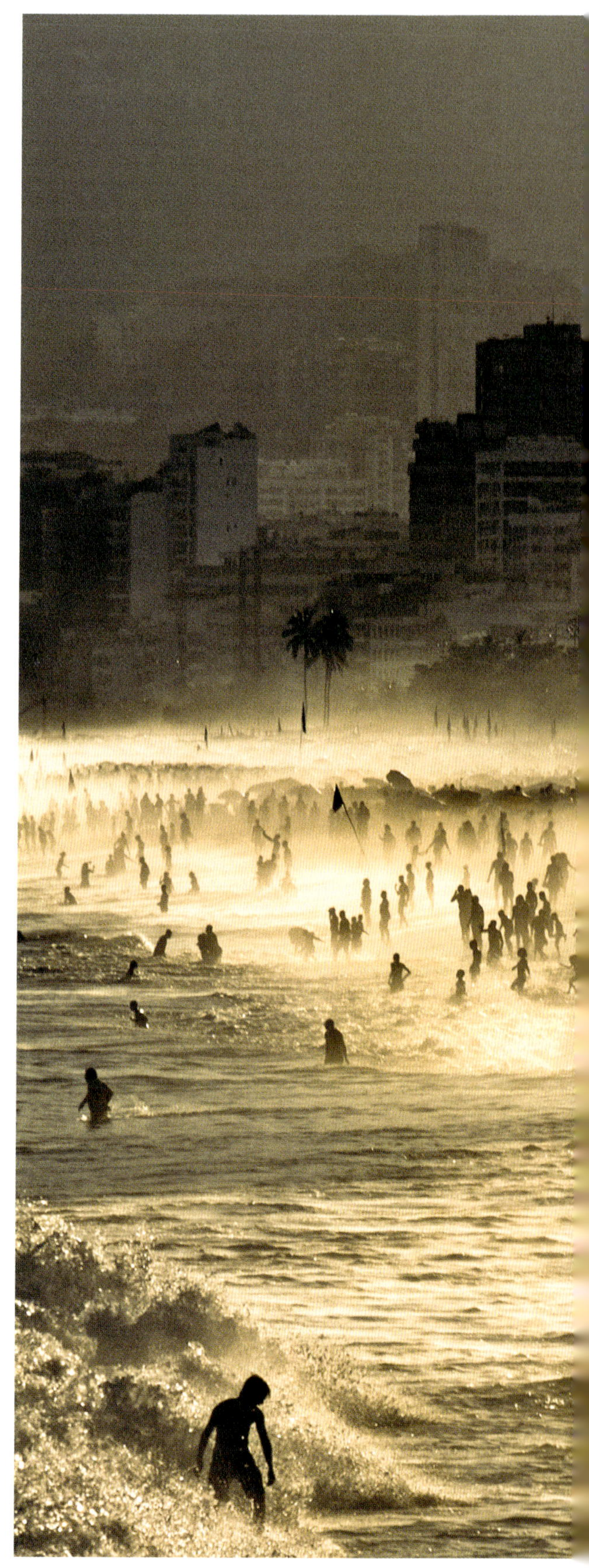

SANDRA CATTANEO ADORNO, Brazilian

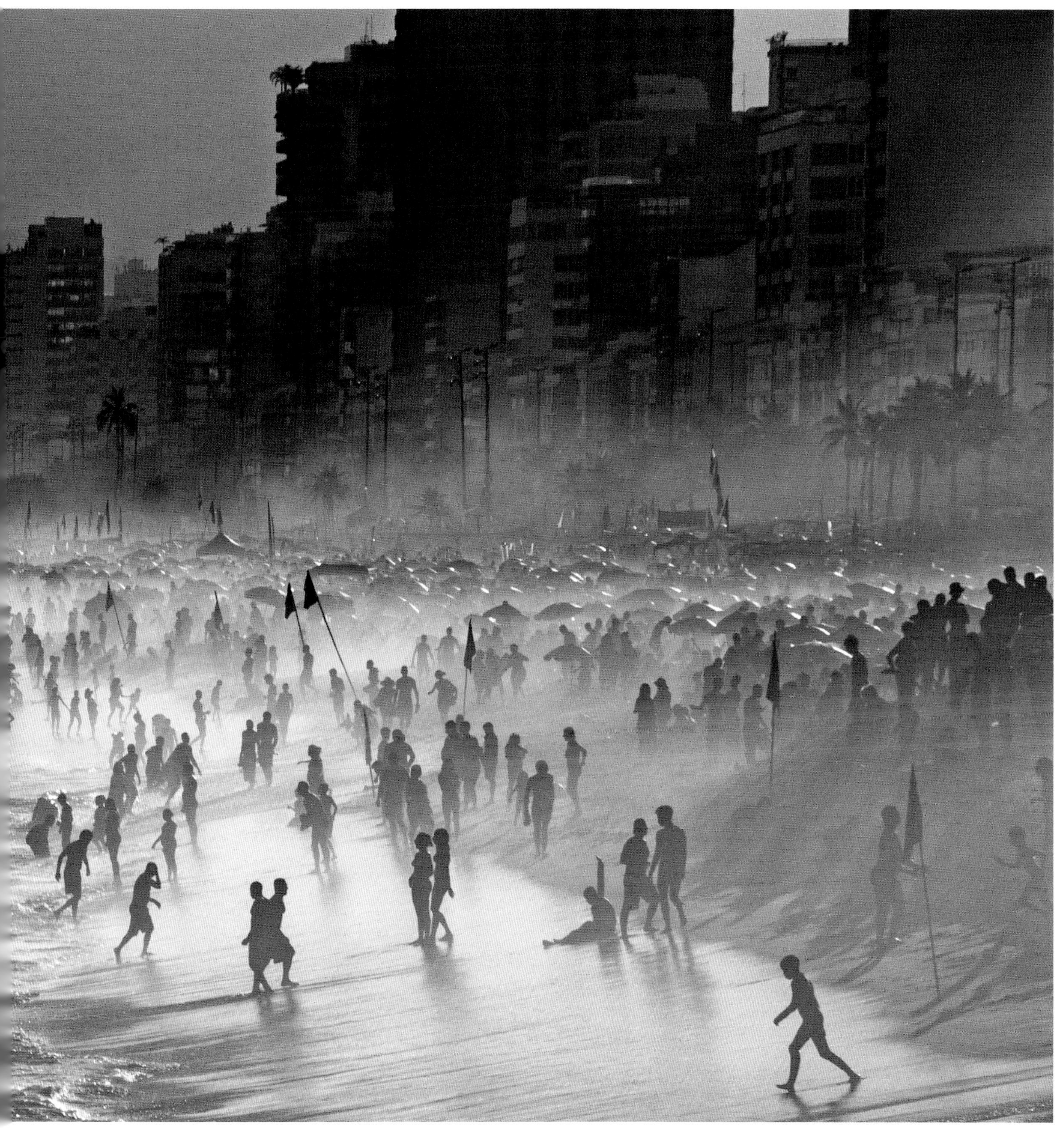

*A Strange Day in Ipanema*, Ipanema Beach, Rio de Janeiro, Brazil, 2016

# Prabha Jayesh

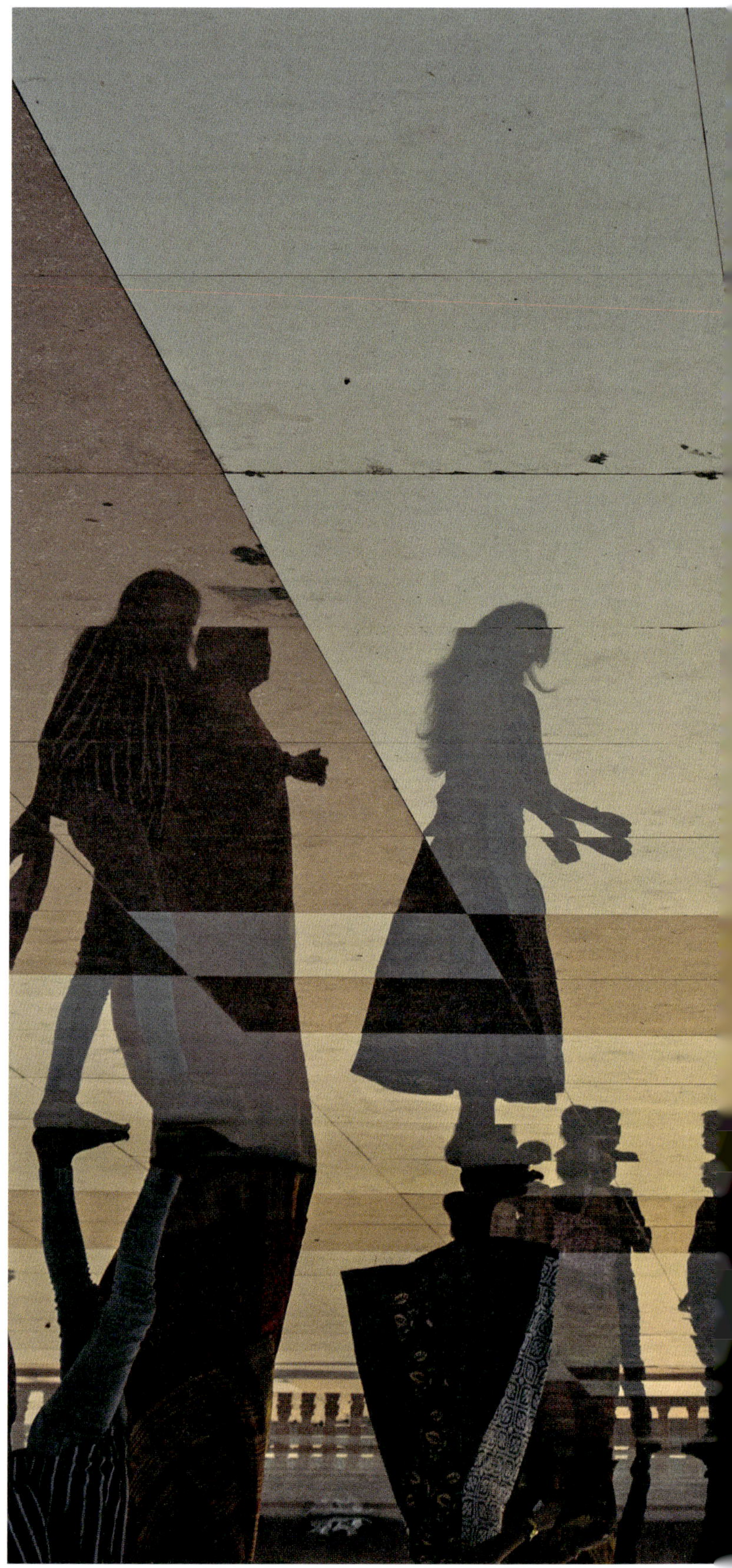

This photograph was taken in a temple outside my hometown Patdi in the state of Gujarat. It frames the reflections of temple visitors on the polished floor in the evening light. The photograph captures the emotions of the people and the evening activities of the visitors at the temple. As the author Peter Drucker once said, "Follow effective action with quiet reflection. From the quiet reflection will come even more effective action."

*Prabha is a street and documentary photographer based in Ahmedabad, India. Her current work relates to education, environmental issues, social taboos, and the life of visually impaired people.*

PRABHA JAYESH, Indian

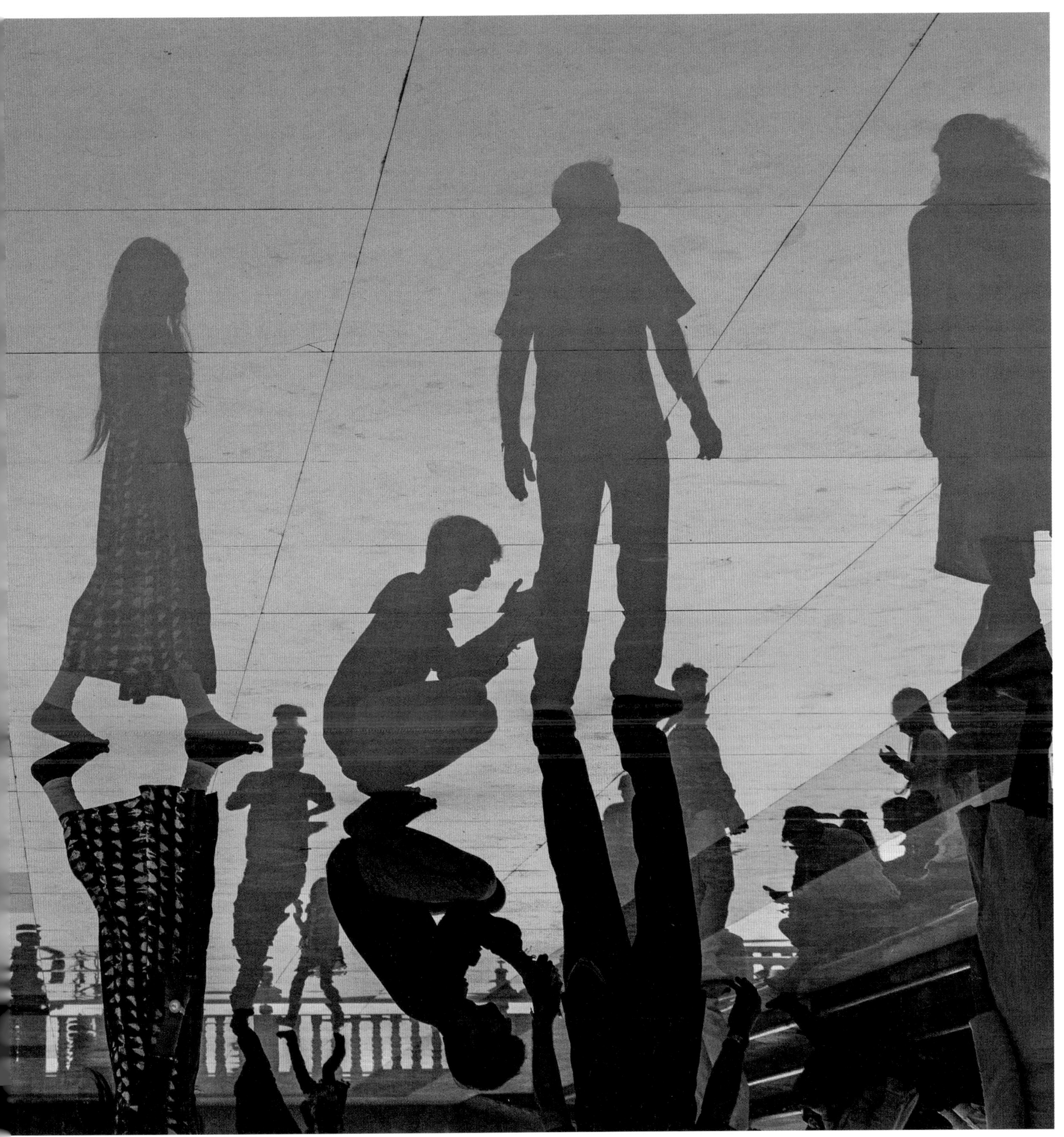

*Stories in Reflection*, Patdi, Gujarat, India, 2017

# 97

# Margarita Mavromichalis

I took this image during the Kumbh Mela in Allahabad, India, in 2019. Millions of people gather for almost a month in the biggest religious celebration in the world. Worshipers bathe in the river Ganges to wash away their sins at all hours of the day and night. I saw this beautiful young woman coming out of the water; she seemed profoundly spiritually engaged. The white clothes she was wearing sparkled through the darkness and added to her beauty.

*Margarita is a London-based photographer. The human presence is extremely important in her frames, as is documenting current events that she feels strongly about. She was a Prix Pictet 2019 nominee.*

MARGARITA MAVROMICHALIS, Greek

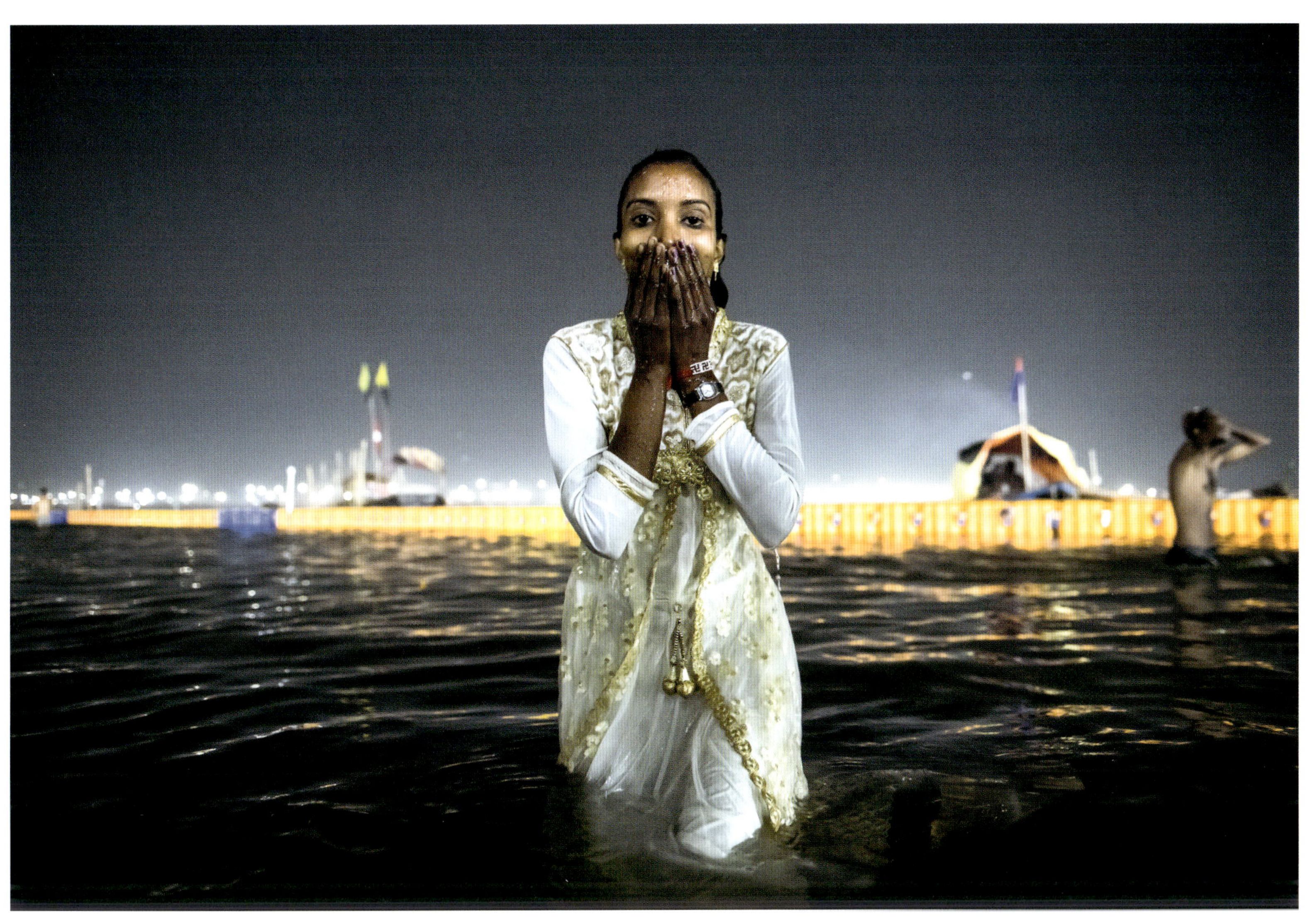

*Untitled*, Allahabad, India, 2019

# 98

# Ximena Echague

Varanasi, Benares, or Kashi is probably the oldest continuously inhabited city in the world. It is the holiest city for both Hindus and Jains, and is also very important for Buddhists. It is bathed by the holy Ganga (Ganges), the mother of India, and a lifeline for hundreds of millions of Indians who come every day to purify themselves in its sacred waters.

Holy men and holy cows interact in a mystic dance. The human and animal worlds closely coexist, naturally sharing in the sacred river. A bathing woman, a holy cow, and the Ganges synthesize India's eternal soul.

*Ximena is a documentary and street photographer based in New York and Brussels. Her work has been published and exhibited all over the world and is in the collection of the Museum of the City of New York.*

XIMENA ECHAGUE, Argentinian

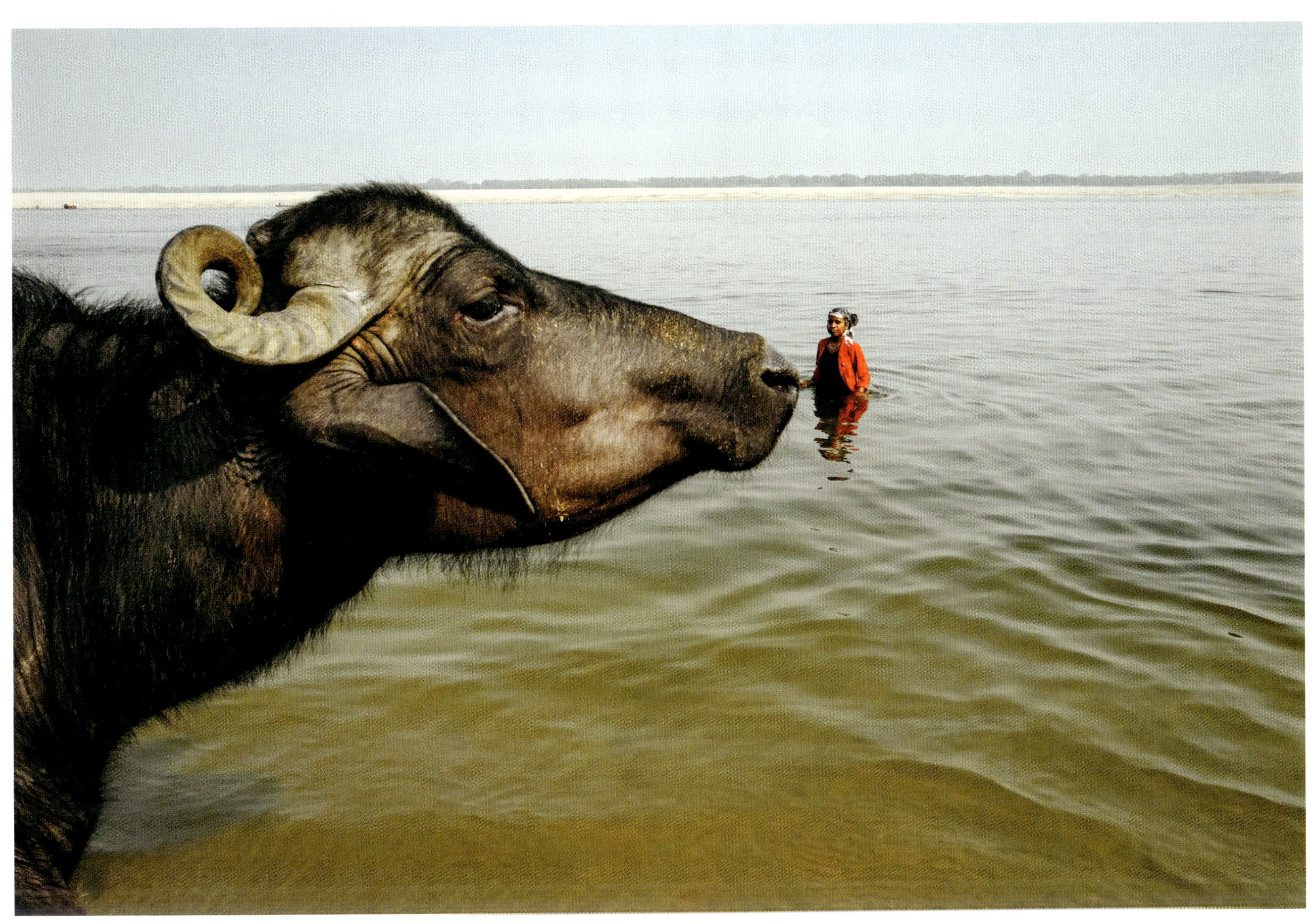

*Soul of the Ganges*, Varanasi, India, 2019

# 99

# Niki Gleoudi

The ancient Greeks didn't write obituaries. They asked only one question after someone died: "Did he have passion?"

I was walking on the beach trying to find a good subject for my ongoing series *Beach Stories* when I saw this man with an amazing, passionate expression. The miracle happened when the kids at the back threw the inflatable unicorn up into the air. I felt so lucky and grateful!

*Niki is an award-winning and published street photographer. She uses color to express emotions and the energy that underlies them.*

NIKI GLEOUDI, Greek

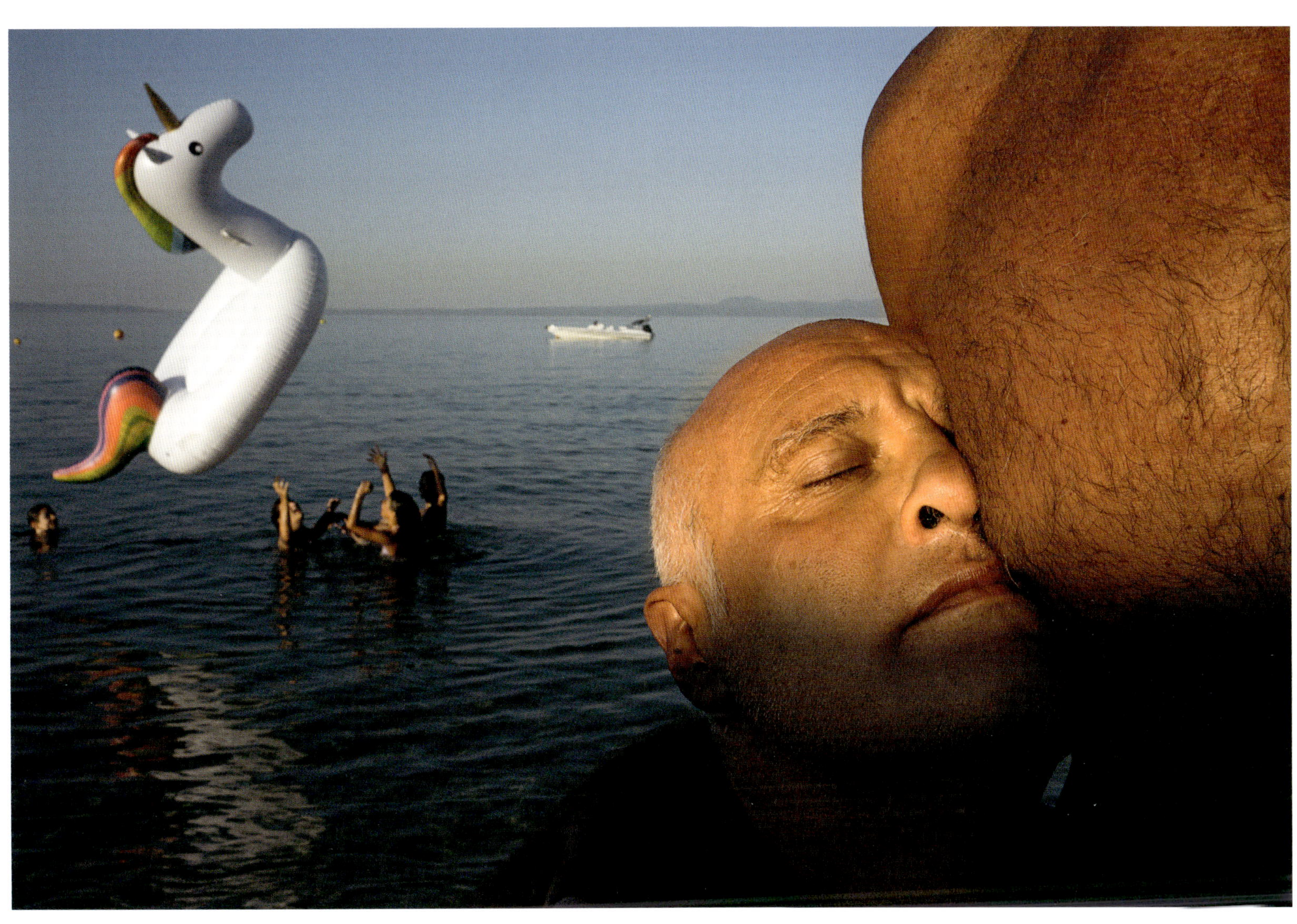

*In a World of Unicorns*, Halkidiki, Greece, 2017

# 100

# Bruna Rotunno

The photo was taken when I was shooting for my book *Women in Bali*.

The daughter of a maid who worked in some villas nearby was tempted by the pool and since it was raining, no one else was swimming. So she shyly looked around and dived in, sure that no one would see her …

I felt the magic of the moment when she completely surrendered to the water, in a surreal instant of daily life.

*Bruna is a photographer and video maker based between Milan and Paris. Her work explores cultures and social themes, focusing on street photography and storytelling.*

BRUNA ROTUNNO, Italian

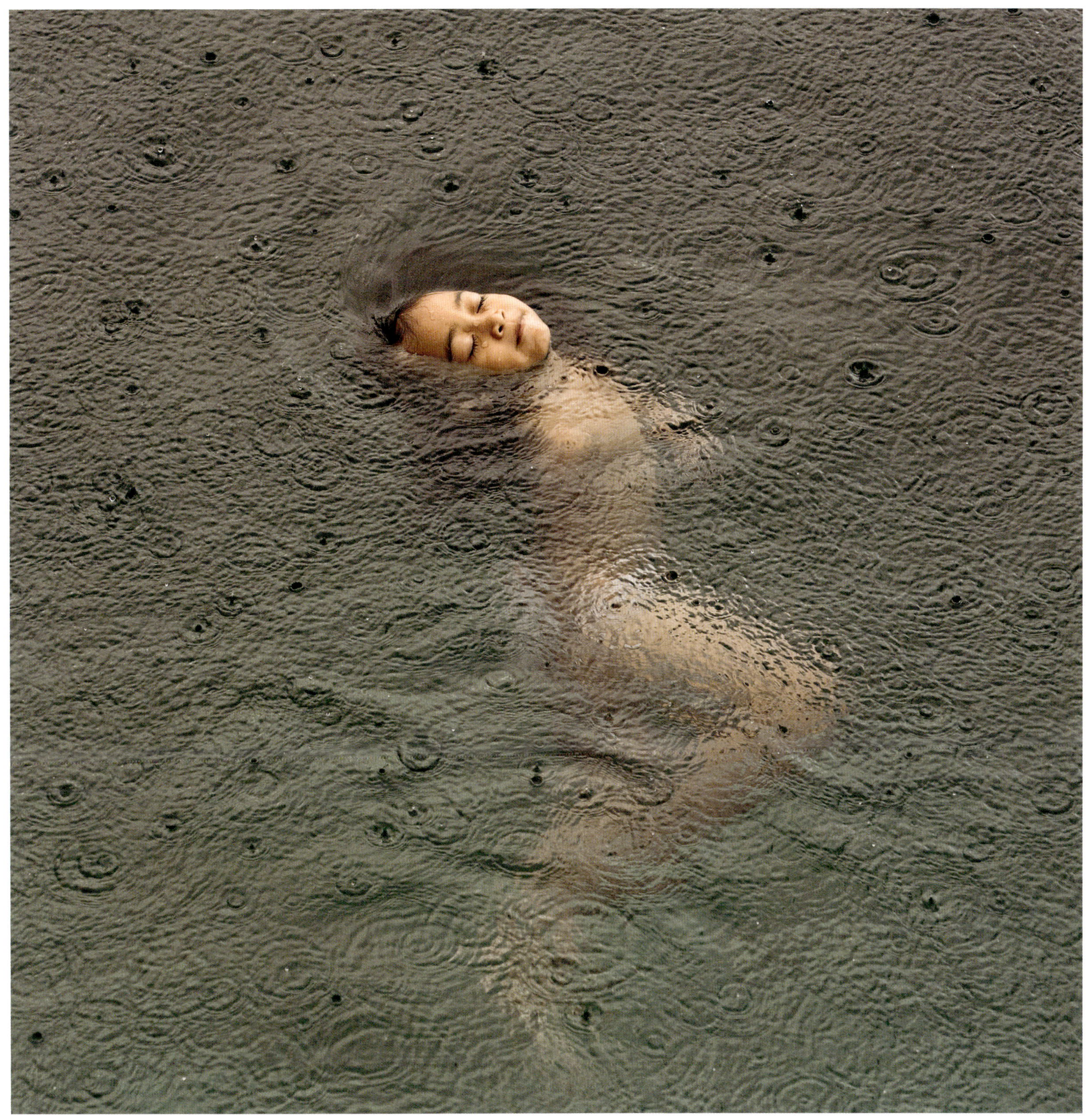

*Materic Water #1*, Bali, 2011

# About the Authors

Before moving to New York City in 1992, **Gulnara Samoilova** was the only female fine art photographer in Ufa, Russia, where she was born. Gulnara is a former Associated Press photojournalist who received national and international acclaim for her photographs of 9/11, including first prize in the World Press Photo competition. She founded the Women Street Photographers traveling exhibition in 2018—which begins each year in New York City— and the associated Instagram feed (@womenstreetphotographers), which acts as a platform for amateur and professional photographers who identify as women.

**Melissa Breyer** is a writer and award-winning photographer whose work has been featured in publications including *National Geographic* and the *New York Times*. She has been photographing strangers on the sly since the 1990s and her images have been shown in exhibits around the world. Breyer has been involved in the Women Street Photographers group since its earliest days; she was an artist in the group's 2018 inaugural exhibit in New York City and successive shows since. She can usually be found roaming the streets of New York City.

**Ami Vitale** is a Nikon Ambassador and *National Geographic* magazine photographer who has traveled to more than a hundred countries, bearing witness not only to violence and conflict, but also to surreal beauty and the enduring power of the human spirit. She is a five-time recipient of the World Press Photo prize whose recent work focuses on compelling wildlife and environmental stories.

# Image Credits and Acknowledgments

The publisher would like to thank the following individuals and institutions who have kindly given permission to reproduce their images in the book's foreword and essay section:

Opposite contents page: Lola Alvarez Bravo, *Los gorrones*, 1955. Collection Center for Creative Photography © Center for Creative Photography, The University of Arizona Foundation

p.i: © Ami Vitale

p.iii: Alice Austen, *Street Cleaner, Twenty-Fourth Street,* 1896. From the Album 'Street Types of New York', copyright 1896 by E. A. Austen, Albertype Company, New York from the Collection of The Alice Austen House

p.iv: Marianne Breslauer, *Défense d'Afficher,* Paris, 1937 © Walter & Konrad Feilchenfeldt / Courtesy Fotostiftung Schweiz

p.vii: Vivian Cherry, *Third Avenue El.,* early 1950s. Courtesy Daniel Cooney Fine Art, New York

p.viii: Martha Cooper, *Cooper Rock Steady*, 1981 © Martha Cooper

p.ix: Graciela Iturbide, *Mujer ángel (Angel Woman)*, Sonoran Desert, Mexico, 1979 © Graciela Iturbide

The images in the rest of the book are © the respective photographers. The curator would like to thank each photographer included in the book for allowing their work to be featured in this publication.

This book draws on the work of one hundred of the women I've met through Women Street Photographers. It gives a global overview of the way in which women are increasingly going out into the world—whether it's their local town or city, or through travels in other countries—and photographing the life that they see. I broadly define street photography as unplanned photos taken in a public space, whether that's a village road, a city subway, or a local beach. The photos capture moments that are variously brash, funny, intimidating, tender, and unnerving, reflecting the complexity of the photographers themselves.

This book, and the Women Street Photographers Instagram on which it's based, is a celebration of the increasing number of women able to work in this field. I'd like to thank Ximena Echague, who has been a crucial part of Women Street Photographers' success and to dedicate this book to the memory of Mary Ellen Mark, who encouraged me to follow my passion. I'd also like to thank the women who have worked on this book, in particular Melissa Breyer and Ami Vitale for their powerful writing, Anna Godfrey, the commissioning editor who led the project, and Shaz Madani for her wonderful book design.

—Gulnara Samoilova, founder of Women Street Photographers

Library of Congress Control Number:
2020046191

A CIP catalogue record for this book is available
from the British Library.

In respect to links in the book, the Publisher
expressly notes that no illegal content was
discernible on the linked sites at the time
the links were created. The Publisher has no
influence at all over the current and future design,
content or authorship of the linked sites. For this
reason the Publisher expressly disassociates itself
from all content on linked sites that has been
altered since the link was created and assumes
no liability for such content.

Editorial direction: Anna Godfrey
Copyediting: Martha Jay
Design: Shaz Madani
Production: Luisa Klose
Lithography: Ludwig Media, Zell am See
Printing and binding: DZS Grafik, d.o.o., Ljubljana
Paper: Profibulk

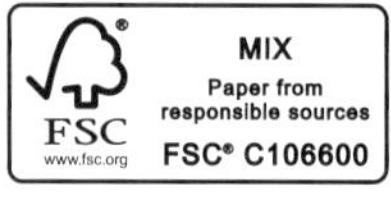

Penguin Random House Verlagsgruppe
FSC® N001967
Printed in Slovenia

ISBN 978-3-7913-8740-6
www.prestel.com